Montessori for Toddler

3 books in 1:

A PARENT'S GUIDE TO DISCOVER AND UNDERSTAND THE MONTESSORI METHOD - MORE THAN 100 MONTESSORI LEARNINGS ACTIVITIES FOR TODDLERS AT HOME - HOW TO CREATE A MONTESSORI TODDLER ENVIRONMENT AT HOME

Olivia Orlando

Table of Contents

Montessori Made

Knowledge and Activities to Create, Guide, and Excel in Learning

Introduction

Montessori Made is an educational and in-depth book for teachers and parents alike to assist their children through self-development. Although primarily intended for teachers in a Montessori school environment, the exercises and activities in these chapters can be applied by yourself as a parent or guardian at home.

Montessori, as we explore in chapter 1, aims to direct learning towards your child. The main principle with this approach to learning is that your children are given choice and freedom to decide their own learning activities. There are basic rules and guidelines, however fundamentally the founder of the Montessori method learned - through her observations - that giving a child choice enables a greater willingness to learn, in addition to enhancing performance, development, and ability.

This book is ideally for children aged 3 - 5 years old and can be taught and applied with just your own children at home, or within any group setting. Equally, if you are a teacher, all of the methods and practices can be expressed in your classroom. You will find the activities, information, and exercises are easily implementable, practical, and down to earth, and are all drawn directly from real Montessori approaches and systems of learning.

Chapter 1: Introduction to Montessori

Montessori is a type of learning approach which is child-centric. It focuses on hands-on learning as well as activities which are directed by the children themselves. Scientifically speaking, this method is based on the developmental stages of children from the time they're born to the time they become adults. It's designed to nurture and support the interests and needs of children by giving them learning experiences which are appropriate to their current developmental stage.

Any Montessori classroom must be beautifully crafted in order to make it a suitable environment to meet the needs of children. As a teacher (or a parent) your role within this environment is to observe the children and guide them as they embark on their own developmental journey. The focus of this method is for children to lead their own learning instead of the teachers teaching them what they "must" learn. Also, another important task of Montessori teachers is to present the activities in the classroom to their children. In doing this, the children learn how to perform the activities by themselves and they have the freedom to choose which activities they want to do in the time they're given.

The beauty of Montessori classrooms is that children are allowed to choose independently, they're given the freedom to move around the room, and they are gently guided allowing them to acquire a love of learning. Children can work on their own or they can work in small groups. Either way, they make use of the educational materials in the Montessori classroom which is self-correcting. What's incredible about these materials is that they are specifically designed so that children learn one concept or skill at a time. They have a self-correcting quality which allows the children to explore the outcomes of their choices on their own and at their own individual pace.

All Montessori materials in the classroom are also designed to match the interests of different kinds of children with the five major curriculum areas which are Mathematics, Language, Practical Life, Culture, and Sensorial. In some classrooms, they also include a Music and Arts area which is also very interesting to children. Since children are given the opportunity to have experiences based on their interests, they learn and develop in the most relevant knowledge areas. The skills they acquire from their Montessori experiences assist with their emotional, physical, cognitive, and social development. So basically, the materials in the Montessori classroom teach children how to work together, self-correct, and solve problems.

Although Montessori classrooms contain only Montessori materials, the great thing about this method is that you can also apply it in your own home. As a parent, you can come up with your own materials and prepare a room in your own home to serve as your child's own personal "Montessori classroom." As long as you learn the basic principles behind Montessori, you will have a better idea of what you need to prepare for your child's learning environment. We will be learning more about this later on. Now, let's learn more about the Montessori method and how it began.

Montessori History and Essence

"I observed little children; I sensed their needs, I tried to fulfill them; they call that the Montessori Method."

~Maria Montessori

Montessori is a unique educational system that originated in the late 1800s through the work of a medical doctor and physician. This physician was Dr. Maria Montessori, a passionate observer and studier of psychology. Dr. Montessori researched and observed children with learning disabilities, specifically autism, and subsequently came up with a universal set of principles and teaching applications which could be applied to all children, to expand and enhance self-development. Fortunately, this means you yourself, as a parent, can implement these teachings and practices at home for your child's best development.

Dr. Montessori was not only a medical doctor and physician but she was also a scientist and experimental psychologist. The first school she opened was called Casa dei Bambini, Italian for 'Children's House.' Maria Montessori found that, despite being chaotic and disruptive at first, the children at her school became calm and peaceful and were able to concentrate for long periods of time. They also developed a sense of order and care for their environment, which all arose from their interest in working with different puzzles, learning how to prepare meals properly, and engaging in the maintenance of their environment, and its orderliness.

Although a traditional Montessori education in a school environment would be ideal, it is not a necessity. All the exercises and knowledge in this book are based on carefully conducted research, and first-hand experience, so you can feel confident applying the processes with your child.

Originally the Montessori method was created for younger children, specifically ages 3-5, however, over time it became adapted for adolescents also. In addition, Montessori herself lived through two world wars, therefore an educational aspect for peace and social justice became and remained an integral part of the system. Combined with this is the emphasis on the importance of culture and community.

In 1929 the Association Montessori Internationale was created, to make sure the philosophy and intentions were passed on through time.

Before going into the essence of Montessori methods and practices, it is useful to look at some recent modern research and findings into the benefits of the Montessori approach to education. A study posted by The Guardian reports, Montessori as - "a method of schooling that focuses on personal development rather than exams produces more mature, creative and socially adept children, scientists have found. Psychologists in the US found that across a range of abilities, children at Montessori schools outperformed those given traditional education."

The article further goes on to say that, "Five-year-old Montessori pupils were better prepared for reading and maths, and 12-year-olds wrote significantly more creative essays using more sophisticated sentence structures. Some of the biggest differences were seen in social skills and behavior. Montessori children displayed a greater sense of justice and fairness, interacted in an emotionally positive way, and were less like to engage in rough play during break times."("Research shows benefits of Montessori education", 2019) [1]

It is also interesting to note that the study shared in The Guardian reported and found that the home environment's effect on a child's self-development was particularly remarkable and that children who were subject to a Montessori framework showed a greater sense of community at school. These children were also more likely to choose positive assertive responses in unpleasant and difficult social situations. The researchers concluded that Montessori education develops social and academic skills equal or furthermore superior to a large spectrum of all other types of schools. Hooray for Montessori Made, then!

Before going into the details and exploring some of these topics further, let's look at some of the benefits of Montessori in brief.

---

1 Research shows benefits of Montessori education. (2019). Retrieved from https://www.theguardian.com/education/2006/sep/29/schools.uk?fbclid=IwAR0UnG60Z2qrhea6xQhmMEowTgxxNaMWgk9LgvCl7R6BDc_Ezzasa886sps

1. The Encouragement of Cooperative Play

Montessori encourages cooperative play through the principles of the teacher or parent acting more as a guide than a boss. The teacher or yourself as the parent do not dominate or 'run' activities in a way which takes away from a child's self-autonomy. This helps your youth learn to explore, question, and share with other children in ways rooted in community and cooperation.

2. The Natural Acquisition of Self-Discipline

It is easier for children to learn self-discipline within a Montessori framework as they are allowed to choose their own activities and for how long. There are of course ground rules and a basic structure, however, they are also provided freedom for their own individual learning which ultimately leads to self-control, concentration, and inspiration. Children are more likely to be motivated to learn when they're treated as independent and sovereign beings.

3. The Focus on Key Development

We explore this in depth in the next section, however, for now, Montessori focuses on key developmental stages which inevitably lead to success.

4. A Highly-Individualized System

Children are allowed to explore activities and ideas at their own pace, which naturally provides time and space for them to attempt challenging and different areas of learning. This, in turn, increases self-development and their learning experience, as when provided choice children are more inclined to push themselves and strive for greatness. In other forms of education, there is a tendency for the teacher or someone in a position of power to push the child. This, unfortunately, creates inner tension and a natural desire to rebel, as it takes the power away from the child. Providing frameworks for individualism and a personal learning journey is, therefore, a key aspect to Montessori educational success. In addition, learning can also be more comfortable for those who need to slow down and absorb new concepts and knowledge at a less challenging pace.

5. A Child-Centered Approach

Extending from the last point is the fact that Montessori is primarily about the child. Unlike in mainstream education where there are frameworks teachers and principal have to abide by, learning and development are 100% child focused. There is no such reality of pushing children unhealthily or unnaturally to achieve certain grades, with the intention of the school or board appearing in a favorable light. Curriculum and activities are centered around the child's specific needs and requirements, not around the school's, teacher's, or some other body's.

6. The Age Range and Peer Mentorship

This may not apply to you directly, but in traditional Montessori education mentoring can come from other students, and younger children are often placed with older ones. It is recognized as healthy and beneficial to allow children of different ages and development levels to interact, as this is one of the key elements to a young human being's development.

7. The Teaching of Order

The Montessori method involves teaching your children order. In other words, all activities and objects have a precise location and 'way,' such as specific location on a shelf, in a cupboard, or any other physical place. This is highly effective at influencing structure and order and can help your child or children with any issues of self-discipline they may be struggling with. An orderly environment creates an orderly inner world, and although the Montessori method encourages great freedom and creativity - order is essential to thrive in the world.

8. "Hands-On Learning"

One of the main benefits of Montessori is the hands-on approach to learning involved. Many activities include language, math, and practical life lessons merged with the important emphasis on a child's freedom to learn and be creative, which is an essential component to learning and development. This can be seen as a key reason as to why Montessori is so successful. Hands-on learning enables greater practicality and concrete learning and activities, as opposed to abstract learning (although this is not omitted completely). Hands-on learning also means that children are discouraged from interrupting one another during activity time until the task is properly mastered, also increasing patience, attention to detail, and focus.

9. The Facilitation of Learning by the Teacher (or Parent)

Another key point to be aware of is that Montessori teachers or parents wishing to use the Montessori method are guides. You obviously do hold a natural position of authority due to the adult-child dynamic, however fundamentally it is all about the child's journey. You may take the lead to ensure directions and certain rules are followed, yet you do not influence them in a way which may be detrimental to their learning processes. The goal in Montessori is for yourself or a teacher to remain as unobtrusive as possible.

10. The Importance of Creativity

Finally, the importance of creativity and creative or artistic expression is fundamental to the success of Montessori. Creative expression is all about the process - the journey - and due to the frameworks in place for learning this enables creativity to be a powerful channel for learning and development to occur. Joy and passion are two words which are also highly valued in Montessori learning, so any activity which is seen as fun or enjoyable by the child will naturally enhance their willingness to engage. Linked to this is the teaching of cultural subjects, which is often presented through creative forms, therefore this allows them to expand their thinking and broaden their perceptions about the world.

As you can see from this list, choice is a key feature of the Montessori approach. Your child or children are ultimately presented with a wide range of activities and areas to choose from and they can engage with each for as little or much as they wish. The main role you play is the role of guide and observer to make sure they keep within a set structure to benefit their learning experience.

How Montessori Works

No matter what age the Montessori class has been prepared for, each class operates on the principle of the Montessori method of "freedom within limits." Therefore, Montessori teachers set ground rules based on the age or age group of the children they will be teaching. All of these ground rules are also based on the core beliefs of the Montessori method which are respect for the environment and for each other.

In Montessori, children have the freedom to work with the materials and activities of their own choosing and at their own pace. They have the choice to work with other children or to work by themselves. Then the teachers observe the children as they move around the classroom watching out for those who need guidance when working with a new activity. In some cases, the teachers may also try to determine whether they can introduce the children to new materials or activities.

But how exactly does Montessori work? What makes it different from other educational or learning approaches? These are some important questions any parent wants to learn the answers to, especially if they plan to start their child on the Montessori path.

Since Montessori encourages active learning that's self-directed, it not only benefits children academically. It also builds the social and real-life skills of children, both of which are essential to their overall growth and development. Whether you have a young toddler or an older child, Montessori will work wonders on them as they learn through the materials and activities they've chosen for themselves.

Montessori works so well because it approaches children in the best way possible. Have you ever tried observing children as they play? As long as children are having fun, they become totally engrossed in the activities they are doing. And this is a lot more evident for children who choose their own toys or activities on their own. It's very common to see children move from one activity to another as they play. This is fun for them and this is what keeps them engaged in what they're doing. And as children play, they are also learning essential skills and concepts without anyone teaching them.

In this sense, the Montessori method is a lot like learning through play. Children are brought into a prepared environment that's full of activities and materials at their disposal. They are guided and observed by their teachers all throughout the time they spend in the Montessori classroom. And if they ever need help or guidance, their teachers are always around to introduce activities and the proper use of materials to them. Here are more reasons why Montessori differs from other educational approaches and why it's so effective too:

- **Montessori isn't just a trend**

When it comes to education, a lot of educators tend to jump from one trend to another. Schools and districts often spend a huge chunk of their budgets on new learning programs only to discover that there are better programs out there. Then they spend on these new programs again much like "fashionistas" purchase clothes and accessories according to the trends.

Of course, this doesn't apply to Montessori schools. Ever since Maria Montessori began this learning approach over a century ago, even the modern Montessori schools retain its tools and philosophy today. Unlike other learning approaches, Montessori schools don't make frequent changes between programs and curricula because there's no need to. Whether you apply the Montessori method to public or private schools, it has proven its effectiveness.

- **Montessori encourages and fosters independence**

Every single thing in a Montessori classroom is aimed at independence. From the way teachers prepare the environment to how they allow the children to explore the environment, it's all about independence. If you try to observe a Montessori class in action, let's say a class with 3-5-year-old children, you will see some kids washing dishes, folding clothes, sweeping the floor, and doing other real-life activities which their parents normally do for them. Then you will also see other children working with materials which are more academic in nature, those which prepare them for their next levels in their education.

Just seeing these children working independently without having to ask for help from their teachers, who are observing them, is amazing. And if, as a parent, you try to apply the same method to your own home, you can also see this independence developing in your own child.

- **Montessori is self-correcting**

As aforementioned, the Montessori materials are designed to be self-correcting. This means that their teachers don't have to teach them what to do or tell them that what they're doing is wrong. This is because the materials themselves allow the children to identify their own mistakes. This aspect helps build their confidence as they don't have to listen to adults telling them that they've made mistakes.

The more independent children are allowed to be, the more they start realizing their own abilities and intelligence. This, in turn, inspires them to keep doing things on their own. Montessori has the potential to empower children, raise their self-esteem, and teach them how able they are in a world where they can feel so small. Although this doesn't happen in an instant, watching the entire process where your child learns how to become independent is a wonderful experience in itself.

- **Montessori helps children understand the "why" behind concepts**

Another reason which sets Montessori apart from other learning approaches is that it helps children understand why things happen. In other words, they are able to understand concepts and skills more profoundly as they become aware of the reasons behind them. Unlike memorization which a lot of programs encourage, Montessori focuses on comprehension as they work with the different materials and activities prepared for them in the environment.

- **Montessori allows children to learn at their own individual pace**

When it comes to Montessori, you don't have to worry about your child "falling behind." The Montessori method involves learning which is completely individualized. This means that your child can learn at his own pace instead of having to keep up with the curriculum set by his teachers.

- **Montessori makes learning fun**

Finally, Montessori makes learning fun! Whether the child is interested in reading, numbers, animals, shapes, colors, music, and more, there is something in the Montessori classroom for every little learner. The hands-on activities are extremely interesting for children and the more they practice, the more they gain proficiency in the concepts and skills they're trying to learn.

Things to be Mindful of!

There are also some things you need to be mindful of before beginning due to the fact that, like with any system, there are naturally occurring weaknesses. The Montessori method is one of the best educational systems in play, however, it is not perfect (what is?!). The main aspect which often comes up for criticism is the fact that the structural approach and framework to learning may be perceived as too free. In other words, there should be more structure.

Of course, this works in two ways, as freedom allows for greater self-expression and willingness to learn and try new activities. It also paves the way, however to tendencies of the child 'doing nothing,' engaging in 'excessive play,' and 'uncontrolled creative expression.' This can be overcome simply with knowledge and awareness, and greater action and guidance from yourself.

You may also want to adapt or expand Montessori teachings by integrating some elements from traditional schooling, such as assigning homework. Homework is not usually given by Montessori teachers, therefore including this may help to provide more structure and increased discipline. This should, however, be done in a way that doesn't compromise from the nature of Montessori and its success in a child's development. These successes are of course disagreeing with traditional competitive methods of achievement, such as tests, grades, and exams.

In this way, individual progress and development is still the number 1 priority.

The Stages and Planes of Development

"It is the sensibility (sensitive periods) which enables a child to come into contact with the external world in a particularly intense manner. Every effort marks an increase in power."

~Dr. Maria Montessori

The Montessori method is based on the principles of stages of development. As you are aware by now, your child's development is the priority with the Montessori approach, and school or board image and teacher or principal requirements are not in the equation. This means the focus and priority are on your child's unique journey; what their skills and talents are, where they thrive, and what they enjoy learning about and engaging in.

The planes of development are a stage-based model created from and shaped around age ranges. Each plane or stage relates to specific activities and in a classroom environment, this opens channels for 'mixed classes,' so the older children can help and guide the younger children and the younger children can enhance the older children's learning experience, through reflection, simultaneously. In a home environment, this may not apply but you can still use the stages of development with your children of different ages.

Connecting to this is the element known as sensitive stages or sensitive periods. This links closely to the notion of developmental stages in the Montessori approach. The general, which we will explore in depth in a moment, is that younger children naturally focus on language skills; four-year-olds are prone to working on their motor skills and completing everyday tasks such as cooking, cleaning, and arts and crafts; and older children like preschoolers expand their learning through experience and knowledge of community, culture, and trips and external events. This is not set in stone, however, but does offer a framework to the planes of development you can expect to see in your children.

This image accurately presents the stages of development for you to integrate into your understanding:

Stages of Development for Early Learning from Birth to Age 7

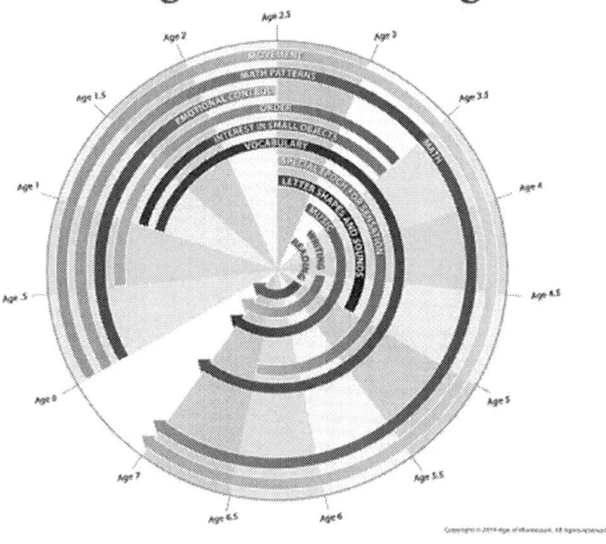

This image has been retrieved from Age of Montessori

"My vision of the future is no longer people taking exams and proceeding then on that certification... but of individuals passing from one stage of independence to a higher one, by means of their own activity through their own effort of will, which constitutes the inner evolution of the individual."("Ages and Stages", 2019) [2]

This quote from Maria Montessori shares the intention of Montessori and why stages of development are so important. She observed that there is a set pattern to stages of development based on a child's age, and used these findings to create a certain specification for the types of activities and learnings your children should be exposed to. These stages are also referred to as developmental milestones and are essential in Montessori education. Let's have a look at these now.

- **Stage 1: 'The Construction of Individuality," also known as the "Absorbent Mind Stage"**

This stage of development is from ages 1 to 6 and is known as these terms as this is when children have an absorbent mind. They learn easily if not effortlessly and can absorb large amounts of information much easier than later in life. This stage is further broken down into the unconscious and the conscious stages and is called constructing individuality as such.

Children aged 3 and under absorb and retain information unconsciously, without conscious effort. They learn through reflection, mirroring, and mimicry; absorbing all

---

2 Ages and Stages. (2019). Retrieved from http://www.montessori-namta.org/ages-and-stages

sounds, sights, tastes, physical sensations, and observations as a part of their unique being. Dr. Montessori refers to this as impressions and observation, which do not merely enter a child's mind - but form it. We are conscious and intelligent beings who respond to a variety of external stimuli and senses, and it is in this age range where children are most able to acquire a sense of individuality based on their new exposure to external information.

From 3 to 6 years of age there is a more conscious stage of development, where experiences and observations become more aware of their conscious mind. They are still able to absorb information easily, like in the unconscious stage, however, the difference is that they actively seek sensory stimuli. Experiences become more enjoyable, and there is a willingness to learn. They expand their newly developed abilities and wisdom and desire increased independence as a result. Maria Montessori referred to this stage as 'help me do it myself,' which is what you should adopt if you wish to provide the best Montessori outlets for your child.

- **Stage 2: "Acquisition of Culture and the Cosmic Plan"**

"Acquisition of Culture and the Cosmic Plan" occurs during ages 6 - 12. It is significantly noticeable as the child transitions from the absorbent mind to the reasoning mind. In other words, instead of just absorbing all external information and sensory data, children transform to actively engaging in reasoning and logical and intuitive processes. There is also a natural progression to group work and learning collaboratively, and with a greater sense of cooperation. Mental processes change from 'what' to 'why' and there is a deepened sense of cognitive functioning.

There is also sparked interest in moral and ethical questions and topics, such as human and animal welfare rights and an interest in the health and care for the planet. Maria Montessori called this the 'Cosmic Plan.'

"The child will develop a kind of philosophy which teaches this unity of the universe; this is the very thing to motivate his interest and to give him a better insight into his own place and task in the world, and at the same time presenting a chance for the development of his creative energy." (Maria Montessori) [3] ("Stages of Development and How Children Learn - Montessori Teacher Training and Parent Resources", 2019)

---

3 Stages of Development and How Children Learn - Montessori Teacher Training and Parent Resources. (2019). Retrieved from http://ageofmontessori.org/stages-of-development-how-children-learn/

- **Stage 3: 'The Development of Personality and Earth Children"**

This stage occurs from ages twelve to eighteen as they develop social or universal consciousness. A new sense of self-awareness increases and interests may turn towards society, the world at large, and humanitarian or community interests.

What is interesting about this stage - and what is in such natural opposition with traditional and mainstream education - is that this stage is where adolescents are less likely to be in their academic prime. Considering that these ages are where children are pushed in school to sit through endless exams, given copious amounts of homework, and are forced to retain large amounts of information, often against their interest and natural passions, this may seem quite worrying. This is the age where your youth are ready to develop their understanding and love for community, expanding their direct experiences, and broadening their horizons and interests.

This is the stage and age range where real-life skills such as cooking, building, creating, learning about budgeting and finance, and getting involved in any real-world practical skills are in their prime to be learned about and integrated. Creativity, artistic expression, and self-discovery are also strong. They may be referred to as 'earth children' as many children during these ages take interest in earth-loving, activist or philosophical pursuits and areas, placing high importance on love and respect for other living organisms, ecosystems, peoples, and cultures.

The following paragraph also shared by 'Age of Montessori' (like the above quote), expands this:

"If puberty is on the physical side a transition from an infantile to an adult state, there is also, on the psychological side, a transition from the child who has to live in a family, to the man who has to live in society. These two needs of the adolescent; for protection during the time of the difficult physical transition, and for an understanding of the society which he is about to enter to play his part as a man, means that there is an opportunity to learn both academically and through actual experience what the elements of social life are. We have called these children the 'Erdkinder' because they are learning about civilization through its origin. They are the 'land children." [4]

Sensitive Stages or Periods

A sensitive period is a child's passion or burning inner fire of interest or excitement, something which really

4 Retrieved from http://ageofmontessori.org/stages-of-development-how-children-learn/

'sparks' their passion for learning, attained during the engagement with a new skill. They are developmental windows of opportunity where your child can learn new and specific concepts more easily and naturally attune to them more than any other period of life. You can always tell when a child is inclined towards a particular sensitive stage as they will show a dramatically increased interest and excitement towards a certain activity, skill or exercise.

This links into the child-based approach to learning which we look into later. It is a fundamental understanding that your child or children learn better when they are given freedom to choose their own activities. Self-discipline hence becomes a natural process of integration and development, as there is no 'overbearing' or dominating authority figure telling them what they can or can't, should or should not do. Sensitive periods are slightly different, however, as the idea with a sensitive stage of development is that, once it is missed, it cannot be re-established. This does not mean that your child will never be able to learn or acquire a certain gift, skill, or ability if they do not acquire it in the sensitive period - just look at some world-class musicians, composers, artists, or experts in their chosen fields who began learning later in life. It does, however, imply that it is crucial to make use of the sensitive periods for your child's best possible journey of learning and development; which were discovered by Maria Montessori herself after years of in-depth research and observation.

The basic sensitive periods of development are as follows:

- Order
- Movement
- Vocabulary
- Interest in small objects
- Emotional control
- Math patterns
- Music
- Reading
- Writing
- Sensations
- Letter shapes and sounds

Let's look at these in more detail.

- **Order**

Children aged 6 months to 3 years have an innate need for order and structure. This is rooted in psychological needs and a basic 'natural law and order' of the world. Just look at nature's design and how everything is inherently designed to achieve homeostasis and work in order and harmony. Many parents don't realize their child's need for order, as it is assumed to be something one develops with maturity and age as they reach adulthood. However, a Montessori environment with the habits for order and structure in place are what is needed for your child's development.

Furthermore, Dr. Montessori discovered that a lot of 'tantrums' were due to the child's lack of order being disrupted, either by a teacher, parent, or the environment!

- **Movement**

Children are born with limited control and sense of movement. As they learn to use their bodies and connect to them consciously, they are able to learn and gain fine and gross motor control. Cognitive abilities also link to movement, as the better able a child is to control their motor senses and reflexes, the more able they are to develop cognitive abilities.

In the words of Maria Montessori - "The hands are the instruments of a man's intelligence."

- **Vocabulary**

We explore vocabulary in later chapters, however, in short, the acquisition of language is easiest for children under 6 years of age. This is why it is suggested to teach your children different languages from a young age, as they are best able to learn and retain them. The ability to learn vocabulary is tied in with many other skills, such as reading, writing, music, and the interest in sensations.

- **Interest in small objects**

Children experience an intense sensitive period for small objects between the ages of 1 and 4. This leads to the development of fine motor control and skills and what we know as the pincer grasp - essentially strength in the fingers and hands. A child's interest in small objects is essential for writing and many other important skills. The fact that Montessori encourages certain activities other systems frown upon portrays why it is so successful!

- **Emotional control**

Infants and babies learn about emotional connection and control from the moment they are born. They are constantly in a state of learning, observation, and development and pick up on sensory stimuli and external cues from their environment. They also acquire emotional senses before they leave the womb, as they have spent 9 months listening to their mother's and other loving voices supporting them and encouraging their healthy and happy growth. Emotional control is the basis of an educated and well-developed mind.

- **Math patterns**

Babies are actually born with mathematical minds and are hardwired from birth to be mathematically inclined. It is interesting that many autistic children have incredible and advanced mathematical, musical, or unique skills which far transcend 'the norm.' Many people believe and are aware of the power of binary, and there being natural geometric shapes and patterns found in a physical and energetic universe. Exposing your child to math patterns and sufficient levels of learning at the correct age will help their growth and development significantly.

- **Music**

The age for development for music is at age 3, where children begin to develop particular sensitivities for learning rhythm, pitch, melody, tone, harmonies, and more. Music is intrinsically connected to academic, emotional, cognitive, and social growth and any child who thrives in musical ability and skill will most likely excel in areas such as math, writing, and creative storytelling.

- **Reading and Writing**

Both reading and writing are skills acquired early on in life. Just like learning a new language or being musically inclined, the earlier on your child can develop these necessary skills, the better able they are to thrive academically. Early literacy development is about the preparation of a child's mind, cognitive functioning, and emotional maturity and connection. It may not appear at first that emotional control and connection is linked to such literacy-based learning aspects, however, they fundamentally are.

Younger children are open to information and sensory and external stimuli during their sensitive period. By providing your child with the correct materials, activities, lessons, and structures for learning, their learning is natural, effective, and in continuous progression. This continuous progression is what is aimed for and why the Montessori approach is so beneficial to children of a young age.

- **Sensations**

Physical sensation and hands-on engagement are extremely important, especially for younger children, as we live in a world of senses. Watching, observing, or listening act as great tools, however ultimately the best way to learn is to actively engage in sensational learning. Practical learning is an integral part of Montessori and something we explore in depth in chapter 2.

- **Letter shapes and sounds**

Children also become very interested in letter shapes and sounds between the ages of 2 and 5 years. This is because they are naturally curious and have a 'childlike innocence' to them. They want to learn and explore through touch as sensation, such as playing with shapes of letters, attempting to place them through cut out holes, and matching the sound of a letter with its shape.

A key component of all sensitive periods is the importance of repetition. When a child is given the freedom to engage in an activity for as long as they like, they naturally develop a certain 'mastery' in that skill. Unlike in traditional school environments, which state you must read this chapter for 12 minutes, then write this specific story for 15, and then go over the chapter and look for a, b and c for precisely 10 minutes; Montessori allows the child to engage in one activity for as long as need be. There is little to no sense of limitation with the time or exercises provided, which ultimately enables your child to engage in something to such an extent that they become expertised in it.

Your child can then repeat an action until there is little to nothing left to be learned or until they become disinterested in it. This disinterest then sparks a passion for interest in another activity. The period of repetition is all dependent on the child and their interests, for example, repetition can last a few hours to a day, a few days, weeks, or even months. There is not limited structure to how long it can take for your child to master something or integrate the skill for long term learning success.

Now, this may appear intense, and there is something intense to it. But this is what makes Montessori as an education system so unique and why it is recognized worldwide as one of the most prestigious and effective educational systems. This quote by Dr. Montessori herself shines some light into sensitive periods of development: "It is this sensibility which enables a child to come into contact with the external world in a particularly intense manner. At such a time everything is easy; all is life and enthusiasm. Every effort marks an increase in power."

Sensitive Periods and the Brain

As briefly mentioned, cognitive abilities and functioning are something in which sensitive periods greatly develop and expand. In sensitive periods of development, the brain is provided signals and cues of how long something takes to complete or accomplish. The child learns about linear time and developmental processes through their own subconscious learning, and the brain records these learnings. Each developmental task or activity, therefore, becomes integrated into the young child's understanding of how and when to apply the particular skill gained and the environment in which it can be applied.

For example, say your four-year-old has spent two weeks attempting to place shaped letters in a building block exclusively for the shapes. Your child may not be consciously aware of it, but with each attempt, your child's brain is recording how long it takes, how they feel each time they fail and succeed, and how and where this activity can be applied in real life. The experience becomes stored in both the unconscious and subconscious, and it is the repetition of acquiring the skill which transforms the knowledge of how to complete the task into something conscious. Thus, your child can complete the task with greater or perfect ease in future situations.

It may sound simple but as an infant or young child, any new skill takes considerable effort and patience, in addition to self-discipline and a sense of order. Being allowed the time and space to succeed greatly helps with your child's ability to learn.

Sensitive Periods and Freedom of Expression

Finally, the last important point to share in this section is the link sensitive stages have to your child's energy.

Sensitive periods are crucial as they provide children space to express themselves. This ties in with temper tantrums, disruptions, and frustrations or outbursts of anger. Simply put, if a child is made to repress or suppress their natural feelings during the learning process, they become blocked. It is highly important that your children are allowed to feel and be themselves without shame or reaction, so they can grow and continue on their course. There is a major difference between responding and reacting. When you respond, you do so from a calm, wise, and empathic place which seeks to guide and direct in a helpful and nurturing or supportive way. When you react, you often 'mirror' the negative energy and emotions being displayed, being of no help to anyone.

Learning to respond, therefore, and embodying the guiding principle of the Montessori method, can enable your child to learn and grow at their own pace and without repressing their natural outburst that comes with self-development. Their energy needs to flow, and it can only flow when you are not preventing it through your own behaviors and actions.

Sensitive periods come and go and this is the beauty of a child's development. By learning about sensitive periods and important cycles of growth, behavior, and development you can be a major catalyst in your child's journey.

Chapter 2: The Montessori Approach

The main aspect which characterizes the Montessori method is the prepared environment. Teachers prepare their classrooms so that they're neat, tidy, pleasing to the eye, real, and simple before they welcome their children to come inside. A reason exists for each of the elements within a Montessori classroom and they are all geared towards the development of children. In the classroom, you won't just find children of all ages. The classroom integrates children of different periods of 3 years in order to promote respect, solidarity, and socialization among the children naturally.

The Montessori approach encourages educators to "follow the child." This is an excellent approach as it recognizes the evolutionary characteristics and needs of each child at each age. Through this approach, educators build for the children an environment that's both spiritually and physically able to meet the needs of these children. Because of this, their progress and development emerge as a need to adapt to their environment.

Each child has a need to give meaning to the world around him. Then he constructs himself in relation to his world.

The materials you would find inside a Montessori classroom each have a purpose as well. These materials are scientifically designed to pay special attention to the interests of children based on the developmental stages they are at when they enter the classroom. They are also created with the belief that when children are able to manipulate concrete objects, this helps develop their abstract thinking and their knowledge. The Montessori materials give children a chance to explore and investigate in an independent and personal way. They promote concentration and they allow children to master concepts and skills through repetition.

No Montessori classroom is complete without an adult who is usually an educator, such as a teacher or a directress. Each teacher observes the children individually taking note of their interests, capabilities, and needs. Then they offer the children opportunities to perform activities and use the materials with a specific and concrete purpose in mind. As the children learn to work with purpose and in an intelligent manner, they also learn how to care for themselves and for their small community which, in this case, is the classroom.

The Montessori approach also allows children to explore different areas of learning. From the time they start their Montessori journey, children are introduced to these areas which we will be discussing in detail later on. These areas of learning focus on teaching children different concepts and helping them develop different skills. Since children have the freedom to explore these areas and work on the materials and activities found within them, they don't feel pressured to learn as fast as everyone else.

As a parent, learning all about the Montessori approach and everything it entails allows you to create your own prepared environment at home. You also learn the kind of materials and activities you can prepare for your child in order to follow the Montessori approach at home. This provides your child with consistency which, in turn, helps him learn more profoundly.

Fences, Not Mazes: The Abstract and Philosophy

This is the philosophy that structure is created so that children can get their educational needs met, whilst simultaneously feeling free. Connected to this are liberty and its subsequent balance with discipline. Unlike in other schooling and educational systems, freedom and discipline don't have to be counter to each other. Liberty and discipline are two sides of the same coin, both necessary for learning and development.

Discipline is defined in a different way to mainstream education. In many schools, discipline is a type of punishment, a tool used to give a child detention, limitation, or some sort of 'telling off,' as if they have done something wrong. Yet in Montessori discipline is seen and treated as a positive thing, a form of self-discipline to enhance learning. This is the fundamental difference between discipline in schools and normal educational frameworks and the self-discipline you find in the Montessori approach; the latter focuses on positivity and reward.

Your child's environment is also an integral part of the philosophy's success. 'Fences, not mazes' suggests that you as the guide (teacher/ parent) provide fence-sufficient borders or boundaries for safety and protection, however not mazes. A maze, as you are aware, is a puzzle or a structure one may become lost in by taking many wrong turns. A fence provides a boundary and framework to keep one enclosed in. This philosophy still allows for the freedom of choice aspect to Montessori education - your child is still allowed to possess creative, artistic, and academic freedom as it is primarily their own learning journey; however there is a priority of boundaries or structures to work within, over endless choices or mazes which can take them down a wrong route.

Other important aspects to Montessori's philosophy which we have covered and cover in other sections are:

- Freedom of choice
- Learning through practical life activities and skills
- The teacher or parent acting as a guide
- The importance of order
- Nature, community, and culture
- Development stages and sensitive periods
- Processes, not results
- 'Help me to do it myself'

Open Systems and Approaches to Learning

This approach is contrary to the status quo. It requires much more preparation ahead of time and gentle guidance as the process unfolds. The open and prepared environment is an integral part of the systems and approaches to learning. In a prepared and open environment, activities are laid out; there is some form of coding - such as color, shapes, or numbers and the objects, furniture, and materials in the environment are shaped to the child's needs. The environment is created to be 'open' - a place where the children feel free to move and walk around and choose each activity as they wish. In traditional Montessori classrooms, there are only child-sized tables and chairs present. It may be interesting to know that Dr. Montessori had her own furniture created when she was in search of child-sized furniture for her classrooms and there were none to be found.

Fortunately, this is not the case now and you can find a child-sized version for anything you wish to provide for your child within a Montessori framework. There is an abundance of materials and activities to make your open system and approach to learning as creative and limitless as possible. It is important to prepare your children's environment so they have the foundations, educational materials and set up necessary for development. Anything 'closed,' such as in mainstream or traditional classrooms, may seriously impact your child's learning and put a limit on to how much freedom and choice they have.

The key to remember is that the open environment is based on your child's development. It is designed to offer activities that match the sensitive periods and development stages, offering a wide interest of variety and skill introduction to your children. Due to the openness and element of choice, every activity may not be used because providing an open system gives your child or children the opportunity to choose what may or may not resonate. In an open learning environment, it is also significant to shape structure around the different types of activities presented. For example, you may choose to order activities into the areas of practical life, sensory, math, and language. You may also have a unique area or section on culture or one exclusive to water or food-related activities. This complies with the sense of order necessary for your child to thrive, yet within the open system framework.

Providing Purposeful Activities

Parents who have the chance to observe a Montessori classroom would see how quiet or calm it is. Often, these parents wonder how they can make their own children be the same way, both at school and at home. In the Montessori classroom, children work independently, they move around the classroom carefully, and they speak softly. Most if not all children in the Montessori environment do this because they are performing purposeful work.

By design, Montessori classrooms provide the children with purposeful or meaningful activities which are aligned with their needs at their current developmental stages. Much like adults, children are able to reach a state where they are calm and highly focused as long as they are able to find purposeful work where they can direct their energy.

Apart from giving them confidence and a sense of accomplishment, providing purposeful work to children is an excellent method to redirect undesirable behaviors. No matter how much energy a child has (and there are A LOT of children who seem to have boundless energy) when they're given work which they find interesting and meaningful they will be able to calm down, focus, and start their learning journey.

In "traditional classrooms," teachers often find it extremely challenging to redirect misbehaviors because all they do is remind the children of the rules, give the children work which they aren't interested in, or try to negotiate with the child by offering rewards. Although some of these methods may work with some children, these aren't long-term solutions. Instead, they should take a few tips from the Montessori method and provide these "misbehaving" children with tasks they enjoy, thus giving them a purpose.

For instance, if a child is interested in animals, the teacher works with this interest. In the Language area, the teacher can give the child the large moveable alphabet, or LMA, along with animal pictures or objects. Then the teacher can present the activity where the child would match the animals with their beginning sounds which they can take from the LMA. In the Culture area, the child will find a lot of activities about animals. Anyone of these can serve as purposeful work for the child. It's all about being creative in terms of providing activities to children which they will find interesting and meaningful.

While Maria Montessori worked with children, she observed how happy children are when they're performing purposeful work, especially when they have chosen the work themselves. In this way, children see their work more as play, but with a purpose. Of course, this doesn't mean that when the children start breaking the rules, the teachers just watch them.

Children must also be guided so that they know what's right and what's wrong. Remember, children may enjoy as much freedom as they need as long as they're not causing harm to themselves, their environment, or to others. When all of the children follow the rules of the classroom, all of them will be able to focus on the meaningful work which they have chosen from the environment.

Although Montessori teachers are trained to guide and facilitate children in the classroom, parents often find it difficult to just let their children be. Often, parents have the tendency to try and make suggestions as an attempt to make them "smarter" or to give them an academic edge over others. However, when you try forcing an activity on children, they won't find this meaningful. Challenging as this is, learn how to trust your child. Children know what they need and once they find it, the work becomes purposeful for them.

Adult Supervision: Guidance, Not Absolute Authority

This brings us to adult supervision and guidance. The best way to see yourself in your child's learning journey is as the director or directress. You are merely a guide, providing the correct structures and frameworks and making sure you are a gentle force in your child's educational life. The whole purpose of Montessori is for your child to have the liberty to learn and to express themselves. There needs to be a sense of freedom for them to move around the room or classroom space you have created and this can best be done when you are taking on a guiding and observing role.

As a director or directress, you are directing your child's energy without controlling it. Control can have a negative and destructive effect on your child's natural developmental urges and instincts, such as imposing a false sense of superiority or authority when it comes to their learning choices. Each child is different, and between the ages of 1.5 to 6 you still can't truly know where your child thrives. If you have a precomposed idea as to where you want your child to excel, this could take away from their true path and their own needs and desires. You may be a math buff, for example, and have little personal interest in art, practical life skills, or cooking. You may be highly musical and see your own kin as having a musical path ahead too, yet they may be inherently drawn to something highly academic, like math.

The key is to allow them freedom by observing their choices and gently guiding their way. You can offer input and suggestions, directing them towards activities they may have been neglecting; however, you should never force them into anything and especially if this force or 'telling' results in any form of distress, tantrum, or extreme display of negative emotion. This would clearly be telling you the activity is out of alignment and in disharmony to their natural interests at the time. Remember, Montessori is a journey and your child has many years to experiment with all the activities presented. The best thing you can do, as the parent and guide, is to have patience and redirect their energy when you best see fit.

If you are ever in doubt, the best thing to do is to look to Montessori's opposite. Traditional schooling has many positive points, of course, however, the fundamental difference is in the approach to the role of the adult. Many children grow to develop resentments and feelings of restriction or limitation through their educational experiences. Sometimes an imposed sense of authority can inhibit the learning process and the teacher may come to be seen as the tyrant or authoritarian figure no child resonates with. Observing these patterns may be able to assist you in shifting any blocks or limiting fears as to the role you play in your child's journey, looking at what you don't want to be or embody to help you become who you do want to be.

Simultaneously, you can seek inspiration from the positive aspects of traditional and mainstream schooling. The authority element to teaching is useful when used in balance and moderation, and when used as a tool solely to help your child's development.

This passage by Dr. Maria Montessori in 'The Child in the Family' portrays these notions accurately:

"The adult must acquire the sensitivity to recognize all the child's needs; only this can give the child all the help that is necessary. If we were to establish a principle, it would be that what is necessary is the child's participation in our lives, for in that period in which he must learn to act, he cannot learn well if he does not see how - just as he could not learn language if he were deaf. To extend to the child this hospitality, that is, to allow him to participate in our lives, is difficult, but costs nothing; it depends solely on the emotional preparation of the adult... Dust cloths ought to be multi-colored, brushes brightly colored and soap interestingly shaped. Attractive objects invite the child to touch them and then learn to use them; he will be attracted to a brightly colored cloth and learn that it is used to dust tables, or to the brush for his clothes, or to the soap with which he must wash his hands. In this fashion, beautiful things will attract him from every corner and instruct him practically by themselves. Now it is no longer the teacher who says to the child entrusted to her, 'Carl, brush yourself off,' or, 'John, wash your hands.' Any self-sufficient child who is able to tie his own shoes, dress or undress independently, shows his sense of achievement and joy as an image of human dignity, which he acquires from a sense of independence." [5] ("An Introduction to Practical Life — Montessori Guide", 2019)

---

5 An Introduction to Practical Life — Montessori Guide. (2019). Retrieved from https://montessoriguide.org/an-introduction-to-practical-life?fbclid=IwAR16uKr4748nHG3qpsQxdLX5ZPVa3KFqK0ZaJ6HWXF4lhxL7H6DBVkzyXNs

Ways to supervise your child while he performs Montessori activities

Although children get the most authentic experience of the Montessori method in an actual Montessori classroom, this doesn't mean that you can't apply the Montessori at home. Using similar activities and materials, you can reinforce your child's learning even in the comfort of your own home.

Of course, you must remember your role as the adult in the Montessori environment. As much as possible, you must refrain from telling your child what to do. Keep in mind that the Montessori approach encourages independence and freedom. Therefore, the role you will play in your Montessori setup is the same role played by Montessori teachers and directresses.

You should observe your child and merely supervise him as needed. Facilitate your child's learning instead of directing it. In doing this, you will be able to successfully reinforce the Montessori method in your home. To help you out, here are some ways you can supervise your child as he performs Montessori activities at home:

- **Allow your child to perform practical life activities in the form of daily tasks and chores**

When you learn more about the Practical Life area of the Montessori classroom, it's all about learning how to do real-life skills. Only in the Montessori classroom, everything is child-sized. The sinks, tables, and chairs are lower, the sharp utensils have dull blades and points, the washcloths are smaller, the brooms and mops are smaller, and so on. All of these are part of the Montessori materials which have been specially designed and which are part of the prepared environment.

Of course, you don't have to purchase all these special items for your child just so he can use them at home, especially if you're on a budget. Instead, you can just show your child how to use the real materials in your home to perform daily chores such as sweeping, washing dishes, cutting soft fruits and other soft food items using a dull knife, and more.

If your child shows interest in a chore you normally do, you can present how it's done the right way. Start by showing your child how to take the material, how to use it, and how to put it back when he's done. From there, observe whether your child was able to follow everything you've taught him or he finds a different way to use the material. Children absolutely love doing the same things their parents do. So, as long as the chore or activity is safe for your child, show him how to do it!

- **Instill a love for language in your child**

In the Language area, there are so many different things you can do with your child. Although learning the alphabet is a huge part of Language, there are other activities you can do as well. From talking to your child, telling stories, reciting nursery rhymes, and singing songs, there are endless possibilities!

Of course, you can also come up with your own materials similar to the ones in the Montessori classroom. For instance, you can easily recreate Object Drawers or the Object Boxes. Simply place small objects which have the same beginning sound in small boxes or drawers. Then print out cards with the alphabets on them, laminate the cards, and stick them on the boxes or drawers. Then you can introduce them to your child and make them part of your materials.

If your child wants to play with these materials, let him. Try to observe how he works with them. Does he sort the objects according to their beginning sounds or does he do something else? If he comes to you and tells you a story about the objects in the box, listen with a smile and make eye contact as he is talking to you.

- **Provide your child with manipulatives to learn the concrete side of mathematics**

The best way to provide mathematics materials and concepts to your child at home is by providing concrete materials or manipulatives. Children absolutely love these materials because they're able to do so much with them. Again, if you prepared or created a material based on the real Montessori materials, learn the method of teaching it too.

Then when your child shows interest in the material, present it to him, step back, and see how he works with it. As long as he doesn't damage the material or he isn't in danger of harming himself, give your child the freedom to work with the material as he sees fit. Then when he asks you how to use it correctly, present the proper method once again.

- **Allow your child to explore freely and discover things on his own**

These are crucial to the Montessori method. If you plan to create a Montessori environment in your home, you must familiarize yourself with the approach as well. Since you're reading this book, it means that you're really interested in learning all about Montessori and how you can apply it to your own child so that's a great start!

After learning about Montessori, you must also practice restraint when it comes to supervising your child. Always remember that Montessori encourages independence. Therefore, when it's Montessori time at home, you must also assimilate the roles of a teacher which are to observe, supervise, facilitate, and make sure that your child doesn't harm himself or the materials in the prepared environment.

Possibly the most challenging thing you would have to face is to restrain yourself from stepping in. As parents, you always want to teach your child the right way to do things. There's nothing wrong with this, of course. But if you really want to practice the Montessori method, you must also practice. Supervision gives your child the freedom to do his own thing and have fun while learning. So when he steps back into the Montessori classroom, he doesn't have to adjust to how things are done there. When you do the same things as the teachers in the Montessori classroom, you're providing your child with the consistency he needs to continue his Montessori learning.

Chapter 3: Discovery Through Montessori

Discovery is an important part of the learning process. Even children must be given opportunities to discover things and one of the best ways to do this is by allowing him to learn through the Montessori method. As we've described Montessori, children are given the freedom to explore the prepared environment as much as they want. As long as they aren't harming themselves or causing damage to the materials and activities in the classroom, the teachers allow them to discover the whole environment.

Through the years, discovery through Montessori has proven to be an excellent and effective way for children to learn. As the children go through the different learning areas of the Montessori classroom, they learn the concepts and skills they need to help enrich their education. As you watch any child go into such a classroom, you will marvel at how they are able to learn without much help for their teachers.

For some parents, when they observe children in a Montessori classroom, they don't really see the "learning." Unless, of course, a teacher is presenting or facilitating the learning of the children. This is how most parents understand the concept of learning. Where a teacher leads the process and the child listens. So for new parents, seeing children do their own thing in the classroom makes them think that the children are merely playing.

But even if the children in a Montessori classroom see the activities they're doing as play, is there anything wrong with that?

The short answer is no. As a matter of fact, play is a powerful thing for children and it's much more important in their lives than parents realize. Play is actually one of the most important aspects of learning.

When parents see the materials in the classroom, all they see are colorful toys. Sure, they may approve of some of the more "academic-looking" materials such as the Spindle Box in the Mathematics Area, the Sandpaper Letters in the Language Area, the Continent Map in the Culture Area, and so on. Such materials look like they're meant for learning but there are plenty of others which, to the untrained eye, may look like expensive toys.

By now you should already know that this isn't true. All of the materials in the Montessori classroom are specially designed to encourage learning in children. Each material has been carefully considered, designed, and created for the purpose of teaching a specific concept or developing a certain skill. Then all of these materials are sorted into the different learning areas to make it easier for the teachers and the children to evaluate and explore.

Now think about it. Since everything in the Montessori is meant to encourage learning, how much do you think your child will be able to learn by exploring and discovering inside the classroom? No matter how you look at it, the answer is A LOT. This is why the Montessori method is so effective and this is also why children love this method of learning. Each time they enter the classroom, they go on a quest of discovery which is both fun and educational.

How Does Montessori Differ from Constructivism?

The Montessori method is one of the most famous types of educational approaches and it's one of the oldest too. It was designed around the enacting principles of constructivism. Back in the 1900s, Maria Montessori started investigating the nature, education, and learning of children. She did this as she worked with children who were considered "learning disabled" and "troubled." Montessori developed a technique wherein she cultivated the sensory-motor skills of the children which, in turn, enhanced their cognitive development. This technique proved successful as she was able to help children who were deemed "beyond help" and even "idiots."

Back then, a child-centered approach to education was very rare and hard to imagine. But it was this approach which proved to be extremely helpful, especially for children who couldn't be helped by the more traditional approaches. The more she employed this approach, the more success she experienced. From there, she started designing developmental tools (which we now know as the Montessori materials) and activities which worked with her child-centered approach to teaching.

Although the Montessori method may have been designed around constructivism, they are now two different learning methods. The Constructivist Theory was proposed by John Dewey who is also known as the "father of modern education." He came up with this theory as an attempt to correct the mistakes of a didactic approach which was more traditional. In Constructivism, the teacher helps students think of their own opinions and questions while also helping them explore then interpret the results they've acquired from research. For those who follow this learning method, they go through a three-step process:

- Discovery
- Introduction of concepts
- Application of concepts

Also, the Constructivist Theory has the following major tenants:

- All of the lessons children learn must be relevant to them. Teachers structure their lessons around a specific question which they know sparks the interest of the children. From there, the children start forming a hypothesis.
- The lessons learned are focused on the concept of "less is more." Children begin learning the basic concepts before they learn more specific details. Then the children formulate their own meanings in a manner which they best comprehend.
- Teachers perceive and value the point of view of the children. Teachers must be aware of how well their children understand the concept by

asking them questions, listening to their answers, and asking them to elaborate.

- The tasks included in the curriculum are adapted for the purpose of addressing the suppositions of the children. So that learning takes place, teachers must start a conversation to see if the questions asked by the children match the concepts which they're able to cognitively understand.
- Teachers assess and mediate the children instead of teaching and testing them. This encourages interdisciplinary inquiry which, in turn, allows children to come up with open-ended and broad questions.

Now that you have more information about Constructivism, you may already see that it does, in fact, differ from the Montessori method even though they do have some similar aspects. The main difference, however, is that a Montessori classroom promotes independent learning more voraciously. Here are the other most notable differences between Montessori and Constructivism:

- In Montessori, the primary classification of materials is focused on sensory attributes; while in Constructivism, it's focused on organization and meaning.

- The materials in the Montessori classroom are self-correcting; while in Constructivism, the children depend on their teachers for correction.
- Montessori promotes "error-filled experimentation"; while in Constructivism, teachers don't attempt to discourage the answers of children even if they are wrong.
- The emphasis of Montessori is on personal choice and individual work stresses; while for Constructivism, the focus is on cooperative group discussions and group projects.
- In Montessori, teachers must create the classroom's social dynamic with an emphasis on courtesy and grace; while in Constructivism, they believe that suppressing conflicts is counterproductive to children in terms of their inner guides and their ability to think about other viewpoints.
- In Montessori, the teachers guide their children as they work; while in Constructivism, the teachers are guides and companions who try to create equal, personal relationships with them.

These are the most significant differences between Montessori and Constructivism. Although both methods are effective, Montessori is clearly more child-centered.

As you can see, in Montessori, the focus is less on the right answer and more on the process of getting to the answer. This provides a sense of continuity and freedom of expression, which we have already covered. Your task as the parent is to be constructive and helpful, not domineering and disruptive to your child's personal journey of development.

Decision-Making: Allowing Children to Make Their Own Choices

Decision making and a child's choosing are integral elements to the Montessori method. You are aware that you as the parent act as a guide, simply a way-shower and support system for your child's journey. Allowing your child to choose their course of action and activity engagement opens up new pathways for individual skills, talents, and gifts to shine through. If choice is taken away and they are made to conform to a rigid structure and 'one way' way of doing things, children are less likely to step fully into their individual self-expression and personal special qualities. Everyone is unique, and Montessori aims to bring this to the forefront.

Your child may be a musical genius yet struggle with math and arithmetic. Simultaneously, they may excel in life skills and individual activities which require skill, such as tying shoes, making bread, or creating order based on color or shape coding. Your child may be incredible at storytelling and writing yet not so strong in reading. The power of choice allows your child to align with the activities they enjoy and can thrive in, so they develop and master a set of skills. This, in turn, helps the other skills they are less strong in, even if unconsciously.

The point is that not all children are the same and you can either hone this knowledge and practice for your child's benefit or try and push more traditional schooling methods with potential detrimental effect. Sticking to a Montessori framework, however, will almost certainly set your child up for success.

Another way choice is presented is through the types of learning. Let's look at these different types of learning to help you understand them better:

- **Visual Learning**

Visual learning is learning through visual representations, such as images, written material, video, or whiteboards. Visual learning involves taking in a range of sensory information through the sense of sight.

For instance, when you present your child with graphs, pictures, diagrams, and illustrations, he's able to remember concepts better. These learners are more technically-oriented than others. Most of the time, visual learners are considered the best types of learners because most learning involves the sense of sight. If you have a visual learner, you may see him enjoy the Language area a lot because it contains a lot of visual materials.

- **Auditory or Musical Learning**

Auditory learning is learning through sound. Auditory learners process information and concepts best when heard or listened to. They are also the types of learners who learn best using rhythm or melody thus, they are also known as musical learners. For instance, musicians learn best by listening to a specific musical piece. Then they try playing the same piece from memory. These learners may also learn more effectively when there's music playing on the background or when they're whistling, humming, toe-tapping, and doing some sort of musical or rhythmic action while learning.

If you notice that your child is a rhythmic or musical learner, you may want to play soft background music during his Montessori time at home. You can also suggest this to your child's Montessori teacher if the music won't be a distraction to the other children. In the Montessori classroom, these types of learners would love the Sensorial area as it contains a lot of auditory materials.

- **Kinesthetic Learning**

Kinesthetic learners understand and process information best when actively engaged in, such as through touch or using their bodies and movement to acquire knowledge. These learners love interacting with the world around them as this is how they learn. They are scientific in nature and they enjoy hands-on learning which is perfect because Montessori is all about hands-on activities.

So if you have a kinesthetic learner, make sure to prepare a lot of concrete materials and activities for them to explore. Therefore, in the Montessori environment, kinesthetic learners would enjoy practically any material which they can touch, manipulate, and explore.

- **Linguistic Learning**

Linguistic learners are the ones who learn best when they're able to use linguistic skills such as speaking, listening, writing, and reading. It's even better when they're able to learn through a combination of these different skills and methods.

For instance, if your child is a linguistic learner and you want him to learn a new concept, you may read a story about the concept skill to him. For older children, you can ask them to listen to an audio recording about the concept while they take down notes about what they're hearing. To make the learning more concrete, start a conversation about the concept and, again for older children, you may ask them to write an essay or even a story about the concept they've just learned.

A lot of professors and teachers are linguistic learners, especially those who teach English, literature, and similar subjects. After all, language is in the nature of their profession. But when it comes to children, linguistic learners are the ones who love learning through words and communication. For children who are linguistic learners, you would find them frequently in the Language Area of the Montessori classroom.

- **Naturalist Learning**

Naturalist learners are the ones who learn best by experience and working with nature. When you think about naturalist learners, an image of a scientist may come to your mind. This would be quite accurate because a lot of scientists are naturalist learners. They love to observe the world around them, they love experiencing their world, and they learn more effectively through experimentation.

In the Montessori classroom, children who are naturalist learners may frequent the Culture or Practical Life areas but they may also be interested in the other areas as well because they love learning in general.

- **Mathematical or Logical Learning**

Mathematical or logical learners are those who love categorizing and classifying things. They're very good at understanding patterns, relationships, equations, and numbers more than other children. Therefore, you would find this type of learner spending a lot of time in the Mathematics area of the classroom.

So if your child is a mathematical or logical learner, you should look for a lot of activities related to math and logic. You can also get creative and come up with other types of materials to teach other concepts but wherein you still incorporate the math skills we've mentioned.

- **Interpersonal Learning**

These types of learners are those who learn best by relating to other people. In the Montessori classroom, you would notice these children are the ones who strike up conversations with other children or those who love coming up to the teachers and asking them questions.

Such learners work well with teams, love sharing stories, and they also love comparing their own ideas to the ideas of other children. By nature, these children can lead well and can be great followers too. So if your child is this type of learner, you may want to invite your child's friends to your home once in a while to have

Montessori time in the environment you prepared at home.

- **Intrapersonal Learning**

By contrast, these types of learners are those who learn best when they're left on their own. These are the most independent types of learners who may flourish in the Montessori classroom. Intrapersonal learners are intrinsically motivated and they are usually introverts too.

They're creative and they might not immediately ask for help from others. So if you notice your child struggling with an activity, approach him and gently ask him if he wants you to show him how to work with the material.

Most children under the age of 5 are kinesthetic learners as they need to learn through touch. This is why toddlers are always picking things up and trying to put objects in their mouths. The brain begins to develop in terms of processing and analyzing as one grows older, therefore your child's learning style will be unique to them. All children learn through visual, auditory, and kinesthetic learning, however, there will be one type which is stronger in each individual.

Through observation in the Montessori method, you can discover which learning type is predominant in your child and act according. You can see this as 'playing to their strengths,' or simply being the best guide and supervisor you can be to support their unique developmental journey. If you observe your four-year-old, for example continuously drawn to activities that involve touch, yet they respond positively to sounds; then this suggests they are still in the kinesthetic stage with a strong inclination towards auditory learning. Simultaneously, if your child enjoys observing and learning through sight (visual learning) then this implies they may be primarily visual learners. The beauty with Montessori is that there is such a wide range of activities, each with their own unique assets, that whatever your child's individual learning style, there will always be something perfect for them.

It is usually very easy to determine a child's primary learning type, simply by being attentive and observant to their needs and learning.

This information from The Age of Montessori is very beneficial and has been shared here to help you better understand the principle of a child's choosing.

"Maria Montessori understood all these learning differences and created an environment for children where they come in each day and choose what they want to work on. At the beginning of their first year in Montessori they might choose between doing a puzzle, stringing beads, or looking at a book. Each day the teacher shows them new lessons and soon they have a larger choice. Eventually, the choices include writing and reading, addition, subtraction, multiplication, and division with concrete materials. It includes biology and geometry, art and music. The free will of each child is gradually being educated. Each choice they have is constructive, developmentally appropriate, and interesting. Montessori's biographer E.M. Standing had suggested that freedom of choice doesn't mean a freedom to whatever you want, but the freedom to what's right. For children, what's right is what he needs to fulfill the next step in his development at any given stage. When a child chooses his work instead of doing what he is told to do, he often develops a more genuine interest and learns to follow the direction of what we call the "Inner Teacher." The child begins to value the inner satisfaction he gets from doing the work that corresponds to his inner developmental needs and he is calm and joyful in his learning.

Not every child chooses to do every lesson. But that is OK. Each child chooses what he needs. There are multiple ways to teach essential skills, so a child who does not want to do one lesson, may choose another that gets him to the same goal. But in Montessori, we realize that not every child reaches those goals in the same way or at the same time. Montessori gave a series of lectures about freedom of choice. She makes a powerful argument that the roots of tyranny are in adults forcing children to obey their commands. When a child spends his entire day, year after year, following the instruction of adults and has no right to follow his own interests, he may come to believe that his own interests are unimportant. He may come to believe that his thoughts are not as important as the thoughts of the adults who are teaching him. Montessori believed in discipline. But she realized that the way to reach it was by creating environments where children found engaging materials to use. When they are fully engaged in the work that appeals to them at their particular level of development, they become self-disciplined. You see in Montessori classrooms a group of three-, four- and five-year-olds hard at work. No teacher could command such discipline, yet the children freely give it to their own self-chosen work.

Freedom of choice becomes a habit of mind. Freedom to explore your own thoughts and interests can open the floodgates to creativity, as it has with such Montessori alumni as the co-founders of Google, Wikipedia, and Amazon.com – all Montessori graduates."(The Age of Montessori)

Empathy and Compassion

Unlike traditional educational systems, Montessori places a high emphasis on empathy and compassion. This is because real life practical skills and culture and community are taught, which both involve real interaction and learning through connection. This is not suggesting that traditional or mainstream school does not teach the importance of empathy or compassion, just that there is a fundamental difference between the applications of the curriculums.

Social interactions and emotional connection are an integral part of Montessori, meaning that morals and ethics come naturally into approaches to learning. Even academic subjects like math, reading, writing, and language have an empathic and moral tone, as in everyday life - which is portrayed and expressed through practical life activities - human connection is present. This brings an element of authenticity and community to Montessori education and the approaches to learning and development in place.

Furthermore, a substantial element to a child's development is defined in the stage 3 developmental cycle, 'Development of Personality and Earth Children,' suggesting that empathy and compassion towards others is an inherent part of a child's true nature.

Let's look at some of the ways empathy and compassion can be brought into your home Montessori classroom.

- **Teach compassion**

Teaching compassion through activities and exercises which involve love and respect for animals and ecosystems is a great and effective way to enhance your child's empathic nature. Many children are already naturally empathic - it is the world and some of the societal practices and structures in play which make them less so. We are born with a natural sensitivity and compassion towards sentient creatures and this is often displayed through many acts of compassion shown by young children. Feeling genuine sadness and empathy towards animals, questioning the consumption of eating them, and being able to feel plants and other nature on a deep level are all common occurrences. The Montessori framework is ideal for developing this natural compassion and connecting to a child's empathic nature.

- **Practicing kindness**

Practicing and acknowledging kindness in the classroom or environment you have created for learning and activity is another main way to develop empathy. This can be done by offering praise, where appropriate, and words of support and encouragement, such as 'that was nice of you,' 'that was very thoughtful and considerate,' or 'it was very kind of you to do this.' Remember, you are a guide for your child or children, so being supportive of efforts through verbal recognition will further increase the kindness and compassion they are already exhibiting. Try and not to overdo it though, as too much attention to natural kind and empathic displays can actually have the opposite effect, bringing focus to your child's pride and praise as opposed to the acts they are engaging in.

- Being respectful

It is very true to suggest that learning by example is one of the most effective ways to learn. Showing respect and treating your child as a young adult, or an equal, is possibly one of the most powerful ways to be an example of empathy. Showing respect to objects, learning material, things in your environment, and other humans, plants and animals will be a direct influence of your child or children. Young children are natural sponges until the age of 6 as they are still very much in the 'absorbent mind,' picking up on all sensory and external data and information. They learn through observation and reflection, mirroring back your actions, speech, and approach to life and others. A little bit of courtesy and compassion goes a long way!

Look to Dr. Montessori's teachings: In the words of Maria Montessori: "The study of love and its utilization will lead us to the source from which it springs, the Child." [6]

- **Learn to apologize**

There is nothing more humble and compassion building than learning to apologize and admit your mistakes. No one is perfect and being an adult does not exemplify you from the principles of humility. Apologizing for your mistakes or wrongdoings naturally increases empathy, connecting you more to your emotional connection and maturity and developing emotional intelligence. As children learn through connection and emotional control, this in turn helps develop their own empathy and understanding towards how connection and compassion work. It also is an important life skill both in the classroom with other children during learning and external to it.

To expand from this further, this is a helpful extract written by a Montessori teacher and taken from her website. A link can be found in the reference page!

---

6 Retrieved from https://quotefancy.com/quote/981067/Maria-Montessori-The-study-of-love-and-its-utilization-will-lead-us-to-the-source-from

How do we teach empathy?

There are many effective ways to teach empathy and I have shared some of my ideas below.

- **Name the feeling**

Teachers talk with the child about what feelings they are experiencing, what feelings are and give them names. "I see you are feeling sad/angry/happy/confused". Giving a name to a feeling a child is displaying, is the first step in helping young children identify feelings.

- **Define that feeling**

"I see you are feeling sad. I can see and hear you are crying".

- **Offer a solution**

"I see you are feeling angry. I can see and hear your angry words. I would like to help you feel happy again, let's find a solution so you can get there". Naming feelings is a good start to helping a child develop emotional empathy and it will promote understanding of their feelings and how to cope with them.

Why is empathy so important?

As stated in my in my introduction, empathy plays a big role in a child's social and emotional development. A child developing empathy is also more likely to show compassion. A compassionate human being will always be more motivated to help others because they have a good balance of emotional and cognitive empathy. A very special moment I won't forget came a few months back when my mother left to go back to where she lived. I had told my students the day before that I felt sad because I had to take my mother to the airport and I would not see her again for a long, long time. The next day, many of my students asked me how I was feeling, they drew me pictures, they gave me hugs, they did all their little 3 and 4-year-old bodies could do to make me feel happy. I was overtaken with emotions because I saw, for a split moment, the power of empathy. I was relieved to see that all our hard work with empathy, of preaching and repeating with much love, kindness, and care was helping build compassionate and kind human beings.

One thing that traveling has gifted me, apart from opening my eyes to this amazing world we live in, is empathy. And now, as a Montessori teacher, I have a very special duty that at times feels more important to me than teaching numbers and words to my students. I make it my duty to help every child that walks through my doors, leave with empathy in their hearts and being compassionate human beings." [7] ("Empathy: A True Lesson in the Montessori Classroom - Montessori Rocks", 2019)

7 Empathy: A True Lesson in the Montessori Classroom - Montessori Rocks. (2019). Retrieved from https://montessorirocks.org/empathy-a-true-lesson-in-the-montessori-classroom/

Chapter 4: Activities and Areas of Learning

Although a lot of parents may have heard about the Montessori method, most of them don't really know what it's all about and what happens inside a Montessori classroom. While some parents simply put their children in Montessori schools because they've heard how great these schools are, other parents actually learn more about this learning approach in order to understand better what they're putting their children into.

Just like you, there are some parents who invest in their children's education by learning more through different means. Valuable resources (such as this book) can help you become more knowledgeable in the Montessori method which, in turn, allows you to help your child learn more effectively. By learning more about Montessori, you will be able to reinforce your child's learning at home by following the principles and by coming up with activities much like the ones found in the different areas of learning which are:

- **Mathematics**

This area involves the utilization of concrete materials for the children to recognize number symbols and quantities too. Through the materials found in the Mathematics area, children learn how to the numeric symbols relate to the quantities and vice versa. The activities in this area are broken down into different categories including:

  - Counting
  - Geometry
  - Arithmetic Tables
  - Decimal System
  - Concrete Abstraction
  - Memory Work

Some examples of activities and materials in this area are the sandpaper numbers, spindle box, number rods, beads, games, and more.

- **Language**

This area encourages children to develop their early literacy skills through the utilization of phonetic sounds. In this area, children are able to use activities which encourage their phonetic awareness in order to build a strong foundation for their literacy learning. These materials are meant to improve your child's listening skills, vocabulary, and ability to differentiate between pictures and objects. Some examples of activities and materials in this area are the sandpaper letters, word lists, large and small moveable alphabet, and more.

- **Practical Life**

This area is important for children to build a strong educational foundation for their Montessori journey. Here, children develop their fine motor skills, self-confidence, concentration span, and also, to develop a love of learning. The activities and materials here are those which children also see naturally in their daily life. They're designed to help children learn "real-life skills" which help them in the real world. The activities here are broken down into different categories including:

- Grace and Courtesy
- Care of Self
- Care of the Environment
- Control of Movement

Some examples of activities and materials in this area are the pouring exercises, dressing frames, scooping exercises, and more.

- Culture

This area of the Montessori involves different subjects which are supplementary to the whole educational approach. The subjects included in this area are:

- Zoology
- Geography
- Science
- Botany
- Foreign Languages such as Mandarin and Spanish

Some examples of activities and materials in this area are the continent map, puzzles, animal families, and more.

- **Sensorial**

This area prepares children and makes them more aware of small details which are frequently overlooked. Each of the activities focus on important qualities such as shape, texture, smell, sound, weight, color, and size. The activities also develop the children's senses of discrimination and perception as they explore and notice differences in the details. Here, they develop their concentration and their fine motor skills as well. Some examples of activities and materials in this area are the pink tower, knobbed cylinders, brown stairs, color tablets, and more.

- **Music and Art**

Not all Montessori classrooms have this area but for others, they create a special area in the environment for children who are interested in music and art. Most of the time, children flock to this area because they get to express their creativity here. This also happens to be the easiest area to replicate in your home because all you need to do is come up with creative activities for your child.

The Montessori Curriculum

In this chapter we will be looking at Montessori curriculum and the types of activities you can share with your children. In this chapter we will cover Mathematics, Language, Practical Life, Culture, Music and Art, and Sensorial.

Before going into implementation and application it is important that you have the right environment set up. Let's look at how you can create the best possible Montessori environment for your child at home.

1. Declutter!

Putting too many toys, books, or activities on display at the same time can create chaos and disharmony, first in your child's mind and then reflecting outwards. A child's inner world is a reflection of their outer world and vice versa. Keep a limited selection of activities out in the classroom environment and stick to the 'one activity' rule expressed earlier. You can rotate the activities every few weeks, or the like, or after you have observed your child's sensitive period and when he or she has moved on to something different. As you are aware by now, children learn best in environments that feel uncluttered, orderly, and organized.

2. Read, and then Read some More

Due to the sensitive periods and timeframes for development, having books and keeping a focus on reading will set up the perfect homeschool environment for your child. Create and maintain reading activities by having a range of books which all relate to different parts of the Montessori curriculum. Appeal to your child's empathic, compassionate, and community driven side with books which warm the heart and are authentic. Display book themes in color or number coding, and make sure there is a range for all different age ranges (one of the key developmental milestones in the Montessori approach to learning) and for each of the sections explored next. The best way to achieve success is to merge and balance short reading periods of just 5 - 15 minutes with longer ones of 'reading time.' We go through this in the Language section.

3. "Help me to help myself'"

Remember the key philosophy and principle of Montessori, 'help me to help myself.' Find ways to integrate this into your home classroom environment and into daily life activities. This can be done through a number of ways, such as actively assisting during play, learning and activity time, and introducing concepts and activities which draw on this principle to engrain in your child's subconscious. Story time, writing, and practical life skills are effective ways to apply this.

4. Keep things Within Reach

Having a 'child-friendly' area in at least one space or as many rooms of your home as possible provides a safe and nurturing learning environment for your children. Provide low shelves, baskets and trays for storage, the correct sized furniture, and coat and towel hooks within reach. Remember, a huge part of Montessori is the practical life approach, so even if you believe you are just in your own home and it is unnecessary, having sections for coats and jackets after coming in and correct facilities for kitchen, water or food activities is highly beneficial. Place a few age-appropriate learning materials like children's books, art supplies, and instruments in at least one room, and smaller and easily accessible practical-life items such as dishes, utensils, tools, and towels.

The more your child can do for him or herself the better able they are to learn and develop independence.

5. Create an Environment of Independence

Linking to the last point is the necessity of creating an environment of independence. By keeping things in reach, providing the correct materials and furniture and adopting the 'parent as a guide, not boss' approach; your child is best able to thrive in such an academically and creatively charged learning environment. Don't underestimate how much children are capable of, even from a young age. Also, shift your mindset from doing things for them to doing things with them. You are merely a director and a guide supporting them for their own learning journey. Their development should be based on the awareness that we are all human beings, not human doings; they should be in a constant state of flow, engagement, and self-development through learning and activity. This is contrary to the mainstream education belief and classroom set up that there is always some end result or external curriculum goal to work towards and achieve.

Children acquire confidence, self-esteem, and skills through participating in everyday life and become the master of their own pursuits. Just like them being highly attuned to the like of order and organized material and environments- naturally, and contrary to any distorted beliefs we may hold, children also have a natural desire for independence. Resist the temptation to do everything for them and recognize you are merely guides in their evolutionary cycle of development.

6. Expand Your Own Learning and Education

One of the most effective things you could do as the parent and acting teacher for your child's journey is to enhance your own understanding and educational awareness. By learning about Montessori curriculum in your own time and going on training or learning courses, you are setting your child up for the best possible learning environment. Build on your existing knowledge and gain a deeper understanding of your child's stages of development. There are many online materials and courses you can align with and with many who have years of knowledge and experience. Of course, Montessori Made is a great basis and framework, however there is nothing quite like embarking on your own personal training course.

Developing your own 'inner teacher' can also help you gain friendships and connections with other like-minded parents and peers in your community, either online or in person. Research some online courses in Montessori teaching, learning, or development and check to see if there are any training courses local to you. Your child will truly appreciate you for it!

7. Have a Nature and Garden Learning Area

Finally, it can be very easy to forget or overlook the importance of nature and an outdoor learning area, especially with such a wide range of indoor activities to choose from and a great focus on maths, language, writing, creativity, and culture. But nature is essential and a significant part of Maria Montessori's philosophy. The 'earth children' is an integral stage in a child's development and an aspect of our shared consciousness simultaneously. Without nature we would not be alive - it is her very breath which supports and sustains us. The acceptance of nature being feminine in nature is supported by the recognition of our planet being 'mother earth,' a feminine and nurturing principle. It is the energetic qualities of nature and the natural world which can support your child's development, providing a grounding and safe haven for learning to take place. Nature also has a variety of sounds, scents, colors, and textures all supplying your child with the sensory experiences and external data needed to grow up healthy and harmonious, and with a deep understanding of the world in which she or he lives.

Introduce a nature area to your Montessori approach by setting up something special in your garden. This may include an outdoor play area, a treehouse, a learning structure where your child can engage in learning outside or any other creative outdoor activity. You may buy a telescope to engage in night time star gazing, or binoculars to observe the birds and clouds. Remember that Montessori education is both academic and creative, connecting to 'real world' applications and practices.

8. Storage Solutions

It is also important when setting up your environment to make sure you have sufficient storage solutions in place which is important for the organizational and orderly aspect to Montessori learning.

Plastic storage drawers are perfect for helping you organize many different aspects of the language curriculum, including 3-part cards, phonetic objects, phonogram cards, puzzle words, and language material. A label maker is also a useful tool for you to find the materials in these storage solutions more easily. It is important to maximize the space in your language area and using storage drawers and clear plastic boxes can help you do this. Creating a learning environment which ensures success for your children is essential for their development!

The Three-Period Lesson

One of the most important parts of teaching through the Montessori method is the Three-Period Lesson or 3PL. Montessori teachers use this so frequently that it becomes their second nature. Of course, parents don't really know what the Three-Period Lesson is and how it is done. Even new Montessori teachers must learn how to perform this method because it's essential in all the areas of the Montessori classroom.

Basically, the Three-Period Lesson is the very basic approach teachers use when they introduce new concepts to children. They use it to move the children from a state of basic understanding to one of mastery.

A physician from France named Edouard Seguin developed the Three-Period Lesson. Just like Maria Montessori, he also worked with children with special needs both in the US and in France back in the later part of the 19th century. As he worked with these children, he was able to discover ways to enhance the cognitive abilities of children. He also believed in the significance of developing the independence and self-reliance of children. Maria Montessori found the writings of Seguin to be extremely inspiring. Therefore, she used them as one of her sources for several of her most practical concepts.

Remember that the role of teachers in the Montessori classroom varies from the role of trained educators. Montessori teachers approach teaching in different ways, one of which is through the 3PL. The Three-Period Lesson is very simple yet highly effective. It follows this structure:

- Point to an object, such as a book. Say to your child: 'This is a book.'
- Ask your child: 'Show me the book.'
- Point to the object and ask, 'what is this?'

This sequence of the Three-Period Lesson creates a repetition and different perspective teaching through the approach taken. The different angles for learning allow your child's cognition to develop and thinking to evolve. Advanced children may appear bored, restless, or irritated at the simplicity of the task presented, however over time, this simple yet powerful structure will aid in the more complex activities given later. To help you understand the sequence of this technique, let's break the periods down:

- **Period 1: "This is..."**

For the first period, you must isolate the object when introducing it to your child. For instance, if you're teaching him numbers using flashcards, only show him number 1 then say, "This is ONE... ONE." Then set the flash-card aside so that your child doesn't see it.

Then show him number 2 and say, "This is TWO... TWO." Repeat the word a couple of times while pointing to the symbol or tracing it with your fingers. If your child wants to hold the card or trace the number, allow him to. When you allow your child to experience the material you're introducing to him through his different senses, his learning becomes more profound. Some teachers stop here, especially if they're introducing a concept which is totally new to the child.

- Period 2: "Show me..."

The second period is all about association and recognition. You can continue with this period right away (usually for easy or familiar concepts) or as a separate lesson. Basically, the purpose of the second period is to familiarize the child with the concept you introduced in the first period.

For this period, you don't have to ask the child to verbalize or repeat the name of the object, symbol, or picture you've shown. The most common mistake adults do during this period is rushing through it. Even without enough practice and repetition, they ask the child to identify the object, symbol, or picture verbally.

The second period is the most important one thus, it must last for the longest time. Here, you reinforce the concept you've introduced while trying to see the connections the child has made with everything else he knows.

Going back to our previous example, you would lay out both flashcards you've introduced to your child. Then ask him to show you the numbers. You can say things like, "Show me number one. Point to number two. Give me number two. Place number one in my hand," and so on. If your child makes a mistake, go back to the first period where you isolate and name the numbers.

- **Period 3: "What is This?"**

This is the final period in the sequence and during this period, teachers can ask the children to verbally identify the object, symbol, or picture. However, teachers must only move to this period when they're sure that the children have grasped the concept well and that they will be able to answer correctly.

This is why teachers remain in the second period for a long time, up until they know that their children have mastered the concept. Remember that in Montessori, the main goal is to help children master concepts and skills by themselves. So if the teacher moves the child to the third period too soon, there will be a need for correcting.

During this final period, you would lay out the flashcards again. But this time, you point to either of them and ask the child, "What is this?" After he answers correctly, point to the other flashcard and ask him again, "What is this?"

Simple as the Three-Period Lesson may seem, it does take a lot of practice even for teachers and parents. You must learn how to observe your child in order to see how well he is able to gain proficiency in the concept you're teaching.

Montessori Areas of Learning

We've already had a quick rundown of the different learning areas of Montessori. Each of these areas is special in its own right. They contain unique materials which teach a wide array of skills to the children. Let's review these learning areas and discuss them more:

Mathematics

All infants are born with mathematical minds. They are hardwired to learn mathematics as we are all born with a core sense of cardinal number. In The Mathematical Brain, professor of Cognitive Neuropsychology Brian Butterworth explains how babies grasp 'number module,' the ability to recognize groupings and quantities of the same amount. After a time, the names and symbols of numbers are acquired. This suggests that numerological and mathematical concepts are instinctual and present from birth.

Developing these natural skills with the correct frameworks, therefore, will allow your child to thrive and develop a mathematical mind. Stimulating the math aspect of the brain and thinking as early as possible will have a positive effect, not only on your child's ability to solve and engage in math, but to organize, remember information, and engage in other areas such as reading, writing, and music. It also enhances cognitive functioning and ability.

Dr. Montessori herself recognized the importance of math and in some of her writings compared it to being 'par excellence (with) the science of precision, order, and intelligence.' She stated that "great creations come from the mathematical mind, so we must always consider all that is mathematical as a means of mental development. It is certain that mathematics organize the abstract path of the mind, so we must offer it at an early stage in a clear and very accessible manner, as a stimulus to the child whose mind is yet to be organized."

Here are some of the practical activities mathematical concepts can be expressed through:

- sorting
- stacking
- handling
- touching
- organizing
- playing
- measuring

Engaging in the above with various materials can help your child learn about quantities, sequence, and patterns. They provide a hands-on approach to math and help learning, specifically if your child is a visual or kinesthetic learner.

"The hands are the instruments of the man's intelligence… The human hand, so delicate and so complicated not only allows the mind to reveal itself but it enables the whole being to enter into special relationships with its environment. We might even say that man takes possession of his environment with his hands." (Maria Montessori.)

Although the mathematical mind is present from birth, the ability to engage in math skills and practices come through learning and development. It is a product of gradual and social development, your child interacting with his or her environment to learn through direct experience, awareness, and observation. For example, an activity may be to count the number of books in each section on the book shelf; seeing how many books there in cooking and food, culture and community, and language and storytelling. This not only introduces your child to number and quantity but also to coding and grouping, learning through direct participation, sight, and touch.

Going outside to observe how many species of birds they see, or the different colors of the leaves fallen to the ground, also creates an inner recognition and can be further used to solve more complex math issues. This is the main principle with math and Montessori - to learn through experience and direct, hands-on engagement.

Arithmetic deals with shape, space, numbers, and time and their relationship to the real world in addition to abstract. It is all very well learning a theory however applying it to something useful and concrete is what will transition your child from learning to integration. Numbers and symbols are very useful to include in your curriculum and numerological or mathematical patterns can be very beneficial in enhancing your child's academic ability. We find patterns everywhere, from nature to the geometric shapes often found when cutting open fruit. We also engage in patterns daily, even when we are not consciously aware, such as waking up at a certain time in sync with the rising sun or eating at a specific time that is naturally best for our body clocks.

The areas of math taught, therefore, are as follows:

- Arithmetic (addition, subtraction, multiplication, and division)
- Geometry
- Statistics
- Calculus
- Numeration/Numerology
- The decimal system
- The number system (whole numbers, fractions, positive numbers...)

There is an emphasis in Montessori math to differentiate between left and right brain thinking and to engage in them simultaneously, and separately. The left brain is responsible for spatial and creative ability, music, art, and a sense of intuition, and the right brain relates to language, logic and reason, and rational thought. Each hemisphere (left/right brain) has its own functions, yet together they make the whole brain. Montessori interacts with both hemispheres.

This is the main difference between non-Montessori approaches to learning - they tend to be predominantly right brain. Yet Montessori has proven to be one of the, if not the most, successful system in play for a child's development. This is because it recognizes the importance of the left brain in academic subjects like math. Creativity and spatial awareness are integrated and balanced with rational thinking in mathematics, providing a holistic approach to learning.

Here are some activities to try with your children. You can of course adapt and expand and be creative!

- **Number cards and Counting cards**: Number cards and counting cards provide a great visual learning journey for children and can be adapted to a number of topics and themes.
- **A Math Bead Cabinet**: A math bead cabinet will allow your child to experiment with beads and numbers whilst learning about arithmetic.
- **Playdough Mats, Sandpaper Numbers, and Magnets**: These are all different outlets your child can use to learn about numbers and mathematical principles. Variety in Montessori is widely taught and embraced as is the use of various materials for learning.
- **Advent Calendars**: Advent calendars are a fun and engaging way to teach math, also helping the child learn about patience and periodic time.

- **Object or Number Matching**: Any activity which helps match an object to numbers is in alignment with the Montessori approach to learning and engaging with mathematics.
- **Sorting Sizes**: Sorting different sized objects will help your children learn math principles such as numbers, grouping, and sequencing. It can also be used in addition, subtraction, multiplication, and the like.
- **Math Puzzles**: Puzzles involving math or numbers are a great way to introduce math concepts into your child's life, from the age of 2. It is best to start with simple puzzles up to 20 pieces.
- **Practical and Sensorial Activities**: Any practical life or sensorial activities focusing on math will aid greatly in their ability to learn and understand concepts and information. Engage in a practical way with numbers such as counting food items, glasses, number of spoons, etc.

Math in Montessori is very 'hands-on,' allowing your child or children to learn directly from real life and everyday experiences. Cooking is a great way to get your child involved in math as many young children enjoy counting and measuring ingredients!

Language

This is one of the human tendencies to communicate with other people. This notion is portrayed from birth. Before even arriving into this world a baby has spent 9 months in their mother's womb. They have listened to loving, kind and supportive words, felt their mother's touch and love through the skin merged with soothing words, and listened to the subtle intentions radiating through. Language is one of the primary and initial sources of sensory information received, therefore is an integral part of a person's development.

Due to the sensitive periods of development, it is important that the correct language systems are put in place from an early age. Reading, writing, storytelling and all forms of communication are integral to a child's development. Language itself evolved thousands of years ago, when images and symbols were merely ideograms. These images and symbols later became words, words evolved to letters and vowels, and one apparently meaningless symbol become associated with certain sounds, which subsequently became associated with specific meanings. Thus, the alphabet was created and complex words and language systems have further evolved over time.

Emotional and collective intelligence comes into this. Some words don't exist in certain cultures or languages, and in other cultures new words and modes of expression arise with each new generation. What may have originally been a universal set of symbols and speech is not just 'one' set way of communicating. Through evolution, society and culture have given rise to new ways of speaking, thinking, and conversing. We use language to convey information, connect with one another, and understand the world at large. Language is an integral part to life.

So, how does this relate to your child's development in a Montessori framework?

When a child enters a Montessori environment they have already become absorbed in their culture's language. Your child has already constructed a spoken language subconsciously, which is expanded and enhanced through various forms of written language. Articulation, enunciation, and punctuation all need to be honed and expressed, and as the parent you need to assist your child's developmental language journey. Because language is intrinsically connected to thinking and mental processes, children need to be spoken to, listened to, and engaged with regularly. There is not just one way, so speaking often but not listening will not do your child much good, nor will taking a step back and listening but not engaging with them directly. In Montessori, it is important to create a multi or holistic language experience, engaging with your child through interaction and conversation whilst simultaneously being the respectful and helpful listener and 'silent guide.'

The most important thing to be aware of is that a child needs to feel free, non-judged and safe to express themselves, make mistakes, and learn through direct engagement. Up until the age of 6, a child is still very much in their 'absorbent mind,' taking in all sensory data, sounds, and speech. At first everything is unconscious, however over time our child's mind begins to operate more consciously and they become aware that sounds and words have meaning and can apply meaning to them simultaneously. Expanding from this is the knowledge and awareness that these words can be articulated through writing, and further from this in more advanced forms of communication, such as storytelling. Once they leave the Montessori classroom or environment, your children should have such a sound knowledge of both the written and spoken language that daily communication becomes enjoyable and exciting, a real passion for interaction and new vocabulary being expressed.

Dr. Maria Montessori goes on to say, "Language is the central point of difference between the human species and all others. Language lies at the root of that transformation of the environment that we call civilization." [8] Maria Montessori spoke lots about the absorbent mind of which you are already familiar. Language acquisition embodies this concept. You can aid in this acquisition and your child's transformation of simply hearing and absorbing speech and sounds, to the conscious learning and participation stage. The best way to do this is to allow for your child's self-discovery.

"The child must create his interior life before he can express anything; he must take spontaneously from the external world constructive material in order to 'compose'; he must exercise his intelligence fully before he can be ready to find the logical connection between things. We ought to offer the child that which is necessary for his internal life and leave him free to produce." ~ Dr. Maria Montessori. [9]

Language Materials

One of the main components of the Montessori environment relating to language is the creation of a 'writ-

---

8 Quote retrieved from http://www.markedbyteachers.com/gcse/health-and-social-care/language-lies-at-the-root-of-that-transformation-of-the-environment-that-we-call-civilization-how-is-language-encouraged-in-montessori-prepared-environment.html

9 Quote retrieved from from http://montessoritraining.blogspot.com/2010/06/montessori-language-arts-curriculum.html

ing center,' or better yet - multiple writing centers. Writing centers are designated spaces your child knows they can go to to write and express, practice vocabulary, or document their skills and the experiences acquired. It is essential to have everything already on display and ready, including paper, pens and pencils and perhaps some different colored material such as crayons or watercolor pencils. This allows your child complete freedom to move around as they wish and become drawn back to the skill and activity of writing.

A writing center is easily accessible and readily available, enabling your child to stay in complete flow and active participation with their own learning journey. Without a writing center, they would have to wait and could lose interest. Writing centers keep their language interests sparked and in a passionate flow and availability.

A writing center may also include labelling, tracing, image cards, booklets, and material on a range of specialist subjects, such as botany, math, culture, history, and geography. By having these all present there is an option to learn at their own pace, keeping learning in a state of 'open development.' By allowing your child to discover reading and writing, he or she becomes a lifelong reader or writer (as opposed to teaching them, which may cause a loss of interest).

Songs and poems are also an important part of the material available. Having song cards and poems readily at hand can help your child learn about sounds in relation to the symbols (words) on the page/in written form. Songs and poems are particularly effective in integrating new vocabulary and language knowledge, as they provide a certain rhythm and pattern to learning. Music is a universal language and this is often displayed in young children who enjoy dancing or grooving to songs which may randomly play. A poem or written song about nature, for example, will aid in your child's ability to understand what they experience day to day. This is because children are constantly in a state of engagement, listening to bird songs - subconsciously or consciously - and interacting with their natural environment. Songs and poems can help provide the concrete visuals to the sensorial experience, awareness, and interaction occurring.

Here are some ideas into different elements of language and what to use:

- **Enrichment of Vocabulary**: 3-part cards and other materials to increase a child's vocabulary.
- **Development of Writing Skills**: Metal Insets, Sandpaper Letters, and the Moveable Alphabet.
- **The 'Total Reading' Scheme**: Phonetic objects, phonograms, puzzle words, and phonetic

readers.

- **Function of Words**: Montessori grammar symbols defining parts of speech.
- **Reading Analysis**: Sentence Analysis material.
- **Word Study**: Singular/plural, prefixes, suffixes, compound words, etc.

Sequence of Language Material

An exercise particularly useful to share with your children is sequence of language. This provides a pattern for them to learn through, where they have to discover matching, categorizing, and sequencing - what belongs, what doesn't belong, etc. An example of this is to have a list of words with a set vowel sound, where they have to choose which one is out of place. Another example is to use colors and shapes, such as having four colors and one word which is a shape. This allows your child to learn about categorization and grouping in addition to the topic in discussion (colors, shapes, etc.).

The same exercise can be adapted to older children with more complex words and categories.

- **Example 1**: Green - blue - red - circle - yellow
- **Example 2**: Cow - mellow - wow - how - allow

It may seem simple to you, but to a young child this is a very effective exercise in teaching about categorizing and what certain words actually mean. In the second example, word groupings regarding vocabulary show how there is a difference between written material/ words and the sounds (speech). Just because mellow ends with -ow like the other words, it does not mean it sounds or is spoken the same.

The general rule regarding language materials and sequencing is that there is a transition, from concrete to abstract, object to picture, tracing to writing, drawing to writing, and sandpaper letters to moveable alphabet letters.

Language as Preparation for Writing

Ultimately any and all language exercises prepare your child for writing. Writing requires the brain to understand how letters and sounds come together to make words and produce sentences, also requiring fine motor skills and coordination. 'Holding a pencil' may seem effortless to you and I, but this is a new skill which takes practice, effort, and concentration. Phonetic awareness comes with time and language practice and further reflects into writing abilities. In phonetic awareness, the absorbent mind stage needs to become less unconscious and more conscious, your child transitioning into an organizing mental role.

The alphabet is one main example of the organization required for both speaking/language acquisition and writing. You can help with songs, rhymes, poems, and by tracking the words and sentences as you read books to your child. You can also play I-Spy with letters and sounds, encouraging the child to sound out words by him/herself. As they become more and more aware they then begin to understand that putting together letters creates words and putting together words creates sentences. Expanding from this is the moveable alphabet, a tool used in Montessori to aid in language learning.

The moveable alphabet guides the child towards writing as he or she visibly creates words from letters, sentences from words, etc. It is part of the hands-on and practical approach to Montessori learning and one of the main methods used is through the use of sandpaper. Sandpaper is a significant material and approach in Montessori as it provides the child real life materials in use of their learning.

There are important tips and techniques for encouraging writing, which are as follows:

- Use your finger as you read to your child, moving from left to right under the words. This teaches motor skills and helps with the acquisition of learning.

- Sandpaper letters help initiate muscle memory in the hands and fingertips for writing.
- Use salt, sand, and cornmeal writing trays for tracing, as they provide different real life textures.
- Colored pencils, crayons, and drawing materials aid with color memory and grouping.
- Playdough and clay are great for strengthening the hands and improving muscle memory.
- Any type of pouring activity such as chickpeas, beans, lentils or any other dried food source is highly effective at teaching left to right skills.
- Using a chalkboard can aid in the learning of many skills.
- Using tweezers for small objects will help your child acquire the '3 finger grip!'
- Cutting practice with fruits and vegetables is highly effective for aiding in writing and simultaneously teaches about geometry, shapes, and color due to the geometric shapes and patterns inside.
- 'The moveable alphabet.' This can be introduced through a number of different materials.

Language as Preparation for Reading

"To talk is in the nature of man... the letters are a stimulus, which illustrate language already in the mind of the child."~ Maria Montessori.

Unlike writing in which the child has complete control over the language they choose, reading offers something more abstract. Your child must organize and place symbols on other people's words, first studying and analyzing the words before reading and then synthesizing them. Engaging in fun conversations and reading to them are effective methods for language development, as is using flash cards or reading cards. Flash and reading cards provide a visual form of learning for their writing development and reading to them or engaging in conversation and storytelling provides an auditory learning experience.

Mirroring is an effective tool for both reading and speaking as it allows your child to repeat back words said or spoken. They can mirror whatever you say to learn through mimicry.

Practical Life

"When we speak about behavior, we refer to purposeful movements. These behaviors are the center of practical life. It's not just practical life in a home environment such as cleaning rooms, watering planets, etc. that is important, but the fact that each person in our world should move with a purpose and must work; not only for himself but for others too. It's quite strange for some to think that they're doing work as part of a service to other people. But if we don't do this, our work won't be very meaningful. All the work we do is not only for ourselves but also for others. Even something as frivolous as dancing would make no sense if there was nobody to watch the performance. The dancers, keep practicing in order to perfect their movements just so they can dance for the entertainment of others. Tailors spend their time sewing couldn't possible wear all of the garments they make themselves. Yet tailoring, like gymnastics, requires lots of movements.

If you have vision of life's cosmic purpose, that every life which exists is based on this movement with a purpose, you will have a better understanding thus, you can also direct the work of children better. In the beginning, children are urged by nature to be active. They are happy when they are active. they begin to develop the behavior of humanity with its limits and possibilities. Movement is closely connected to psychic life; we must move with intelligence, will, character, etc." [10] ("An Introduction to Practical Life — Montessori Guide", 2019) (Maria Montessori, from the 1946 London Lectures.)

Practical life activities are the activities of everyday life. These can involve cleaning, tidying, engaging in arts and crafts, and organizing. It can also include cooking, baking, and shopping!

There is a large emphasis on the importance and power of practical life activities in Montessori as the child is able to gain real life experience and skills through activities one would experience in a non Montessori environment. There is a sense of purpose and meaning to the activities performed and this can only add to a child's learning and development and understanding of the world. In this respect there is also a notion of culture, defining what it means to be human and part of a community.

Practical life involves the following main areas: Caring for Self, Caring for the Environment, Grace and Courtesy, and Movement of Objects. There are also characteristics of practical life activities, which are as follows.

---

10 An Introduction to Practical Life — Montessori Guide. (2019). Retrieved from https://montessoriguide.org/an-introduction-to-practical-life?fbclid=IwAR16uKr4748nHG3qpsQxdLX5ZPVa3KFqK0ZaJ6HWXF4lhxL7H6DBVkzyXNs

These are important to be aware of, so you recognize the intention of why your child is engaging in the activities. These are as follows:

- **Reality-based**

Reality-based activities are what the name suggests; they are based in reality, such as washing dishes, cleaning and tidying, cleaning shoes, cutting fruit, and tending to plants or the maintenance of environments. There is now 'watered down' activity, for example cutting fruit involves using real knives and polishing shoes involves real materials and real polish.

- **Self-containment**

Materials and exercise activities are contained in set places, introducing the concept of order or structure to your child's learning journey. These may include trays, baskets, boxes, or storage spaces and you as the parent are responsible for ensuring the activity is prepared prior to play and learning. Linking with this is the location of activities and grouping. For example, food activities are in the food area or kitchen, cognitive development activities are all in one place, etc.

- **One activity only**

There is a general rule in Montessori that there should be only one of each activity. This teaches both patience and to not succumb to instant gratification; your child has to wait if the activity is in use by a friend or sibling and there is an increase in appreciation for the exercises available. When there is only one activity that may have to be waited for, its value rises and natural feelings of gratitude are developed over time. This does not take away from having spare or excess activities which can be stored in a different place for your child's access.

- **Unlimited/not limited**

There is a limitless element to practical life activities due to the nature of reality. A number of factors come into effect, such as community, culture, and environment, therefore there is no limit on the number of types of different activities to introduce or choose from. This unlimited aspect also differs from country to country, not just different cultures and communities, so there is great choice for your child or children.

- **Color-coded activities**

Color-coding is highly important in the Montessori method, as it enables children to associate certain activities with color; which is an integral part of life. Other methods related are number coding or shape coding. These can all enhance your child's development.

- **Completion**

Completion is essential as it teaches your child to see something through to the end. This may seem contrary to the idea of freedom expressed earlier, however having completion as one of the fundamental rules and structures means that the child learns how to not give up and stay committed to something and their own development. It also increases self-discipline, patience, and focus and concentration.

- **Sequential, functional, and orderly**

Activities should be sequential - having a beginning, middle, and end. They should be functional, in that they have a clear purpose and intention, such as a learning outcome or skill acquisition. They should be orderly, as this is an important aspect in that it increases the child's ability to learn and keeps things organized and easily found.

- **Child-proportionate and manageable**

You may have heard the saying by Albert Einstein - "Everybody is a genius. But if you judge a fish by its ability to climb a tree, it will live its whole life believing that it is stupid." [11] This applies directly to the Montessori approach. You need to make sure that the materials

---

11 Retrieved from https://www.goodreads.com/quotes/8136665-everybody-is-a-genius-but-if-you-judge-a-fish

you provide are child appropriate and proportionate. There is no use giving your child an adult size knife they don't know how to handle and which may cause safety issues. The same is true for containers, trays, baskets, and all other activity materials presented. Struggle and achievement are important elements to Montessori learning, however things also need to be achievable - there is no point setting your child up for instant failure!

- **Natural materials**

Linking to the previous point is the use of natural materials and objects. These provide a multisensory experience and can teach your child more about real life, preparing them for the real world. Natural materials also often feel or smell nicer and there is nothing stimulating or pleasing about rubbery or fake materials.

- **Order and structure**

As expressed previously, order and structure are necessary (when combined with a child's freedom and choice). Merging with this is the order of easier to more difficult tasks and activities, which can be presented chronologically for the effectiveness of your child's choosing. More complex activities may be placed in one area and easier ones in another. Simultaneously, different groupings can be placed in an orderly way and materials for specific activities can be laid out correctly to show the importance of neatness, order, and presentation.

- **Health and safety**

Like with any educational or learning environment, health and safety are an integral part of Montessori method. The best way to view health and safety is like you would in any normal daily activity. You wouldn't leave a sharp knife sticking out away from the table, or beads or stones on the floor to potentially trip over. Hot water or potential fire spots would have signs and there would be safety precautions for any potentially dangerous or ambiguous situation. The whole intention with Montessori is to not 'molly coddle' your child and to allow them sufficient and healthy freedom and independence. This should be balanced with mindful and appropriate health and safety measures.

- **Community and culture**

Finally, all real life practical activities should have an element of community or culture; where appropriate. Activities should therefore reflect the child's environment, either through specific country, culture, or immediate environment. Religion is something which is also taught in Montessori, but from a holistic and 'all-encompassing' perspective.

a. Caring for Self

Includes dressing, buttoning, tying, zippering, sewing, putting on clothes, hand washing, polishing, and food preparation.

b. Caring for the Environment

Includes table scrubbing, plant watering, dusting, cleaning, cloth washing, towel drying, seed planting, and animal care.

c. Grace and Courtesy

Includes good manners, correct greetings, please and thank yous, correct posture, sitting, silence and stillness, inner calm, listening, patience, and empathy and compassion.

d. Movements of Objects/Basic Procedures

Includes pouring, spooning, cutting, tweezing, opening and closing, folding napkins, walking, hanging towels and coats, sorting, and cleaning.

These elements of practical life can enhance confidence, self-worth and self-esteem, and increase feelings of being respected and appreciated by being given tasks to look after both the environment and one's own self. There is a level of responsibility given through the main areas of practical life activities and tasks and they also prepare your child for the real world.

Try some of the following to include at home:

- Allow your children to dry their own clothes. Hanging clothes helps with developing organizational skills and also aids in fine motor skills.
- Allow your children to pick up their own toys after playing and clean up after themselves. This teaches responsibility, independence, and a sense of autonomy.
- Let your child or children roll up their own mats, put away their cushions, and move objects on their own. The same goes for folding clothes!
- Allow them to develop their fine and gross motor skills through exploring everyday objects freely, such as locks and keys, clothes clips and zippers, buttons, and anything else that is not supremely dangerous. Not only do these develop motor skills but they also provide a feeling of trust and equality, enabling your children to believe they are seen as adults.
- Provide opportunities for 'conscious cleaning,' which allows your child/children to begin looking after themselves and their environment. This is best introduced from age 3.
- Allow your children to water their own plants,

feed the animals and become involved with pet and garden care and maintenance.

- Encourage them to wash their hands, face, and bodies on their own. This may take up more bath time than usual but it will foster independence.
- Get them to arrange books in the book shelf. This will help them to take care of their things.
- Use a variety of different locks and get them to match lock and keys. This activity encourages problem solving behavior.
- Allow the child to help you to put vegetables and fruits in the sink. Prop up a small stool and let them climb up and help you in the kitchen by peeling bananas, carrots or eggs.

Culture

Cultural activities are an integral part of Montessori and are believed to be significantly important to a young child's development. Culture defines us - we are raised in a community, even if that community is a larger society. Societal activities are equally as necessary in the Montessori curriculum and older aged children in traditional Montessori environments frequently go on trips and social events. Walks to local parks or nature spots are common and 'extracurricular' experiences are encouraged. Art, music, culture, and shows are a part of Montessori education yet they are not separate from academic beliefs and perceptions towards learning. Culture, community, and society are seen as equal to math, language and other subjects like science, geography, and history.

As the main focus areas in Montessori are language, math, and practical life skills, however, subjects you often find in mainstream education such as the school system are included in culture and society. Geography, zoology, botany, and the sciences are encompassed and are presented through both written material and books, and images, pictures, puzzles and hands-on activities. Culture encourages children to learn about creation, therefore there are strong creative and artistic ties with the cultural and societal approaches in Montessori method.

Here are some of the positive effects and benefits of immersing your child in cultural and societal activities:

- Encourages creativity and expression.
- Increases awareness of others and the world.
- Encourages tolerance and respect for other cultures, views, and beliefs.
- Embraces multiculturalism.
- Increases compassion and empathy for self and

others.

- Expands a child's mind and perspectives.
- Increases joy and passion for learning, which reflects into other subjects and topics.
- Increases a feeling of connectedness to the world and connection to others.
- Allows for movement and a sense of freedom to explore their community.
- Trips and events can keep energy flowing and provide healthy breaks in routine.

Activities and engagement:

- Allow your child to mingle with other kids. Let them play in a team and share toys with each other. Initially all kids fight over toys but slowly they learn that playing together is more fun.
- Outdoor playing is also important for every child. Take them for walks or play dates in the park.
- Teach him to greet people, to shake hands, and to wish good bye.
- Encourage him to say "Sorry" or apologize for bad behavior.
- Pretend play is another creative method to teach as well as a fun activity. Let them be a

doctor, shopkeeper, teacher, anything of their choice. It is a great way to teach them about team play, money, services, different roles.

Sensorial

Sensorial activities as you may be aware relate to all sensory experiences. They link to practical life activities; however they are not mutually exclusive, as sensorial activities encourage the child to develop their emotional, mental/cognitive, social, and intuitive intelligence, in addition to their practical intelligence and skills. Sensorial activities can increase confidence, self-esteem and feelings of security and connection to others and the world which expand further with an integration of the skills and knowledge involved.

The main point in sensorial activities is that the focus is on the development of your child, with independence and self-sovereignty being in the forefront of priorities. As you know, you are a guide and observer acting as a director or directress for your child's journey. In terms of acquiring sensory knowledge and skills, this ties in perfectly as sensory information and its acquisition is often a personal and unique journey. Children observe, learn, and take in a range of data and information and there are not just the five physical senses (although these are the primary focuses in the first years of development).

In relation to sensorial learning, Maria Montessori stated: "Our sensorial material provides a kind of guide to observation, for it classifies the impressions that each sense can receive: the colors, notes, noises, forms and sizes, touch-sensations, odors and tastes. this undoubtedly is also a form of culture, for it leads us to pay attention both to ourselves and to our surroundings." [12]

The following are aspects to sensorial learning with an associated exercise. Details to some of the exercises can be found at the end of this section.

- Visual - Broad stair
- Olfactory - Smelling bottles
- Gustatory - Tasting bottles
- Tactile - Rough and Smooth boards
- Visual Geometry - Triangle box
- Auditory - Sound cylinders
- Stereognostic - Mystery bag

The aims of sensorial activities are to develop concentration, acquire attention, and achieve visual discrimination. Math, reading, and writing come into sensorial activity, however not directly.

For the Visual Sense Exercises, children learn visual discrimination as they try to spot the differences between

12 Retrieved from https://greenspringmontessori.org/the-childs-absorbent-mind/

differing objects and similar objects. For the Tactile Sense Exercises, children learn through their sense of touch, allowing them to focus on what they're feeling through concentration on a small part of their body. The Auditory Sense Exercises are where your child can discriminate between different sounds. All of these sense exercises enhance the sensitivity of children to everything in their environments.

For the Gustatory and Olfactory Sense Exercises children get to experience their senses of taste and smell. Of course, not all kinds of tastes and smells are provided to the children for these exercises. But they get to learn how to distinguish one taste from another or one smell from another. Then they can apply these sensations to what they experience in the environment. Finally, for the Stereognostic Sense Exercises children learn to feel different objects and recognize them based on what they feel.

- Sensory activities will help the child to explore their five senses – sight, smell, sound, touch, and taste. For sensory play activities, you can DIY (Do It Yourself) at home or buy some minimal supplies from the store.
- The texture of homemade or store-bought play doh is a great sensory activity for toddlers. They can use the rolling pin and cookie cutters to cut

out different shapes. It is a great way to boost their creativity. You can also use food color to make different colored dough.

- Spend a day exploring crayons, color pencils, and paints. Expose your child to the world of colors with finger painting, thread painting, and vegetable painting etc. Let them color, scribble as per their whim. You can also ask your child to color on uneven surfaces like sandpaper or different textured papers.
- Different musical instruments like flute, drums, and keyboard also appeal to toddlers a lot. Let them explore the sound coming from each instrument. You can also start singing songs and ask your child to join.

Music and Art

Music and art are an integral part of Montessori play and learning. Without going into too much depth, here are some fundamental principles you need to know to provide your child with the best Montessori background.

Art

Art can be defined as explorative, creative, child led, and imaginative. Art in a Montessori environment taps into your child's patience, thoughtfulness and mindfulness, and uniqueness; and focuses on the process and not the product. Expressing themselves through art allows your children to tune in to their sensitive and empathic nature, connecting to a range of ideas from nature, culture and their connection to others, whilst tapping in to their academic side simultaneously. A child's art can be seen as a reflection of their beliefs, thoughts, feelings, and inner world or at least a mirror of what they are beginning to discover.

Here are just some of the benefits of including art into your child's life and curriculum:

- Sensory development and perception
- Fine motor development and control
- Cognitive development
- Emotional intelligence and connection
- Empathy
- Freedom of expression
- Creates feelings of joy, happiness, and excitement
- Allows for peace and inner stillness
- It can develop language and vocabulary
- Develops attention to detail and awareness of a range of important topics, such as animals welfare or the environment

- Increases concentration and focus
- Enhances memory and recall through visual imagery

There are many things you can do to enhance your child's ability to engage in art, express themselves freely, and feel passionate about doing so. Some of these are:

- Learning about the impact of creativity on learning and development
- Educating yourself on the power of art and its effect on cognitive functioning
- Being open minded to artistic expression
- Understanding that art is not about perfection or the end result but about your child's progress and sense of fun and engagement
- Providing the correct materials
- Providing variety for your child

Preparing an artistic environment for your child or children can include creating ground rules to be followed, creating specific structures and frameworks; having a designated art space, stocking up on supplies, and ensuring the correct storage methods are in place.

Some of the art supplies you may consider purchasing in alignment with the Montessori method are: cotton balls, q-tips, paint brushes, watercolor paper, watercolor pens and pencils, craft sand, aprons, paint, crayons, sponges, small storage trays, paint trays, small glass jars for water, glue, dispensing bottles.

Finally, to create your own art class do the following:

- Observe your child and determine their needs.
- Determine their likes, dislikes, and passions/areas of interest.
- Establish an aim or intention to work towards (a framework).
- Gather the sufficient materials.
- Create a structure for the exercises and activities.
- Educate yourself on the basics of art.
- Engage in the exercise(s) yourself.
- Present them to your children!

Chapter 5: The Human Tendencies

The human tendencies are a set of characteristics introduced by the approach centered in human development observations by Dr. Montessori. They are unchanging, universal, and individual - they allow us to survive and adapt to our environments. These tendencies are also described around emotional intelligences, creativity, and social and emotional learning and are connected to the planes and stages of development, however not exclusive to them.

Maria Montessori believed these stimulate children within society. The best reference to the human tendencies is found from Ruffing Montessori School and, therefore, will be shared as is written on their website. Some of these you are already knowledgeable of, however it is useful to include them all in this topic to provide the whole picture. The basic human tendencies are:

- Self-Perfection

It is the development of the person to a point that is satisfying to the person himself. As educators, it is the aim of the Montessori teacher to teach the children so that they can control themselves and this is done through the environment itself.

- Order

The tendency for order helps in the understanding of one's surroundings. For a child it means she/he has the need for predictable events in her/his life; for example, an ordered environment where everything has a certain place. As educators, we provide an ordered environment with things in a well-defined place.

- Exactness

It is the desire to be precise and constant so that things are objective. It is a necessary tendency to survive (to maintain stability and prevent accidents). As educators, we give the child the freedom to repeat an activity until it reaches a point of exactness. He/she is shown exactly how to properly use the materials.

- Manipulation

It is the tendency to touch and to handle one's surroundings to give control over an activity. A child has the need to touch, feel, and to experience the physical world. As educators, we must give the child this experience through Montessori materials in language, math, and science.

- **Repetition**

This tendency is the ability to do over and over again an exercise in order to reach perfection and to experience the joy of increased control and understanding of one's world. When a child is not satisfied with her/his performance in one activity or does not get any joy from it, she/he will repeat the same exercise several times. As educators, we must provide materials that are easily accessible and allowable to be used over and over again.

- **Creativity**

This along with creative expression are fundamental aspects to the Montessori approach to learning and development. Spontaneity, joyfulness, and creative freedom are key expressions here. This tendency refers to our natural ability to be resourceful, artistic, innovative, and being able to express this through our words and actions.

- **Abstraction**

It is the ability to reason beyond the limits of the concrete as well as to generalize and interpret. This tendency will not develop in a child unless she/he has had enough concrete experience. As educators, we must allow concrete experiences through the materials in order for these to provide a solid understanding of the concepts intended.

- Exploration

This tendency is the curiosity leading to explore and the desire to understand. It renders living better materially and spiritually. We are all potential explorers with a tremendous desire to learn, research, read, and travel. As educators, we can easily see that children are the best explorers and they must have the freedom to explore as rich an environment as possible.

- Communication

This tendency is the ability for living beings to understand each other as well as to be understood. This takes the three forms of speaking, writing, and reading. As educators, freedom of speech, listening, and storytelling help enable speaking. Research and creative writing help to develop writing. Reading by the child is nurtured through reading to the child by the adult, as well as preparatory exercises in the classroom.

There are other human tendencies which include:

- Orientation

This tendency is the ability to orient oneself in new situations. For a child it means that she/he needs to know where and how she/he fits into a particular time or environment and how to adapt. As educators, we must give the child the freedom and the information necessary to his/her orientation without too much guidance.

- Activity

It is the ability to move which involves both the mind and body. A child is restless and needs constant activity which seems purposeless to the adult. As educators, we must give the child the freedom to move around.

- Work

The tendency to work is related to the tendencies of activity and manipulation. It is the ability to put into reality what the imagination suggests. It enables independence and dignity as well as a feeling of rest. As educators, we realize the child's need for his/her self-construction and we must therefore never judge or stop a child's work, realizing that his/her goals are different than ours. We must also give the child the freedom to work at her/his own pace in a stimulating and appropriate environment.

Spend time noticing these tendencies in your child as well as yourself!" [13] ("Human Tendencies and Montessori | Ruffing Montessori School", 2019)

Other human tendencies which can also be included here are sensory learning, sensitive periods, self-discipline, and concentration. Concentration, when observed, requires a child's total engagement; their attention is usually completely absorbed in whatever they are trying to pursue or achieve. That naturally requires self-discipline and shows how each of the human tendencies are linked to one another. In Montessori, there is an interconnected web of principles and tendencies, arguably making the Montessori method a holistic approach to learning and development.

Developing Basic Human Tendencies through Montessori

All humans received wonderful gifts of love, reason, will, and intelligence. All of us have the power to change as well as to adapt to whatever environment we are in based on what we need. Unlike animals, human beings have evolved in a special way which has

---

13 Human Tendencies and Montessori | Ruffing Montessori School. (2019). Retrieved from http://ruffingmontessori.net/home/about/why-montessori/montessori-articles/human-tendencies/

endowed us with movement, instincts, and intelligence. Basically, there are three fundamental needs which are crucial to our survival: shelter, clothing, and food. In the past, our ancestors always searched for ways to thrive by sustaining these fundamental needs ever since they came into existence. Their ability to satisfy their need for food happened because they searched for, found, and also experimented with that which they needed to live.

But apart from our human needs, we also have human tendencies. In fact, one of the most significant discoveries of Maria Montessori was that all human beings have certain behavior patterns or "tendencies." No matter where you are in the world, no matter what culture you have, or what ethnic group you belong to, you follow the same natural laws as everyone else. Those which lead all human beings to react or act in a certain way.

These human tendencies exist at all ages in our lives. But some of these tendencies are much more evident than the others during the various developmental periods. Also, human tendencies vary in terms of how they manifest in different people and how strong these human tendencies are in them. One thing's for sure, all of these human tendencies are present in one form or another in each human being. And these tendencies guide us as we grow and develop. They direct us to either take or not take a specific action.

In children who are 3 to 6 years of age, you can readily witness these human tendencies. Children at these ages always want to talk and they tend to manifest their tendencies in the way they make use of the new vocabulary that they learn. They have a desire to socialize and so they love being with other children. They also tend to imitate what those around them are doing. They're precise because they want the people around them (especially their parents) to do the same things each and every time. They also want to do the same things which interest them repeatedly.

For young children, these tendencies aren't just a part of them. These tendencies are the masters of the child and he is their slave. Because these tendencies are the nature of the child, he is compelled to follow them. Of course, this isn't an issue since these tendencies actually take us to where we must go. These tendencies drive children to learn, to improve themselves, and to gain proficiency in the knowledge and skills that they are learning. They guide the children and help them learn the truth of their existence.

So how can Montessori develop these human tendencies in children?

When the basic tendencies of children are respected and understood, children become "normalized," a term coined by Maria Montessori. Normalized children have a sense of inner tranquility, joy, happiness, and peace. Because of this, they're able to concentrate on what they want to do and what they are supposed to do. They're able to select a material or activity to work on and keep at it all the way to the end. They're able to make rational decisions and deal with feelings of frustration. They're able to adapt, they have self-control, they have self-discipline, they're independent, and they feel secure. These children also have a positive self-image, adequate self-esteem, they're aware of other people and they show consideration. With all of these good things, let's discuss how Montessori helps develop the basic human tendencies one at a time:

Self-Perfection

This human tendency has something to do with basic physiological needs, basic survival, and psychological and physical safety. Human beings often forget that we're not just a physical body. We are composed of a body, a mind, and a spirit all of which work together. Therefore, we must work in order to assimilate these three aspects.

Whenever you do work which fulfills the needs of your mind, body, and spirit this makes you feel energized, rested, and motivated. A huge part of our humanity is when we feel the need to be loved or to belong to a specific group. Human beings need both emotional and mental support. We need to build a social life in order for us to be able to interact with others and gain the support of our own culture.

When we're able to have a social life, we are able to learn everything we need to so that we can function as a useful part of society. There are collective rules which can help us understand what's right and what's wrong in our society. Fulfilling spiritual needs is also important as this gives us a sense of belonging to our own community as we all influence one another.

Self-perfection as a human tendency is something which we start developing from our early years. In the Montessori setting, children work towards self-perfection by doing work which fulfills the needs of their mind, body, and spirit. As children come into the Montessori class, they explore the environment until they are drawn to a certain activity or material. They work with these and start thinking about what they want the outcome of the activity to be.

Since this activity develops this tendency, the children keep working on it as they also seek for precision and order. They don't feel satisfaction until they feel that they have achieved exactness. With the self-correcting materials, children are able to notice imperfections thus, they're able to control their own errors. They continue working with the same activity repetitively until they've achieved "perfection."

This concept of perfection is in the minds of the children themselves. It isn't something which is assigned by the teacher. When children are given the freedom to do work until they've achieved the results they want, they experience a profound sense of satisfaction from it.

Order

Humans are able to develop this tendency through exploration and order. We gather all of our experiences, take into consideration the discoveries we have made, then we start categorizing these experiences while trying to make sense of them. Through order, humans are able to come up with a sense of security and predictability. Therefore, we're able to establish a sense of order within our own selves. External order is important as it helps us create order within ourselves.

If there is no order, there is also no quality to life. This is because we would always feel completely lost. Apart from security, one of the most essential things you can give children is order. Through this, you will be able to set reference points which, in turn, help the child start making sense of his environment.

As humans, we need two kinds of order, external and internal. When you provide children with an orderly environment (hence the "prepared environment" of Montessori), you will be able to help children develop an internal sense of order as well. Without this order, the children won't feel secure. When things keep changing and there's no order in the environment, children will never know what they should expect and when they should expect things to happen.

It's important for children to internalize the concept of order. When they're able to do this, they will also be able to learn other concepts like logical thinking, sorting, sequencing, and so on. Both children and adults need external and internal order. These help eliminate the chaos in our minds and our lives. Creating systems and schedules in the classroom are great ways to keep the order. Routines allow children to know what happens next and so they start feeling steadier and safer in their environment.

Exactness

This tendency is our ability to get what we need in the quickest and most efficient way possible. Using "control of error," we are able to move towards self-perfection which, in turn, allows us to perform tasks with more efficiency and exactness. And when we're able to accomplish our work faster and in a better way, we're also able to conserve energy. Doing work exactly right provides us with enormous satisfaction. This is important for children too as it enables them to consciously control themselves.

It's a fact that all humans tend to seek precision or exactness. Even children have this innate tendency to seek exactness in the work they do. To achieve this, they utilize other tendencies such as order, repetition, and manipulation in order for them to achieve a sense of exactness that's highly satisfying.

Have you ever observed children when they see someone put something back but in the wrong place? More often than not, children will either feel frustrated or upset. This is because this action contradicts their natural tendency towards exactness. In the Montessori classroom, you will also notice children lining up objects or materials neatly before they start working. This is because they have an instinct to do their work exactly right in order to feel satisfaction from it.

Manipulation

The term "manipulation" has a Latin origin as it comes from the word *manus* which means "hands." This literally means that we humans need to manipulate objects with our hands in order to gain a better understanding of them. This is especially true for children who are very inquisitive and exploratory. When children are born, they have an innate need to hold, touch, and shape the environment they are in. They learn how to use manipulation along with exploration and with how they express their imagination.

As human beings, we must take hold of our environment in order to understand it. This is the next step we must take after we have explored our environment. Children are the same way. After finding something which makes them feel interested, they have the natural desire to use or manipulate it one way or another. For our ancient ancestors, this is how the concept of using "tools" started.

Children love to move. They're often restless and they find immense enjoyment in physical activities. But there is a purpose for these movements and that it to gain self-mastery and self-control. Also, children love to manipulate the things around them constantly. In the Montessori classroom, this manifests as they pile blocks, manipulate gears, sort objects, and more. This manipulation allows them to comprehend how their world works and how they affect the world around them. In effect, this is the "true work" of children which is recognized by the Montessori method. In Montessori, the teachers encourage children to keep on manipulating their environment and the objects in it until they feel satisfied and find other things to manipulate or work with.

Repetition

By definition, this occurs when you keep doing the same thing over and over again. On some level, each individual has a drive to feel interested towards his environment then to reach out and grab a hold of it. After that, he starts concentrating, takes focus, collects energies, and repeats his work again and again. Repetition allows us to master all of the skills we need to survive. The more efficient we become, the more we strive for self-perfection. Although we can't really achieve self-perfection, we constantly strive for it anyway.

Keep in mind that the concept of perfection varies from one person to another, from one child to another. The more important thing is to feel confident about the decisions the person has made. It's also important for people to do what's needed in order to fulfill their own satisfaction. When you look at it this way, it's quite possible to achieve some degree of perfection when you're able to satisfy your needs.

In order to achieve satisfaction, you must achieve conscious self-mastery. Upon doing this, your mind, body, and spirit are satisfied. In turn, you feel fresh, happy, and energized. Think of it this way, if your spirit was behind all of the work you did and you were able to accomplish it successfully, you will feel rested since what your spirit wanted, you were able to achieve. Because of the continuous process of striving for perfection, you become more efficient in terms of the work you do. There are even times when even after you've gained mastery, you keep repeating the activity because it brings you pleasure and satisfaction.

In the same way, children have an innate tendency to repeat tasks which interest them again and again. They keep choosing the same activity as they work towards mastering it. According to Maria Montessori, this repetition only gets completed when children have decided that they're done. This might mean that they feel like they've mastered the activity already. Children who are engaged in repetition are often extremely focused. This helps them master the task at hand. Also, the heightened concentration enhances their sense of accomplishment after they've completed the task.

Creativity

There is a misconception that joyous spontaneity and order and structure need to be seen in opposition. Creativity and contentment in one's learning are not disharmonious to academic order! Meeting the developmental needs of children in a free and orderly environment is joy and freedom of expression. Every child has an inner teacher driving him in his development, picking from the environment those activities which allow him to grow. When the environment is rich in activity and the child is lovingly introduced to them, allowed to move freely to select what he needs, a transformation that leads to joy and contentment can be seen. Life is essentially creativity and expression.

You cannot force a child to be happy or joyous, regardless of your intentions and will. Joy must come from directly inside your child - they must genuinely want to learn and explore through the sheer excitement and new skills creative expression brings. You can of course be the guide and create environments and opportunities for creative freedom and expression, however you cannot force anything. there is an element of spontaneity which comes with the freedom of choice and open nature of the classroom, or home Montessori environment you have created. The child's own personal development is a powerful sense of joy and excitement in itself.

It is important to note that joy in a developmental creative sense is not always supreme uncontrolled giggles or sheer laughter; joy can be calm and serene. There is a sense of inner joy and contentment that comes with learning and your child knows this. This is why creative environments outdoors or in nature are extremely beneficial, and why it is important you look towards 'non-classroom' activities and channels of learning to express Montessori curriculum through.

Abstraction

Human beings have this tendency which comes along with our higher level of intelligence compared to other animals. The only limit to our imagination is our bodies. And abstraction or imagination isn't possible for people who don't have a firm grasp of reality. Through abstraction, people have the ability to visualize situations or events which haven't even happened yet. They can also express feelings or have emotions which aren't tangible. Through this tendency, we can imagine things which don't exist then work towards making them happen.

Even children have the tendency of abstraction or imagination. However, this won't develop in children unless they've had adequate concrete experiences. Therefore, teachers allow children to have these concrete experiences as they work with the activities and materials in the classroom. These provide the children with a better understanding of the intended concepts. With enough concrete concepts, children can start imagining. With the proper tools and enough freedom to express their abstractions, children are able to make these a reality.

Exploration

Exploration is another tendency for the fulfillment of basic human needs. By nature, humans are explorers. Exploration helps us learn more about our environment in order to find the best possible route to take and learn everything we need for survival so that we can live a comfortable and happy life.

Children love exploring as well and they do this to adapt, to feel secure, and to gain a sense of achievement or accomplishment. Children are able to construct themselves through the experiences they have with their environment. Learning to accept and incarnate the world exactly as it is allows children to adapt easily and completely to any kind of society. Children love exploration. They have a natural curiosity which compels them to look for new sensations and new places. The Montessori method encourages this tendency as it allows children to explore freely in a safe environment.

Communication

This human tendency allows people to share their feelings and thoughts with each other. As a species, we are emotional by nature thus, we need to be able to share all of our thoughts effectively with one another. This helps us understand ourselves, the people around us, as well as the world we are in. Communication is closely linked to our need as humans to be active or to work. We must act together with other people, our environment, animals, objects, plants, and even ourselves. This tendency helps us learn and it gives us a chance to think in a different way.

Communication is an essential tendency which allows us to share information from one person to another. Children use communication as well. They make use of speech, gestures, and facial expressions in order to communicate what they need. Ultimately, this tendency allows children to learn reading and the written word. The good news is that in Montessori, communication is also encouraged and it can come in many different forms. Here, children learn how to communicate with each other, with their teachers, and with themselves too.

Conclusion

Applying the Montessori Method at Home

The Montessori method was developed over 100 years ago by Maria Montessori, the Italian physician. This method of learning focuses on the belief that all children have the capacity to independently initiate their learning experiences. Montessori schools and classrooms contain a compelling combination of activities and materials which are specifically designed to develop learners who are well rounded. This means that the children who learn through the Montessori method are challenged emotionally, socially, physically, and cognitively.

Montessori isn't an unknown term in the world of education. Even though parents may not know what Montessori is all about, they must have already heard of it. One of the best things about Montessori is that children can learn through this method even in the comfort of their own home. From the Introduction of this book all the way to Chapter 5, you have learned a lot about Montessori.

When it comes to applying the Montessori method and its principles at home, there are some things you must do. Now that you've learned more about the different areas of Montessori, you have a better idea of the types of materials and activities you can create (or purchase) for your child. But the Montessori method isn't just about the materials and activities. Before we end our book, here are some final tips to guide you:

- **Prepare the environment**

When it comes to the prepared environment of Montessori, keep in mind that there's always a place for everything and everything must always be in its place. Assign one of the rooms in your home as your child's Montessori learning environment. If there are Montessori schools in your area, go ahead and visit them to have a better idea of how to arrange this room.

You may also go online and search for Montessori classroom ideas on Google or Pinterest. Either way, having a visual image of what Montessori classrooms must look like will give you a better idea of how to arrange the room you've assigned in your own home. One thing to keep in mind though is to make sure that everything is child-sized and at your child's level so that he won't keep asking you for assistance when he wants to take something.

- **Plan all the materials and activities to include in your child's environment**

After planning the environment, it's time to think about the materials and activities to place inside that environment. You can go online to search for a complete list of Montessori materials in each of the learning areas. Then you can either purchase similar materials (actual Montessori materials are very expensive) or create them on your own. For instance, you can easily create sandpaper letters and numbers using thick cardboard and sandpaper.

Arrange these materials and activities according to their areas of learning and make sure that all of them are accessible to your child. You may want to include a combination of easy materials and those which are a bit more challenging or unfamiliar to your child. Also, you may want to rotate these items regularly so your child doesn't get bored. If you see that he's not interested in some activities or he has already mastered others and he's not using them anymore, take these materials out and replace them with new ones.

- **Focus on life skills**

As previously mentioned, activities and materials which teach life skills are the easiest ones to replicate. It's important for children to learn life skills early on. With these skills, children learn how to care for themselves and their environment. This sets children up to become capable and considerate adults when they grow up. Providing the proper materials to teach these skills even makes your life as a parent a lot easier! Soon, your child will start volunteering to help you around the house because he already knows how to do these chores.

Of course, you must always match the activities and materials to the abilities and age of your child. Introducing activities which are too difficult for children is never a good idea. Obviously, your child won't be able to do these activities and if you force him, this might weaken his self-confidence and his willingness to continue with the rest of the activities you've prepared.

- **Help your child learn concentration and inner motivation**

These skills are essential if you want your child to get the most out of the Montessori method. In order for a child to master a skill, concept or activity, he must concentrate while doing it. If you have prepared the environment well, your child will be able to concentrate on the activities you have prepared for him. This means that there should be no distractions such as gadgets, electronic devices, and random toys which don't really have a purpose inside the room.

Also, avoid giving your child rewards when he does something good or gains proficiency in something. Try to observe your child at the moment he realizes that he has finally been able to master a puzzle or a practical life activity. You will see a sense of accomplishment in your child. This is much more valuable than extrinsic rewards because this sense of accomplishment becomes the driving force within your child to keep on going in order to master the other activities in his environment.

- **Take on the role of a Montessori teacher**

Finally, learning how to facilitate the Montessori method for your child is also essential. Rather than teaching everything to your child, allow him to discover, explore, and choose the materials and activities on his own. If your child asks for help, oblige. If not, observe.

You may also step in if your child picks up a material and can't figure out how to use it. Again, he will probably ask you to help him out. These are the best and most appropriate times to step in when it comes to the Montessori method. Then when your child celebrates his mastery of a skill, celebrate with him! There's nothing more satisfying than to see your child grow, develop, and improve at his own pace and through his own efforts.

Montessori is truly a wonderful learning approach. Whether it's done in school or at home, children love learning through this method mainly because of how it's done. Now that you've learned all the basics about Montessori, you may start planning how you will apply this in your home. Then step back and watch your child learn in the best possible way!

Biblography

Berkshiremontessori.org. (2019). *The Montessori Difference / Planes of Development*. [online] Available at: https://www.berkshiremontessori.org/Page/76 [Accessed 25 Apr. 2019].

Burke, M. (2019). *What is a Montessori School? 5 Benefits of a Montessori School.*. [online] Carrots Are Orange. Available at: https://carrotsareorange.com/montessori-school-benefits/ [Accessed 25 Apr. 2019].

Education.com. (2019). *10 Benefits of a Montessori Preschool | Education.com*. [online] Available at: https://www.education.com/magazine/article/10-benefits-montessori-preschool/ [Accessed 25 Apr. 2019].

Guidepost Montessori. (2019). *What Makes Us Different—Why The Montessori Method Is Unique | Guidepost Montessori*. [online] Available at: https://guidepostmontessori.com/blog/why-montessori-method [Accessed 25 Apr. 2019].

Internationalschool.info. (2019). *Special Teachers: The True Essence of Montessori Schooling | LittleStar Magazine Online*. [online] Available at:

http://www.internationalschool.info/special-teachers-the-true-essence-of-montessori-schooling/ [Accessed 25 Apr. 2019].

Montessori Education. (2019). *Montessori Sensitive Periods And How To Implement Them At Home Sensitive Periods - Daily Montessori*. [online] Available at: http://www.dailymontessori.com/sensitive-periods/montessori-sensitive-periods/ [Accessed 25 Apr. 2019].

Montessori-namta.org. (2019). *Ages and Stages*. [online] Available at: http://www.montessori-namta.org/ages-and-stages [Accessed 25 Apr. 2019].

Montessoritrainingusa.com. (2019). [online] Available at: https://www.montessoritrainingusa.com/sites/montessoritrainingusa.com/files/Six%20Sensitive%20Periods.pdf [Accessed 25 Apr. 2019].

Motherly. (2019). *Montessori at home: Giving your child 'purposeful work' could be a game-changer*. [online] Available at: https://www.mother.ly/montessori-at-home-giving-your-child-purposeful-work-could-be-a-game-changer [Accessed 20 Apr. 2019].

Mpswaco.com. (2019). *STAGES OF DEVELOPMENT IN A CHILD | Montessori Preparatory School*. [online] Available at: https://mpswaco.com/stages-of-development-in-a-child-2 [Accessed 25 Apr. 2019].

Omni-montessori.org. (2019). *Planes of Development*. [online] Available at: http://www.omni-montessori.org/montessori-education/planes-of-development/ [Accessed 25 Apr. 2019].

Prince George Montessori Education Society. (2019). *History of Montessori - Prince George Montessori Education Society*. [online] Available at: https://pgmontessori.ca/history-of-montessori/ [Accessed 25 Apr. 2019].

Rasmussen.edu. (2019). *The Pros & Cons of Montessori Education | Rasmussen College*. [online] Available at: https://www.rasmussen.edu/degrees/education/blog/pros_cons_montessori_education/ [Accessed 25 Apr. 2019].

Thinkamajigs. (2019). *All About Montessori's 4 Stages Of Growth*. [online] Available at: https://www.thinkamajigs.com/blog/all-about-montessoris-4-stages-of-growth/ [Accessed 25 Apr. 2019].

This Toddler Life. (2019). *MONTESSORI SENSITIVE PERIODS BIRTH - 3 YEARS - This Toddler Life*. [online] Available at: https://thistoddlerlife.com/montessori-sensitive-periods/ [Accessed 25 Apr. 2019].

Edutrends is about everything related to good practices in education. (2019). *THE SCHOOL AS AN OPEN SYSTEM*. [online] Available at: https://euniceacheampong.wordpress.com/2014/11/26/the-school-as-an-open-system/ [Accessed 25 Apr. 2019].

Lifetimemontessorischool.com. (2019). *Making Choices | Lifetime Montessori School*. [online] Available at: https://lifetimemontessorischool.com/making-choices [Accessed 25 Apr. 2019].

Managementhelp.org. (2019). [online] Available at: https://managementhelp.org/misc/orgs-open-systems.pdf [Accessed 25 Apr. 2019].

Montessori Academy. (2019). *How to Recognise and Support Sensitive Periods in Your Child's Development - Montessori Academy*. [online] Available at: https://montessoriacademy.com.au/how-to-recognise-and-support-sensitive-periods-in-your-childs-development/ [Accessed 25 Apr. 2019].

Montessori Academy. (2019). *Montessori Philosophy of Education | Montessori Academy*. [online] Available at: https://montessoriacademy.com.au/about/montessori-philosophy/ [Accessed 25 Apr. 2019].

Montessori Academy. (2019). *Montessori Philosophy of Education | Montessori Academy*. [online] Available at: https://montessoriacademy.com.au/about/montessori-philosophy/ [Accessed 25 Apr. 2019].

Montessori Guide. (2019). *An Introduction to Practical Life — Montessori Guide*. [online] Available at: https://montessoriguide.org/an-introduction-to-practical-life?

fbclid=IwAR16uKr4748nHG3qpsQxdLX5ZPVa3KFqK0ZaJ6HWXF4lhxL7H6DBVkzyXNs [Accessed 25 Apr. 2019].

Montessori Teacher Training and Parent Resources. (2019). *The Significance of Sensitive Periods - Montessori Teacher Training and Parent Resources*. [online] Available at: http://ageofmontessori.org/significance-sensitive-periods/ [Accessed 25 Apr. 2019].

Montessori Teacher Training and Parent Resources. (2019). *Montessori and Freedom of Choice*. [online] Available at: http://ageofmontessori.org/montessori-and-freedom-of-choice/ [Accessed 25 Apr. 2019].

Montessori Teacher Training and Parent Resources. (2019). *Top Ten Helpful Montessori Tips for Parents*. [online] Available at: http://ageofmontessori.org/top-ten-helpful-montessori-tips-for-parents/ [Accessed 25 Apr. 2019].

Montessori-esf.org. (2019). [online] Available at: https://montessori-esf.org/sites/default/files/downloads/files/180811StanFerguson.pdf [Accessed 25 Apr. 2019].

Ourkids.net. (2019). *Montessori Education | Montessori Method & Philosophy*. [online] Available at: https://www.ourkids.net/montessori-education-philosophy.php [Accessed 25 Apr. 2019].

Step By Step Montessori Schools and Child Care Centers. (2019). *Sensitive Periods in Child Development - Step By*

Step Montessori Schools and Child Care Centers - MN. [online] Available at: https://www.stepbystepmontessori.com/2018/07/25/sensitive-periods-in-child-development/ [Accessed 25 Apr. 2019].

Winans, S. (2019). *What is the Montessori approach to education?*. [online] Bundoo. Available at: https://www.bundoo.com/articles/what-is-the-montessori-approach-to-education/ [Accessed 25 Apr. 2019].

Yonkerspublicschools.org. (2019). *Montessori Philosophy / What is Montessori Education?*. [online] Available at: https://www.yonkerspublicschools.org/domain/2908 [Accessed 25 Apr. 2019].

Antigonishmontessori.com. (2019). *Make Good Choices! | Antigonish Montessori*. [online] Available at: http://www.antigonishmontessori.com/2015/03/05/make-good-choices/ [Accessed 25 Apr. 2019].

Arborland Montessori Children's Academy. (2019). *Building Compassion and Empathy in Children*. [online] Available at: http://www.arborland.com/building-compassion-empathy-children/ [Accessed 25 Apr. 2019].

Carrots Are Orange. (2019). *The Ultimate Guide to Montessori Math*. [online] Available at: https://carrotsareorange.com/montessori-math/ [Accessed 25 Apr. 2019].

Carrots Are Orange. (2019). *The Ultimate Guide to Montessori Language*. [online] Available at: https://carrotsareorange.com/montessori-language/ [Accessed 25 Apr. 2019].

Chitwood, D. (2019). *Montessori Math Activities*. [online] Living Montessori Now. Available at: https://livingmontessorinow.com/montessori-math-activities/ [Accessed 25 Apr. 2019].

Infomontessori.com. (2019). *Montessori - Mathematics - Introduction*. [online] Available at: http://www.infomontessori.com/mathematics/introduction.htm [Accessed 25 Apr. 2019].

Meadow Montessori School. (2019). *Making Good Choices - Meadow Montessori School*. [online] Available at: http://www.meadowmontessori.com/making-good-choices/ [Accessed 25 Apr. 2019].

Montessori Nature. (2019). *Secrets of Clutter-free Montessori Home*. [online] Available at: https://www.montessorinature.com/clutter-free-montessori-home/ [Accessed 25 Apr. 2019].

Montessori Print Shop. (2019). *Language Training in the Montessori Classroom*. [online] Available at: https://www.montessoriprintshop.com/language-training.html [Accessed 25 Apr. 2019].

Montessori Rocks. (2019). *Empathy: A True Lesson in the Montessori Classroom - Montessori Rocks*. [online] Available at: https://montessorirocks.org/empathy-a-true-lesson-in-the-montessori-classroom/ [Accessed 25 Apr. 2019].

Montessori Teacher Training and Parent Resources. (2019). *5 Excellent Ways to Teach Empathy - Montessori Teacher Training and Parent Resources*. [online] Available at: http://ageofmontessori.org/5-awesome-ways-teach-empathy/ [Accessed 25 Apr. 2019].

Ourkids.net. (2019). *Montessori curriculum | OurKids.net*. [online] Available at: https://www.ourkids.net/school/montessori-curriculum [Accessed 25 Apr. 2019].

Psychology Today. (2019). *Montessori: A Good School Choice for Smart Kids?*. [online] Available at: https://www.psychologytoday.com/ca/blog/going-beyond-intelligence/201701/montessori-good-school-choice-smart-kids [Accessed 25 Apr. 2019].

Wbms.org. (2019). *What is the Montessori Curriculum?*. [online] Available at: http://www.wbms.org/blog/what-is-the-montessori-curriculum [Accessed 25 Apr. 2019].

Whattoexpect. (2019). *The Montessori Curriculum | What to Expect*. [online] Available at: https://www.whattoexpect.com/family/the-montessori-curriculum [Accessed 25 Apr. 2019].

Chesapeake Montessori School. (2019). *Elementary Programs Series: Art & Music | Chesapeake Montessori*. [online] Available at: https://chesapeakemontessorischool.com/art-music/ [Accessed 25 Apr. 2019].

Children First Montessori School. (2019). *Cultural Areas - Children First Montessori School*. [online] Available at: http://www.cfmontessori.us/practical-life/cultural-areas/ [Accessed 25 Apr. 2019].

Chitwood, D. (2019). *Montessori Sensorial Activities*. [online] Living Montessori Now. Available at: https://livingmontessorinow.com/montessori-sensorial-activities/ [Accessed 25 Apr. 2019].

Guidepost Montessori. (2019). *The Importance of Practical Life Activities Within the Montessori Method | Guidepost Montessori*. [online] Available at: https://guidepostmontessori.com/blog/practical-life-activities-montessori-method [Accessed 25 Apr. 2019].

Hart, L. (2019). *Montessori Learning Through Sensorial Work - Silverline Montessori*. [online] Silverline Montessori. Available at: https://silverlinemontessori.com/montessori-learning-sensorial-work/ [Accessed 25 Apr. 2019].

Infomontessori.com. (2019). *Montessori - Language - Introduction*. [online] Available at: http://www.infomontessori.com/language/introduction.htm [Accessed 25 Apr. 2019].

Infomontessori.com. (2019). *Montessori - Practical Life - Introduction*. [online] Available at: http://www.infomontessori.com/practical-life/introduction.htm [Accessed 25 Apr. 2019].

Infomontessori.com. (2019). *Montessori - Sensorial - Introduction*. [online] Available at: http://www.infomontessori.com/sensorial/introduction.htm [Accessed 25 Apr. 2019].

Montessori Guide. (2019). *An Introduction to Practical Life — Montessori Guide*. [online] Available at: https://montessoriguide.org/an-introduction-to-practical-life [Accessed 25 Apr. 2019].

Montessoricompass.com. (2019). *Art, Music, and Movement – Montessori Compass*. [online] Available at: http://montessoricompass.com/art-music-movement/ [Accessed 25 Apr. 2019].

Montessoriservices.com. (2019). *Geography & Culture - Montessori Services*. [online] Available at: https://www.montessoriservices.com/geography-culture [Accessed 25 Apr. 2019].

Montessoriservices.com. (2019). *Geography & Culture - Montessori Services*. [online] Available at: https://www.montessoriservices.com/geography-culture [Accessed 25 Apr. 2019].

Msow.org. (2019). *Cultural | Montessori School of Waukesha*. [online] Available at: https://www.msow.org/our-school/overview/cultural/ [Accessed 25 Apr. 2019].

St. John the Baptist Catholic Montessori School. (2019). *How Music Education is Integrated into the Montessori Classroom*. [online] Available at: http://www.stjohns-excelsior.org/school/Current-Families/News/entryid/29/how-music-education-is-integrated-into-the-montessori-classroom [Accessed 25 Apr. 2019].

Brainmass.com. (2019). [online] Available at: https://brainmass.com/sociology/sociology-of-education/constructivism-and-the-educational-practices-of-maria-montessori-58457 [Accessed 18 Apr. 2019].

FAMM. (2019). *The Montessori Method*. [online] Available at: https://www.fundacionmontessori.org/the-montessori-method.htm [Accessed 18 Apr. 2019].

how we montessori. (2019). *The Five Key Learning Areas of Montessori*. [online] Available at: https://www.howwemontessori.com/how-we-montessori/2016/07/the-five-curriculum-areas-of-montessori-.html [Accessed 18 Apr. 2019].

Irinyi, M. (2019). *Parenting for Independence the Montessori Way: Fostering Self Discipline and Confidence*. [online] Montessoritraining.blogspot.com. Available at: http://montessoritraining.blogspot.com/2009/06/parentin

g-for-independence-montessori.html [Accessed 18 Apr. 2019].

Irinyi, M. (2019). *Why Choose Montessori? Montessori vs. Constructivism: An Explanation of Montessori Philosophy*. [online] Montessoritraining.blogspot.com. Available at: http://montessoritraining.blogspot.com/2007/07/why-montessori-part-i.html [Accessed 18 Apr. 2019].

Mead, S. (2019). *How Do Children Learn Through Play?*. [online] Whitbyschool.org. Available at: https://www.whitbyschool.org/passionforlearning/how-do-children-learn-through-play [Accessed 18 Apr. 2019].

Montessori Academy. (2019). *Montessori Education | An Introduction to the Montessori Method of Education*. [online] Available at: https://montessoriacademy.com.au/montessori-education/introduction-montessori-education/ [Accessed 18 Apr. 2019].

Montessorischools.org. (2019). [online] Available at: http://www.montessorischools.org/montessori-overview/how-does-montessori-work/ [Accessed 18 Apr. 2019].

My Little Moppet. (2019). *How to Start Montessori at Home*. [online] Available at: https://www.mylittlemoppet.com/how-to-start-montessori-at-home/ [Accessed 18 Apr. 2019].

Pilzner, A. (2019). *Top 5 Reasons Why Montessori Works - Montessori Rocks*. [online] Montessori Rocks. Available at:

https://montessorirocks.org/top-5-reasons-why-montessori-works/ [Accessed 18 Apr. 2019].

Skillsyouneed.com. (2019). *8 Types of Learning Styles | SkillsYouNeed*. [online] Available at: https://www.skillsyouneed.com/rhubarb/fingerprints-learning-styles.html [Accessed 18 Apr. 2019].

Time4Learning. (2019). *Learning Styles*. [online] Available at: https://www.time4learning.com/learning-styles.shtml [Accessed 18 Apr. 2019].

Austin Childrens Academy. (2019). *Human Needs and Tendencies in Montessori - Cedar Park Montessori*. [online] Available at: https://austinchildrensacademy.org/the-montessori-theory/needs-and-tendencies-in-montessori/ [Accessed 19 Apr. 2019].

Danmont.com. (2019). *The 5 Areas of a Montessori Classroom | Danville Montessori School*. [online] Available at: http://danmont.com/the-5-areas-of-a-montessori-classroom/ [Accessed 19 Apr. 2019].

Irinyi, M. (2019). *The Three-Period Lesson: A Key Part of the Montessori Method Explained*. [online] Montessoritraining.blogspot.com. Available at: http://montessoritraining.blogspot.com/2007/09/montessori-method-three-period-lesson.html [Accessed 19 Apr. 2019].

Jones, E. (2019). *Human Tendencies | Mead Montessori School*. [online] Meadmontessorischool.com. Available at: http://meadmontessorischool.com/human-tendencies/ [Accessed 19 Apr. 2019].

Maitri Learning. (2019). *Montessori Human Tendencies – Maitri Learning*. [online] Available at: https://www.maitrilearning.com/pages/human-tendencies [Accessed 19 Apr. 2019].

Montessori Teacher Training and Parent Resources. (2019). *Human Needs and Tendencies - Montessori Teacher Training and Parent Resources*. [online] Available at: http://ageofmontessori.org/human-needs-and-tendencies/ [Accessed 19 Apr. 2019].

Montessoriforeveryone.com. (2019). *The Tendencies of Humans from Montessori for Everyone*. [online] Available at: http://www.montessoriforeveryone.com/Tendencies-of-Humans_ep_73-1.html [Accessed 19 Apr. 2019].

Montessoriservices.com. (2019). *The Three-Period Lesson - Montessori Services*. [online] Available at: https://www.montessoriservices.com/ideas-insights/the-three-period-lesson [Accessed 19 Apr. 2019].

PaperAp.com. (2019). *Montessori - the Human Tendencies Research Paper Example*. [online] Available at: https://paperap.com/paper-on-montessori-the-human-tendencies-261/ [Accessed 19 Apr. 2019].

Ruffingmontessori.net. (2019). *Human Tendencies and Montessori | Ruffing Montessori School*. [online] Available at: http://ruffingmontessori.net/home/about/why-montessori/montessori-articles/human-tendencies/ [Accessed 19 Apr. 2019].

Sapientia Montessori. (2019). *Montessori at Home | How to Create a Montessori-Friendly Home*. [online] Available at: https://sapientiamontessori.com/montessori/montessori-at-home/ [Accessed 19 Apr. 2019].

Wells, K. (2019). *Easy Ways to Use Montessori At Home | Wellness Mama*. [online] Wellness Mama®. Available at: https://wellnessmama.com/60555/home-montessori/ [Accessed 19 Apr. 2019].

Motherly. (2019). *Montessori at home: Giving your child 'purposeful work' could be a game-changer*. [online] Available at: https://www.mother.ly/montessori-at-home-giving-your-child-purposeful-work-could-be-a-game-changer [Accessed 20 Apr. 2019].

Montessori Toddler Activities

Knowledge and Activities to Create, Guide, and Excel in Learning

Introduction

Congratulations on Purchasing the Book "Montessori Toddler Activities". There are many books on this subject and we are glad that you chose this book to guide you in the Montessori toddler journey.

The chapters that follow in this book will:

- Introduce the Montessori method of educating children and Toddlers
- What makes an activity fall under the Montessori category
- How to prepare the Montessori environment for toddlers and students
- Types of Montessori activities
- What these Montessori activities promote

The Montessori Method is a mode of learning which focuses on active learning, cooperation, independence, and following the pace of each child. It advocates for independence and individuality in learning. Because children are curious and want to know more, the Montessori method believes education should follow the harmony of a child. Rushing children to learn new things is not effective because it puts pressure on them. However, focusing on a child's development pace enables toddlers to acquire more knowledge. This method emphasizes every aspect of development instead of getting specific information. Montessori method was developed under the premises of respecting children, prepared environment, and paying attention to sensitive periods. An activity is considered Montessori when it helps children do things alone. It is okay to help a child when he/she does not understand, but they should be allowed to practice it by themselves in the end. Moreover, an activity is considered Montessori if it promotes self-efficiency, critical thinking, independence, and focuses on children's development needs. Children are free to follow their interests at their own pace. Montessori materials are made in such a way that they can control errors. It enables children to identify and correct mistakes without assistance. It promotes independence and self-reliance. Children can only learn by doing, not seeing.

Types of Montessori activities children can practice include:

- eye-hand coordination,
- music and movement,
- arts and crafts

Encouraging children to participate in several activities allows their minds to develop. Montessori is tailored to meet every child's development needs. It also prepares them for the next stage, and this gives it an added advantage.

Chapter 1: Introduction to Montessori

Maria Montessori was the one who developed the Montessori Method. She was a child development expert who was admired and respected by many. She believed that every child passes through a unique development process and learns through his/her capabilities. She emphasized that every child is unique and should be treated as such. She argued that knowledge is more than memorizing education materials. She wanted the education to change focus from memorization to actual learning. Moreover, she stated that knowledge must be specific so that any child can understand it. She did not like the fact that children could not understand specific knowledge because of their age. To solve this problem, she developed a method and materials to integrate changes that she wanted. The Montessori method is different from the rest, which focuses on children learning the same thing. Maria Montessori argued that learning should not be determined by age, but the speed at which children acquire information. Montessori is considered by many as a suitable for toddlers. There are over 5000 Montessori schools in the US.

Maria Montessori stated that educators should follow the child and not vice versa. They should know the specific needs of every child, create a favorable environment to promote learning. Children need to understand the world around them, and the only way to do that is to construct meanings. She noted that there are four periods under which a child goes from infancy to adulthood. Every period is different and has specific needs. Maria Montessori stated that meeting the needs of one period increased chances of success in the next one. The first phase of development starts from birth and moves on until six years. This period focuses on a child's absorbent mind. The child absorbs everything in the environment, whether good or bad. The second phase starts from 6-12 years, where the child develops a rational mind. The child starts imagining things and engages in abstract thinking. From 12-18 years, the teenager develops a humanistic mind which longs to understand the world and make an impact. The child moves from observing to contributing to society. The last phase is from 18-24 years, where an adult uses a specialist mind to explore the world. The adult uses the specialist mind to find his/her place in it.

All parents long to find the best education method for their children. There are many educational programs that parents can choose from. However, most of the programs are not sufficient and do not contribute to a child's development. Early learning has a lasting impact on a child's development. If it is not done right, it can affect future learning. This is why parents are advised to choose education programs wisely. What makes Montessori unique and appealing? Why are many parents using instead of others? Montessori gained popularity around the world more a century ago. Montessori is unique and appealing because contemporary research confirms its effectiveness. Parents are using it because it meets the educational goals they have for their children. One of the reasons why the Montessori Method has grown famous is because it enables children to grow into strong people and allows them to connect with others. It also makes children productive and reliable. Not many education methods can turn children into responsible adults. The Montessori method is also practical because it promotes early growth.

The Montessori method turns children into accountable, responsible and confident people to succeed in the real world. Education plays an important role in what we become. If a child did not develop properly or had issues, chances of failure are high. Montessori is designed to give children an opportunity to discover and nurture their own abilities. It shows children what to do and allows them to practice. Whether it is communicating their feelings or dressing. Montessori inculcate a sense of responsibility. Children learn early on that they are responsible for themselves and others only come in to help.

Furthermore, there are development activities that encourage children to interact with others. An essential component of a child's development comes from interaction. When a child can communicate their needs, it becomes easy to learn other concepts.

Toddlers are free to choose the activities they want to do. Giving them the freedom to choose what they want to do fosters independence. They choose what they want based on what is available. Some may choose to work with others, while some prefer to work alone. Allowing children to make decisions enables them to develop into capable individuals. Montessori also promotes accountability. Learning activities are given to toddlers, and they move at their own pace. They are allowed to practice, assess, and engage in other activities when they want. Moreover, toddlers choose activities based on their abilities and interests. This is what makes Montessori different from other programs. It instills accountability in children and develops reliable people. They are in charge of their learning and decide what to retain or eliminate. Children are assessed daily by looking at a child's interaction with their peers and the environment.

Montessori has an individual learning plan for every child. It does not use one framework to assess performance because it appreciates individual differences. Moreover, it promotes coordination, focus, and independence in children. Montessori activities are designed in such a way that children can educate themselves. Parents usually wonder if they have to buy many materials when using the Montessori method. Note that a few and carefully chosen materials are better than expensive but inappropriate ones. When choosing materials, pay attention to a child's needs.

Moreover, a bad environment can affect the learning process. A child will have trouble learning in a cluttered or crowded space. To facilitate learning, parents should clear the learning area and put things in order. Doing this makes it easy for a child to find materials and concentrate on the task.

You do not have to spend a ton of money to buy materials. The materials come in three categories: practical life, sensorial, and academic. Sensorial materials help children learn through their senses. Studies show that sensory learning plays a vital role in brain development. Sensorial information is useful in building neurological connections that are vital for reasoning. Montessori provides sensorial materials that are active and helps children to connect with their senses. Montessori sensorial materials include Pink Tower and solid wood cubes in different sizes to promote visual understanding of dimensions. Sensorial materials can be expensive because they are long-lasting and can be used by many children. However, parents can make their sensorial materials at home by following instructions from websites. The important thing is to use natural and beautiful materials to evoke a child's sense.

Parents can opt to use practical life materials to facilitate learning. These are real tools children can use to learn everyday tasks. They equip children with skills such as washing, pouring, and dressing. They are sharp, learn fast, and imitate what others are doing. Practical life materials enable children to acquire problem-solving skills, coordination, and independence. The good thing is that you do not have to spend a lot of money to buy practical life materials. Instead, take time to show your child activities in the house step by step. Start by doing things with them, and let them take charge slowly. Do not be the kind of person who wants to do everything for a child because they will never know how it is done.

Guide your child and encourage them to imitate what you did. You can child-size tools to make it easier for your child.

Sensory and practical activities promote brain development, which is necessary for learning math, science, and language. These skills create room for writing, reading, and recognition of shapes and sound. Montessori materials were designed to focus on a child's interests based on the stage they are in. Materials used to enable children to explore and learn independently. Children can repeat steps many times, and this fosters concentration.

The role of a Montessori teacher is to observe the child, identify his/her needs, abilities, and interests. The teacher creates opportunities for the child to explore areas of interests and work intelligently. The teacher is called "directress" and intervenes as minimum as possible. The goal is to allow the child to progress as he/she develops. The child needs to act and think for him/herself. Minimum intervention helps the child to develop confidence and self-discipline. The child is responsible for what happens next, which makes him/her responsible for the actions taken. Furthermore, the directress does not give rewards or punishment but allows the child to find inner satisfaction after completing activities. When a child is ready for lessons, the directress can choose to give him/her new materials or use small groups.

There are five basic principles of Montessori, namely:

- i respect for the child,
- ii sensitive periods
- iii the absorbent mind
- iv auto-education and
- v prepared environment.

The Montessori principle is pegged on respect for the child. Many teachers make the mistake of not respecting children. Children are forced to follow rules they know nothing about. Failure to do what the teacher says leads to punishment. Children who do not follow their teachers are considered indiscipline, and parents are told to straighten them out. Teachers rarely pose to think if they are using the wrong approach.

Moreover, they do not pay attention to their special needs and overbear them with activities. We cannot be rude to children and expect them to be nice. Children imitate what they see so if they detect a harsh tone in your voice, they follow suit. Maria Montessori advised teachers to treat children concerning improve learning. They show respect by helping them do things and learn new concepts. If a child is not comfortable with a particular activity, there is no point in forcing him/her to do it. Instead, give children choices to help them develop the skills needed for effective learning. Children who are respected have self-confidence than those who are forced to do things. Some teachers think that they will lose control when they respect children. On the contrary, it gives them power because children are pleased with what they are doing. Moreover, a respected child is happier and productive most of the time and need minimum supervision. Therefore, parents using the Montessori method at home can make things easier by allowing children to think for themselves. Let them decide what they want to do, and when they make mistakes, they will learn from it as well.

Maria Montessori believed that the most sensitive period takes place between birth and six years. Others define it as a time of opportunity milestones. During the early stages, children pass through some categories of sensitive periods, namely: language, order, sensory skills, social skills, and movement. These periods last for some time and fades away after accomplishing their purpose. It is difficult to recognize your child's sensitive period as most think. Sometimes your child repeats the same song a million times, and it may drive you crazy. What you do not know is that this is one of the symptoms of sensitivity. The child may have high sensitivity when he mimics what you are doing, high concentration and shows obsessive behaviors. Do not interrupt a child during his sensitive period because it results in tantrums. Breaking a routine that a child is used to such as sleeping a certain time or getting a dress may cause an emotional breakdown. The sensitive period for order starts at birth and rises in the second year of development. Children learn how to reason and understand the environment during this time. A child may crave routine or repeat songs during sensitivity to order. It is important to have rules to facilitate the sensitivity period for order.

Children are in a sensitive period for language from birth up to six years. They become sensitive to spoken language, reading, and written language. A child becomes interested in reading between four to five years. Parents can support language development at home by immersing children in an environment rich in language. Children only learn from what they see and hear so if you want to increase sensitivity to language, make it part of your home. You can start by speaking in a clear language and allowing them to say what is on their mind. Some parents have the habit of assuming that they know what the child wants even before he/she speaks. This is not good because it prevents the child from communicating his feelings. The child may become withdrawn altogether. You can also sign or read to your child in the morning or before bedtime. Children are sensitive to movement from birth up to two years and from two years up to five. They start by learning how to crawl, pull up, and eventually walk on their own. From two to five years, children learn the co-ordination of movements. They start using both hands and coordinate movements. The outdoor environment supports movement sensitivity. Taking the child to the park, encouraging him to draw or jump. Children develop an interest in social relationships from two to five years. They learn to pay attention to people and develop the desire to be around people. They develop friendships and group activities. Parents can support social skills sensitivity by taking their children to playgroups or childcare where they meet and play with other children.

Maria Montessori believed that children educate themselves. While a directress acts as a guide, the child does all the work. A child absorbs knowledge into his life and is constantly learning. The role of children is to learn, and the mind makes it easier for them. They are thinking beings who are always on the move. The environment, experiences, and teachers influence what they learn. Montessori emphasizes the belief that children are born learning. Furthermore, Montessori stated that periods influence learning. She argued that children are more likely to learn during certain periods than others are. While all children have the same sensitive period, the timing and sequence vary. Parents and teachers can observe the child know times of sensitivity.

Montessori stated that it is important for a teacher to guide children without letting them feel their presence too much. Some teachers are overbearing. They not only give children too much work but also never give them space to do anything. They want children to do things in a certain way, and those who refuse are termed rebellious. Montessori does not think this approach of learning is effective because it pressurizes the child to act a certain way.

Furthermore, children who are forced to do things are not fulfilled and act based on fear. According to Montessori, the teacher should only give the needed help but never be an obstacle to learning. Children cannot acquire great learning experience if they are not free to do thing by themselves. To facilitate learning, the teacher needs to make the child the center of learning. The role of the teacher is not to talk, but to avail learning materials and prepare a good environment. Parents should assume the same role with their toddlers at home. Instead of talking the entire time, give the child space to do things alone. Another way to promote learning is to encourage children to do better. There is nothing worse than scolding a child for mistakes they have made. Such a child may never have the confidence to do anything in life. Rather than admonishing the child for the mess, he has made, commend him for the wonderful progress so far. A child who is encouraged is more likely to improve than one who is made to feel like a failure. Moreover, encouraging a child to improve his/her self-esteem and builds confidence. You can encourage your child at home by giving him freedom in the prepared environment. Trust your child to learn from his/her mistakes. Refrain from rushing children to act in a certain way.

Montessori believed that children have different learning pace, and it is crucial to give them time. Just because another child learned, a concept fast does not mean every child should do the same. Moreover, just because a child has not mastered a concept does not mean that he/she will never get it. This is where encouragement comes in. Let your child know that you believe in him/her. Parents using the Montessori method should observe their children know if they are doing the right thing. This does not require you to be present all the time. You can review what they did during the day and guide them where they went wrong. Moreover, determining sensitive periods helps to prepare the best environment for your child. It also allows parents to divert inappropriate behavior in essential activities. It might take some time to know a child's sensitive period and requires patience. Another way teachers or parents can increase the success rate of the Montessori method is to prepare the learning environment. Make sure that the learning materials are in the right formats and benefit the child. There is no point in using materials that do not add value to a child is a learning experience. Parents should support their children's learning by being there when needed. Giving the child the freedom to choose activities that interest him does not mean that he no longer needs you. He may be stuck at some point and need your advice. Being there to listen and guide the child gives them the confidence to do the impossible.

The Montessori method emphasizes on the role of a prepared environment for learning. Learning is improved in a prepared environment, where children have the liberty to do things by themselves. Freedom is crucial in the environment because it enables children to decide what they want to do, rather than forcing them to do specific activities. When the child is allowed to explore materials, he/she wants, it becomes easy to absorb information. The environment should enable children to be active and learn new things. Montessori described the ability of children to educate themselves as auto-education. A child who is free to choose activities and is in a prepared environment educates him/herself. However, children who are restricted do not acquire a lot of information. Parents prepare space so that the child can learn alone. It may seem odd at first but makes sense later.

Chapter 2: The Approach that this Book Will Take: What Makes an Activity Montessori and Types of Activities that Qualify as Montessori

This book will explore various activities of Montessori; explain what the Montessori method is, and what makes an activity a Montessori. There are many activities that children engage in, but not all of them are beneficial. Moreover, some activities do more harm than good because they do not foster important tenets of Montessori. This book will also look at the Montessori environment and what can be done to make it suitable for children. Maria Montessori emphasized the importance of preparing the environment and its role in learning. She established that children are not productive in a messy environment and advised teachers and parents to provide a conducive environment for learning. This book explores the Montessori Method in detail and explains to parents why they should use Montessori.

To promote development, but some are fake. Parents need to know how to distinguish helpful activities from those that waste time and resources. Some businesses only waste time and children gain nothing in the end. While some parents do not mind, what their children are doing as long as they get them out of the way, it is important to engage them in meaningful activities. Many because of its benefits use Montessori activities. Several studies have confirmed the benefits of Montessori methods. Therefore, parents must be keen on materials they give their children. Children learn quickly, and it is difficult to get them into a new routine when they are used to another one.

An activity is considered a Montessori when it promotes the "do it myself" philosophy. Maria Montessori argued that there is nothing better than letting the child take charge of the learning process. She stated that forcing your child to learn things they are not interested in, results in failure. Furthermore, children can experience an emotional breakdown because of being overwhelmed. A parent can gauge the efficiency of activity by determining whether it gives children control. Maria Montessori also stated that an activity is considered Montessori when it promotes independence, self-efficiency, and critical thinking. When a child is allowed to think on his own, it empowers and prepares him for the future. He learns from an early age that they can do things by themselves instead of relying on others all the time. When parents allow children to think on their own, it boosts their confidence.

An activity is considered Montessori when it is tailored to a child's development needs and interests. One activity that pays attention to the individual needs of children is better than ten thousand others are. This is because it examines the strengths and weakness of a child and finds ways of improving their skills. Montessori activity is unique because it is not done in groups but at an individual level. A teacher can decide to create small groups for children with the same interests. However, it is majorly done on a personal level. Therefore, an activity must be tailored to the specific needs of children to be Montessori.

Furthermore, an activity that is child-centered is Montessori. Montessori activities are flexible and allow children to move at their pace. An activity that is self-motivated and empowers the child to choose activities is counted as a Montessori. It requires parents to study their children to know their areas of interests. Furthermore, an activity is considered Montessori when it has control of error. Montessori materials have control of errors, which enables them to correct mistakes with assistance. They enable the child to detect and correct errors without help. Parents can tell the joy their children feel when they correct an error without intervention. They start believing that they can achieve anything, and this is what all parents want for their children. Unfortunately, some parents like to take over their children's activities. Instead of encouraging their children, they make it about themselves. Others do activities as the child watches and never allows them to participate. Such parents make it difficult for their children to do anything in life. They grow up knowing that they cannot do things by themselves and must rely on external support. If not corrected, such children may never have hope in life. This is why it is essential for parents to sit back and let their children be at the center of attention. Montessori materials are designed in such a way that children can repeat and practice as much as they want to. Parents and teachers need to understand that children cannot grasp knowledge as fast as they can. This is why a child-centered activity is important because it allows them to do activities that they are comfortable with.

An activity that facilitates sensory exploration is Montessori. Maria Montessori established there is a better outcome in learning when the senses of children are engaged. A child is a sensory explorer, and it is crucial to choose an activity that fosters, rather than limiting their senses. Moreover, an activity is considered Montessori when it encourages children to do, instead of watching. The only way children learn is by doing, not seeing. Therefore, an activity that allows them to express their ideas, interests of tastes is better than one with a lot of explanations. Montessori uses a hands-on approach to educate children. It allows children to be as creative as they can be.

An activity is Montessori if it breaks down concepts into simple steps that children can follow. There is no point in using a complex concept that the child cannot understand. Parents can make things easier by breaking down concepts into simple steps to foster learning. The child should complete each step before the outcome is achieved. Breaking down the concepts makes the child think that it is easy, and they can do anything. It also motivates them to take up similar activities. Activities that promote independence are Montessori. Maria Montessori wanted nothing than to foster independence in children. She believed that this was the only way to raise responsible and dependable adults. She advised teachers to strive to impart knowledge that fostered independence to help children in the future.

Toddlers can do numerous Montessori activities at home. These activities are interesting and practical. They are also ideal for calming super active kids. You take some ideas from the list and incorporate at home too. Let us start by looking at practical activities for toddlers at home. These activities can be set up in the kitchen for children to access and work with any time. These activities include peeling and cutting bananas, washing dishes, pouring water, and spreading crackers. Doing such activities might seem simple to an adult, but captivating to children. They not only keep children preoccupied but also promotes brain development. All the materials they need should be laid on a tray and be attractive. Children love to color, and you should make the materials appealing. Children can engage in, such as washing their hands, wiping windows, arranging flowers, watering plants, and mopping other practical life activities. They can also participate in self-care tasks such as brushing their hair and blowing their noses. Parents do practically everything for their kids because they think that they cannot do anything. However, it is good to use things around the house. Parents can give their children simple tasks in the house, such as brushing their teeth to keep them active.

It is easy to incorporate Montessori activities at home. It requires only a little preparation, and you are set to go.

Moreover, you do not have to spend a lot of money to buy materials because you have everything you need at home. If you do not have particular materials, you can find them easily at any store. Think of everything your child needs and buy them ahead of time. Do not wait until the last minute to buy materials because they may be difficult to find or expensive. Resist the urge to put out all the materials at once because your child might misuse them. Put out only a small amount of materials for your child to practice with. For example, if the activity is spreading butter on toast, only put out a small amount of butter to avoid wastage. Parents should be there to help their children when they are stuck. Alternatively, you can put someone to be in charge in case you are preoccupied with other things. The important thing is to avail materials and guide the child along the way. Some activities parents can incorporate at home include helping with the laundry, putting soap in clothes, bringing clothes to the laundry area, and taking clothes from the washing machine. Parents should take caution when children do somehow risky activities such as putting clothes in the laundry machine. The child might get stuck or get hurt. Parents should refrain from assigning children in dangerous tasks.

Another type of Montessori activity is getting dressed. Allow the child to dress and undress himself occasionally. You should only help when the child asks you to. Parents can make it easier for children to dress themselves by picking out clothes that do not require much effort to put on. Dressing yourself can seem like an easy task, but children view it differently. Once they learn how-to put-on clothes, you can move to a challenging activity to keep them motivated. You can tell them to help with breakfast when they are ready. Use a container with a scoop for them to serve their oatmeal. Include also a cup of milk for them to add to their cereal. Letting the child serve himself breakfast instill independence in him. They can move from serving breakfast to helping with lunch. Have small amounts of items and allow the child to serve themselves.

The child may not get right the first time, but do not pressurize them to be perfect. Instead, allow them to make mistakes and learn in the process. Parents can step in and help when the child seems overwhelmed. The key is to let them learn to do practical activities at home. Once the child is comfortable with serving their lunch, let them prepare with supper. Let them help in the kitchen by preparing vegetables and salads. Look for cutleries suitable for small hands. Children can also set up the table. Parents should let their children get ready for visitors from time to time. The child can be doing tasks like making the bed, tidying up after playing with toys, and getting the towel. Parents should involve children in activities such as baking, going to the supermarket, and cleaning the house. Activities should be fun if you want children to participate. When an activity is overwhelming to the child, tell them to stop and resume when ready. The practice is important in the learning process. If it is washing, have cleaning supplies ready for the child to use. Parents should have child-size materials to make practical life activities fun.

Children are less likely to enjoy activities at home if they do not have tools that fit them. Parents can make learning enjoyable by buying things such as an apron, a broom, or a mop. It is also important to focus on the process, not the outcome. Most parents are too worried about the result that they miss strides their children make. Such an attitude can discourage the child from improving and feel like they are not enough. Remember that involving a child in activities takes longer, and the outcome may not be perfect. What is important is that the child learns and resources or time spent. The child should know a thing or two after doing an activity. The child may not get it right, but they are mastering the skills, which will help them later in life. There are several ways children can help with chores at home. Parents only need to identify tasks that are simple and exciting. Assign younger children simple activities such as carrying a t-shirt while the parent carries trousers to the laundry area. Once they clock two years, children can help with a lot of tasks at home, such as putting on an apron.

Practical life activities should be attractive. Just because they are done at home does not mean that they should not be appealing. On the contrary, Montessori activities done at home should be more attractive to keep toddlers active. Practical life activities can be used in any setting. There are four areas of practical life; self-care, control of movement, care for the environment, and courtesy. There are fun activities that toddlers can engage in to learn courtesy, such as repeating kind words such as "excuse me," and "please." Toddlers are naturally attracted to activities they have seen before. This is why Maria Montessori emphasized on the role of practical life exercises. Most of the time, children repeat what they see their parents doing. Montessori argued that letting the child do practical life exercises enables them to adapt and find his place in society. The duty of the parent to show the right way of doing practical life exercises. These exercises should be done in a way that the child can follow easily. Parents should not move while talking or talk while moving to minimize distraction.

Furthermore, the parent should keep in the know that the goal is to demonstrate actions so that the child can repeat them later. There is no point in showing actions that are difficult for the child to master. Maria Montessori believed that the role of a directress is to show how things are done and minimize imitation. The child should be able to make the exercise their own. The role of parents is to show their children practical life activities in the house and let them do it their way.

Arts and Crafts

Another type of Montessori activity that toddlers can engage in at home is arts and crafts. Parents should not make art class a weekly event. Instead, they should encourage creativity and an active imagination. Toddlers can participate in clay sculpting to engage their fun side. Arts and crafts do not have to be boring or limited to certain tasks. Let the child explore different thinks to discover what they enjoy. Create some people, animals, and other child-friendly materials for the child to use. Non-hazardous tools should be used to avoid injuries. Once the child is done sculpting, encourage them to explain what they have made. Parents can chip in to correct them where necessary. Toddlers can also draw and paint to express themselves. Children are skilled at telling stories through imagery. Rather than telling them to talk every time they have an idea, let them paint or draw. They can use crayons, colored pencils, and paint, which enables them to get comfortable with writing.

Problem-solving games are also part of the Montessori method. Puzzles are a great alternative to boring and redundant games offered by other programs. There are several types of puzzles that allow children to think critically and solve problems. Parents should provide different puzzles to get their children engaged. Moreover, there are many educational apps that parents can use to find enjoyable activities for their children. The child needs to develop new ways of doing practical life activities to make them real. Parents should not be worried or fussy when their children fail to do things exactly like them. Instead, they should be glad that the child could take an activity and make it their own. All toddlers can make activities their own given a chance. What matters is proper guidance on steps to take to achieve desired results.

Most toddlers cannot count numbers, which means that they miss out on board games. They can have fun doing other activities such as identifying colors. Toddlers get excited when they identify or arrange things properly. Parents can incorporate fun activities such as identifying different colors and encouraging toddlers to participate. While some toddlers are gifted to count numbers, which enables them to play board games, most are not so lucky. What makes colors and shapes fascinating is the fact that toddlers do not have to wait until it is their turn to play. It is good to start with non-activities before the child moves to a competitive one. Parents can introduce games such as dice when the child gets older. What matters is that the child is learning and having fun at the same time. We can prepare numerous activities for toddlers using materials readily available at home. It may not seem obvious, but toddlers get bored quickly, hence the need to switch up activities. Instead of using the same color in all activities, opt for a bright hue that will appeal to them.

Another type of Montessori activity toddler can do at home is unpacking the dishwasher. Do not treat the child as though he/she cannot do anything. If you allow them to develop such a mentality at an early age, it will be difficult for them to grow into responsible adults. Moreover, most children love helping around the house and take advantage of every opportunity they get. If you are afraid that the child may break the dishes, remove delicate ones, and let them unpack light ones. You can allow them to unpack their plates and cups from the dishwasher as a start. This will remind them that they are strong and can do anything. Moreover, it turns them into responsible and independent individuals. The next time you want someone to put the dishes away, ask your child to do it. It may seem like a difficult task at first, but soon they will get the hangs of it.

Fine Motor Skills

Another type of Montessori activity suitable for toddlers is fine motor skill work. Fine motor skills have been ignored for the longest time, yet they play a vital role in a child's development. Fine motor skills are used to make movements. Because these movements come naturally to most of us, we often do not pause to think about them. However, fine motor skills are complex and involve coordinated efforts of the muscles and the brain to pull off. Furthermore, they are built on gross motor skills that enable us to make big movements. Toddlers can improve their fine motor skills through activities such as holding a pencil, learning scissor skills, and manipulating play dough. Toddlers can also use silverware while eating to improve fine motor skills. Other exercises include getting dressed with belts, manipulating technology, opening a latch. The important thing is to let the child take over and do what interests them. These skills are simple yet vital in a child's adult's life. A child may struggle moving forward if he/she lacks fine motor skills. Parents have the duty of incorporating these simple but effective activities at home to help their children cultivate fine motor skills. Fine motor skills come in handy when tackling advanced projects or tasks. Children who lack this ability struggle to make things work. Fine motor skills are good but do not go overboard. Introduce one activity at a time and see how your child responds to it. Parents can look for similar exercises, but if he does not enjoy it, change it. Parents should not expect their toddlers to get it right the first time. Instead of putting pressure on the child to draw a straight line, commend them for the good work. Who said that toddlers have to get it right for them to have fun or learn? Let us just make the most of the situation and promote their fine motor skills. Some parents struggle with getting the right exercises for their toddlers. They can ask other parents who are using Montessori activities to get ideas.

Toddlers can practice holding pom poms because they need small movements to hold. Moreover, toddlers will not have trouble picking or moving them. They also promote eye coordination. Alternatively, have the child hold buttons to improve fine motor skills. These are small items that not only promote fine motor skills, but also eye coordination. Picking the buttons works on the toddler's muscle. However, the actual fine motor skills come from buttoning things. When a toddler buttons a shirt, it works wonders for eye coordination and finger strength. A great alternative is a paper clip. Paper clips are great for finger movements and manipulation. A high degree of concentration is needed to slide a clip onto a piece of paper. Other great options include tweezers, pipe cleaners, and rubber bands. Rubber bands strengthen their fingers and play a vital role in developing fine motor skills. Going by this list, parents have many several exercises they can use to promote fine motor skills. They do not have to restrict their toddlers to certain tasks because they will get bored. Playing with dough is a fantastic way of building small muscles. When the child kneads, pushes and rolls the dough, it strengthens them. Another simple but effective exercise toddlers can do to improve their fine motor skills is to peel stickers. Have the child peel stickers from the sticker sheet. In case the child is having a difficult time peeling the sticker, remove the non-sticker part and they will still gain useful fine motor skills. The secret is to take advantage of every activity the child engages in to teach them useful skills. Kitchen tongs are a great option for developing fine motor skills if you do not have access to other materials. Use child-size kitchen tongs to make it easy for toddlers to use. Bring the tongs out for cleaning and your child will be pleased you took the initiative.

Chapter 3: Preparing a Montessori Environment At Home and School

A prepared learning environment facilitates learning. Toddlers are more likely to concentrate in an organized space than where there is disorder. Parents and teachers can take simple to prepare the environment. Maria Montessori stated that a man who lives in a disorganized environment could not develop his faculties properly. Furthermore, it denies a man a chance to know himself well. Most of the time, you will find parents and teachers complaining that children are not performing as expected and they wonder what is wrong. The sad part is that they rarely take time to analyze and prepare the environment. A simple step like tidying the room goes a long and improves learning. As adults, we know the importance of a clean environment. While some people are not entirely concerned about it, others are obsessed with it. To find peace, parents remove things that cause destruction. If they are bothered when the TV is on, they switch it off immediately. This is the same with toddlers, only that they may not communicate their feelings accordingly. Most toddlers lose focus when they are in a messy space. They wish to tell their parents or teachers but lack correct words. Others are scared of speaking because they are unsure of how their parents will react. Instead of scolding the child for complaining about the poor state the environment; be glad that they can communicate their feelings. This shows that they will not cow under pressure or hide their true feelings in the future. The environment mostly affects children under the age of six. If the environment is quiet, they focus more, compared to a noisy place. Moreover, a beautiful place encourages them to do things correctly. Toddlers develop habits and independence in an orderly space.

The goal of the prepared environment is to foster independence. There is nothing more appealing than a self-reliant child is. This does mean that they can do everything by themselves, but that they can make their own decisions. There is no point in putting things where the child cannot reach. A prepared environment does not mean that the child has no access to things.

On the contrary, it is meant to remove irrelevant things from the place and leave the needed materials. The toddler should have access to important activities in an environment tailored to his/her needs. Parents are free to borrow inspirations from other parents using Montessori, but they should consider the child's needs. Do not implement everything you see in another space because it looked beautiful. It sounds like a lot of work to prepare a Montessori environment at home, but this is not the case. Parents only need to put in little efforts now and leave the rest to the child. The child will learn how to do most of the work by him/herself. After all, the prepared environment teaches them self-reliance and how to do things by themselves.

To prepare a Montessori environment at home, start by choosing the place. Chances are there is more than one space you want to set up Montessori because the child is "all over the house." This is not bad because they need access to different areas in the house. Parents need to prepare the bathroom, bedroom, kitchen, living room, and home office area. To make things easier, start by choosing one space. You can move to another place if the child is uncomfortable or wants something different. The environment at some point in life affects everyone. Organizing the learning environment reduces stress and facilitate the development of a creative mind. We all want our children to grow into capable individuals, and there is no better way of achieving this than allowing them to explore their interests. This is why it is important to choose the space wisely. Do not use a space because it has no use, but consider the child's needs. It is good to involve the child in the selection and organization of the place. A child who sees how things are arranged grow into responsible adults. They also learn how to organize the room and does not ask for help when searching for things. Keep in mind that toddlers learn from observing, not hearing.

The next step to prepare a Montessori environment at home is to observe how the child behaves in the space. Before you settle in space, spend some days with the toddler, there to see how he/she reacts. If you have chosen the bedroom, focus on what the child needs, and get it. You also need to consider what the child asks help with, and what he/she can do. If space is in the bathroom, can the child brush his teeth if he had access to the toothbrush and toothpaste? Parents should remove distractions from the chosen space. For example, if you want the child to learn how to make the bed, there is no need in including toothbrush in the room if it will not be used.

Once you have chosen the space and observed how the child behaves, it is time to create a plan. Things rarely go wrong when you have a place, and in case they do, you have a way out. In the plan, consider the routine of the family and how you want the space to be. Establishing a routine makes it easy for the child to adopt wanted behaviors. For instance, every morning, the child uses the bathroom to wash his feet, hands, and brush his teeth if he was playing outside. To make this work, remind the child to the same thing every time he comes from playing, and it will stick. It will reach a point when you no longer have to tell him/her to clean up. After determining the routine, make a plan around it. The child can use the bathroom without help, but it would be nice if he could replace the toilet paper when it is empty. You can store extra toilet papers near the toilet so the child can access it. The child may also know how to brush his teeth, but you have been applying the toothpaste for him. Instead of helping apply the toothpaste every time, show him how it is done and it within reach. It is difficult for the child to use the bathtub to wash his feet. You can make things easier for him/her by putting a shallow plastic bin in the bathroom to use. The child can fill it with sink water and wash his/her feet without help. The goal is to let them do things by themselves as much as possible, provided they are not harmed in the process.

The next step to take to prepare the Montessori environment at home is to collect what you will need. You may have all the items you need at home, but making a list helps you get everything. If the chosen space is the bathroom, you need to check whether you have a step stool, rags, shallow bin, and a towel. You can buy things that you do not have early to avoid a last-minute rush. After getting everything, you need, set up space, and implement the routine. Do not waste time once you have what you need. Set up space and show the child how to use things. Toddlers like knowing what is expected of them. Show the child the routine at the right time. For example, when it is time to brush his teeth, show him how to squeeze the toothpaste and how to hold the toothbrush. Rather than telling them what to do, show them. You can have the child watch you as you put toothpaste on your toothbrush then invite him to do the same. To make the activity fun, set a time limit to challenge the toddler.

Parents can prepare the environment by including physical materials and rules governing the space. A child is introduced to the world at around three years. Instead of rushing the child to adopt things, it is good to provide an environment rich in learning materials. A prepared environment creates interests and widens his/her thinking. Toddlers understand music, art language, and science better in an organized space. The environment plays a significant role in a child's development. To aid proper development and to respect and inspire the child, but good things in the environment. Parents do not have to spend a lot of money because most of the things are already in the house. Toddlers prefer to work on the floor instead of the table. Put all the materials on the floor to facilitate learning. Instead of storing materials in boxes, keep them in baskets or trays. Refrain from putting out all the materials at once. Only provide those that are used by the child at the moment. It is normal for a child to become disinterested in an activity they enjoyed before. This is because the child grows, and his/her interests change. It is important to keep the environment peaceful and uncluttered.

More and more parents are embracing the Montessori method in their homes. However, Montessori cannot work in a disorganized environment. Parents must create a good place to reap the benefits of the Montessori method. Every home is unique, and what works for one home may not work for another. Although home Montessori has its special effects, all Montessori prepared environments have certain elements in common: They are clean, attractive, and organized. The prepared environment should be somewhere; the toddler can store and organize items. Furthermore, it needs to be a place where it is easy to think. It should be easy for children to move around. Parents should ensure that the prepared environment has enough space to accommodate others. Everyone should be able to find a place to sit during group time.

A prepared home Montessori environment should make it easy for toddlers to access materials from bottom shelves without help. Some parents make the mistake of keeping everything away and telling the child to contact them when they need things. This method is not good at building independence in children. On the contrary, it makes them to over-rely on your help to do basic things. Parents normally fear that toddlers will mess things on the shelves, so they deny them access. Toddlers who see their parents organize the room will adopt the same behavior. You will find them cleaning the space or the shelves after playing. A prepared Montessori environment should have child-size tables and materials to make things easy for toddlers. The area should be simple, orderly, and beautiful. Toddlers are attracted to colorful things so parents should consider this. Furthermore, every item in the space should have a purpose. All the materials that are not being used by the toddler should be put away to create space. By now, all parents know that they should use visually appealing materials. Before setting any material in the space, parents should know its purpose. Arrange the materials in working order. Apart from being captivating, materials also need to stimulate the toddler's interests. Moreover, they should accommodate all the social, cognitive, and physical needs of the child. It is difficult to get things right the first time. Parents should be consistent in getting what the child needs for an exercise.

The prepared Montessori environment should be organized based on the primary subject areas: practical life, sensorial, language, and arts, math, and science. Secondary areas to focus on when organizing the room are art, library, and circle time. Space should include the use of tables, low shelves, and an area to keep the child's projects. The more energy parents put into preparing the Montessori environment; the more fulfilling the experience will be for the toddler. Parents also benefit from an organized environment because the child does not ask for help looking for things. They can focus on other things while the toddler participates in an activity. The prepared environment enables the child to learn to the fullest and develops confidence.

There are a couple of steps teachers can take to prepare the Montessori environment at school. Maria Montessori stated that the role of the prepared environment is to make the child independent. The idea behind the prepared environment came from the desire to facilitate independent learning. Teachers play a big role in preparing the learning environment. They should ensure that space is well ordered, calm, and has a lot of activities. Children should be able to move around easily. There are six aspects of the prepared environment teachers should consider, namely: freedom, beauty, structure and order, social environment, nature and reality, and intellectual environment.

Maria Montessori stated that children should be free to follow or explore their natural impulses. A child develops well when he/she is allowed to follow his/her interests. The prepared environment in the classroom should allow freedom of movement, freedom to play with others, freedom of exploration, and freedom to be alone. Teachers should not distract toddlers when they are trying to focus on tasks. Instead, they should give toddlers space to be themselves. Giving the child freedom in the classroom ultimately leads to freedom of choice. Children grow up knowing that they have a choice and should not stay in difficult situations.

The second aspect of the Montessori prepared environment teachers should pay attention to is the structure and order. While structure and order seem to go against the freedom of the child, it does not interfere with independence. Structure and order stipulated in the prepared environment signify the structure and order in the world. Some rules govern how people behave. Just because there are structure and order does not mean there is no freedom.

On the contrary, it promotes freedom because people know what is acceptable. The structure and order in the Montessori environment help the child understand the world better. Maria Montessori stated that the sensitive period for an order is between one to three years. This the time when the child starts making a conclusion about the world and without order, the child's reasoning may go off. At this point, the child does not understand most of the things happening in the world and order set things straight. This does not mean that the classroom routine cannot be changed. It means that any change should be considered before implementation. Moreover, changes should be closely monitored to ensure that toddlers benefit from them. If the teacher notices that implemented changes are doing more harm than good, they should be eliminated.

Another aspect of the Montessori prepared environment in the classroom is beauty. The prepared environment should be beautiful. It does not matter whether your school is old or new. The environment should be visually appealing and stand out. The teacher needs to remove clutter and let the environment reflect tranquility and peace. The good thing with a well-maintained environment is that toddlers are naturally drawn to it.

You will not have to invite them to come, as they will be attracted to its beauty. When preparing the environment, the teacher should consider nature and reality. The Montessori method respects and fears nature. Maria Montessori believed that nature should be used to inspire children. She advised teachers to take children out to interact with nature to inspire creativity in them. The Montessori method does not believe in confining children in the classroom. To preserve the environment, Montessori uses natural materials to prepare the learning place. Teachers can use real wood, cotton, or reeds to prepare the environment.

The social environment plays a vital role in learning. Children develop empathy and compassion when there is freedom of interaction. This is why parents who use the Montessori method at home are advised to take children to playgroups or childcare centers for them to interact with other toddlers. Toddlers become more socially aware as they develop. The Montessori method encourages social interaction in the prepared environment. The intellectual environment also plays a vital role in learning. If the previously mentioned aspects are not organized, it becomes difficult to create an intellectual environment. The Montessori method aims to develop the whole personality of a child. The environment should be tailored to the needs of the child to help him/

her develop properly. This can be done by providing sensorial materials and giving them the freedom to be unique.

Preparing a Montessori environment is not as daunting as most teachers think. It only becomes overwhelming if you have not collected the necessary materials. The first step towards creating a Montessori classroom is to create flow. Arrange the classroom in a manner than creates flow. Ensure that everything is in a child's reach. Moreover, younger children should have access to low shelves to retrieve materials. Older kids should use higher shelves. Whatever you do, do not overfill the shelves. Put materials on trays or baskets if you lack space. Put materials in a sequence of development to make it easier for the child to access and use. Teachers should have a list and check to ensure that all the materials are available. Ensure that all the materials are in good condition and easy to use by toddlers. It might take time to get all the materials, but it is vital in running the classroom smoothly. Go for a welcoming, fresh, and inviting space. Wipe the chairs and scrub the floor to make the environment tidy. The teacher should have a separate shelve from the children. It should be higher up and labeled. Top up your supplies if they are finished and use what is available properly.

The teacher also needs to ensure that all the books are in good condition. Torn books should be repaired before the next use. There are several activities, and great movement in the Montessori prepared the environment. The teacher acts as a preparer of the environment. The good thing about a prepared environment is that it gives the child the freedom to develop to his/her fullest potential. There are simple and complex materials children can use to improve their skills. Montessori classrooms offer activities and lessons that align with the developmental needs of a child. Teachers should know that children will not be interested in the same lesson and this is okay. The prepared environment is a key tenet of the Montessori method.

Many parents wonder what makes Montessori method different from other daycare centers or preschools. The first thing that sets the two apart is that childcare centers tend to be noisy, messy, and lively. When you enter a Montessori classroom, the first thing you notice is the peace, order, and beauty. People wonder why the two systems are different from one another. The difference between the two lies in the prepared environment prescribed by Maria Montessori. She described the key components of Montessori to educate teachers and parents why the environment matters. Montessori classrooms are peaceful and lively. Teachers should prepare many places for children to play and learn in different ways. They can learn alone, in pairs or groups. Instead of the teacher preparing the needed materials alone all the time, he/she should involve children in the process. It is not necessary to designate a specific place for Montessori activities. To make it fun and exciting, teachers should use bright and attractive colors. They should also incorporate cultural materials to improve learning. Children feel an electric touch when they enter the Montessori classroom because they know it is a place set aside for them. Here they learn how to take charge of their social interactions and do things correctly. The teacher can use role-playing exercises to teach children how to handle conflicts. Instead of scolding children when they make mistakes, explain to them why the behavior is inappropriate. Teachers who are sensitive to the needs of toddlers end up with self-regulating classrooms. They also find peace and harmony in the process.

Creating an environment where children can move freely makes it easy for them to access materials. The teacher should only restrict movement in the classroom when it endangers the child or others. One of the guiding principles of the Montessori method is respect. Preparing a good learning environment also shows respect. It informs them that you care about their education. There must be change as the child moves through the stages of development. These changes are respected through the preparation of the environment. It is prepared in a way that facilitates optimal development. The Montessori method emphasized on the environment because it liberates children's learning. The main difference between the Montessori system and conventional education is that the former gives children the chance to discover answers for themselves in a prepared environment. Conventional education helps the child with nearly everything. The child barely gets a chance to explore things they love because of a restricted method. The Montessori method works because it enables children to get more in-depth experience and develop a strong interest in continued learning. The role of the teacher is to link the child to experiences and activities in the prepared environment. For the Montessori method to work, teachers must know and play their role accordingly. Montessori cannot work if unconventional methods are used, and the environment is not prepared. The classroom needs to support the development of creativity and imagination. Children can only be creative in a peaceful environment.

Chapter 4: Types of Activities and What They Promote

There are different types of Montessori activities that aid in childhood development. Eye-hand coordination activities are useful because they help the child develop normally. They also increase strength and enable the child to grow into a responsible individual. Hand-eye coordination exercises allow the eyes to guide the hands in the right movement. Eye-hand coordination is vital because it helps the child at many levels. It helps the child develop good handwriting. Visual-motor integration plays a big role in handwriting and comes from eye-hand coordination exercises. This is because the eye directs the hand in forming letters and letting them stay in line. Toddlers who do not acquire coordination skills have poor handwriting and struggle to put their thoughts or ideas across. Eye-hand coordination activities are recommended because they help the child focus on what he/she is doing. The eye is the one that guides the child, and this eliminates distractions. Eye-hand coordination activities are useful because they help in reading. Coordination skills help toddlers to develop eye-tracking skills, which are useful in reading. They can also acquire eye-tracking skills from games and other interesting activities. Coordination skills also come in handy in sports. A child who has good coordination skills catches the ball better than one without.

Moreover, the child can also hit the ball with a bat and move to demand sports activities. Therefore, parents and teachers should incorporate eye-hand coordination activities to nurture a child's interest in sports. Coordination skills are also vital in life as toddlers use them to stack towers or build with Lego. Having known the benefits of eye-hand coordination, parents should provide the necessary materials to nurture such skills.

There are several activities that toddlers can engage in to develop eye-hand coordination skills. They can partake in suspended ball activities. To make this exercise simpler, suspend a ball in a net to avoid chasing it while the child practices coordination skills. You can use a net bag, pop the ball in, and knot it. Tie it to reach a rope length, and it should be long enough to reach the child's chest. Suspend the ball away from you. You can push and catch or bat it. Parents should show their children how it is done and then let them practice. Another activity that children can do to improve their eye-hand coordination skills is rolling a ball. This exercise is amazing for toddlers because it is fun and different from usual activities. To do this exercise, let the child lie with lets apart, and proceed to roll the ball to them. Ask the child to stop the ball before it hits the body. The child needs to focus keenly on the ball as you roll it to stop it from hitting the body.

Moreover, he will coordinate the hands to stop the ball before it hits the body. This exercise is great for toddlers and preschoolers. Another exciting coordination activity is object relays. This exercise is great because the whole family can join in. It is great for hand-eye coordination and builds endurance. Let the children stand in a line and pass the ball to the one behind them. Start by passing the ball overhead and switch to between the legs. Tell the toddlers to use both hands to receive and pass the ball. Teachers can make the activity fun by putting a bucket of objects in front that will be transferred to an empty bucket at the end.

Another exercise toddler can participate in to improve eye-hand coordination is passing and tossing the ball. It requires a lot of concentration for the child to pass or toss a ball with both hands. Start by giving the child a light object to pass and move to heavier ones when they become stronger. Eye-hand coordination is a neurological process that parents need to encourage from an early age. It goes hand in hand with fine motor skills and gross motor skills. There are several ways to foster the development of coordination skills. For toddlers to master coordination skills, they need to practice for some time. Play forms an essential part in the development of eye-hand coordination skills. From basic activities such as picking toys to complex ones, these skills develop as the child grows. Parents who are concerned about the child's hand-eye coordination should seek professional help. The secret to improving coordination skills lies in doing exercises that do not focus on objects or destinations, but the space in between.

Another activity that toddlers can do to improve their coordination skills is bouncing a ball. Let the child hold a racket in front of them, with the palm facing up. Hold the racket with them if they are unable to do it alone at first. Take a ball, and tell the child to bounce it as many times as possible without missing it. Have them repeat this exercise many times throughout the day. A wall ball exercise is another great exercise that improves eye-hand coordination. It is amazing because the child cannot do it alone. To do this exercise, tell a child to take a ball and throw it in front of the wall and catch it. Repeat this exercise and move far from the wall, the more they practice. Jigsaw puzzles are also great for improving eye-hand coordination skills. They can improve fine motor skills and sharpen visual perceptions. They are also effective in a child's development.

Moreover, jigsaw puzzles improve the child's memory and help them set goals. Parents need to choose an age-appropriate puzzle. Choosing a difficult puzzle leads to frustration and can demotivate the child from using puzzles in the future. There are several options to choose from to enhance eye-hand coordination skills. Parents and teachers have no excuse for not incorporating fun activities to nurture such skills. They do not have to adopt all the activity because a few go a long way in developing eye-hand coordination skills.

The good thing with practical life activities is that parents do not spend money on buying materials. Everything that they need for practical life activities is found in the house. Practical life activities should be encouraged because they give children life skills. These are skills that may not be acquired in the classroom. The teacher can only tell the child how certain things are done at home, but may not show them. For example, the teacher can explain to the child how to make the bed but never show them. This approach to learning is limited because the child only hears, but never sees how it is done. Practical life activities allow parents to show their children how things are done. It works better if there is less talking and more action. It is also a great opportunity for parents to interact with their children as they learn skills that will help them in the future. Moreover, parents get to be part of their children's education.

Examples of practical life activities include making the bed, putting dishes in the dishwasher, wiping the table, and cleaning the house. Parents should give toddlers exercises that they can complete. Some parents think that it is wrong to give children because they are too young, but that is far from the truth. As long as the task is age-appropriate, there is no problem. Parents can start by showing children simple chores around the house, such as wiping the table or putting dishes in the dishwasher. Once they master these skills, move to hectic ones. Buy child-sized materials to make it easy for the toddler to participate. Instead of making their beds every morning, parents should show their children how it is done.

Start by showing them how to spread a sheet and show them another aspect the next day. Remember to slow down when teaching toddlers practical life activities at home or school. Do not overwhelm them with many activities at once because they may get confused. Moreover, congratulate them for doing a good job. Another practical life activity that can be done at home or school is making the flowerbed. Parents can make this activity more exciting by using actual flowers and allowing the child to participate. Start by showing the child how it is done and let them take over. Give them little flowers to use in case you do not have a lot to use afterward. Practical life activities are beneficial because they help parents to form strong bonds with their children. The child becomes attached to the parent when they do things together. It also boosts their self-esteem and confidence. Practical life activities help the child to understand the world and find their place in it. The child grows into an independent adult who can do things by themselves and help others. Practical life activities are important because they prepare children for the real world.

The best way to cultivate a healthy lifestyle is to start young. There are various movement exercises that children can do to stay active. Music is a great alternative for toddlers who have a difficult time finding what they like. There is no doubt that music is an effective tool for learning. Exposing children to music has profound benefits, such as boosting their confidence, boost brain power, and promote social skills. Studies have proven countless benefits of music and movement to toddlers. The best way to get the child to move around is to play music. This concept also applies to adults. When adults go to the gym, they usually have headphones to play music as they exercise. This is because music empowers and motivates them through the workout routine. Similar to how adults play music for motivation, toddlers use the same way. It makes learning enjoyable. Combining music and movement is a great way to help them develop gross and fine motor skills.

There are basic music and movement exercises toddlers can do at home or at school. They can wiggle the toes, flex the feet, clap hands, shake the hips, stomp their feet, or bend their necks. Parents should show the child how the exercise is done and leave them to practice. They should monitor the child to avoid injury because of using a lot of force. Toddlers can also snap their fingers, reach high and low. Toddlers can also practice advanced music and movement exercises to maximize learning. They can do the jumping jacks, dance, squats, and run around. Music and movement are a good way for toddlers to socialize together. It also keeps them active and motivated. Children become more comfortable and thrilled about physical activities, as they get older. A child may not like being part of social events now but will enjoy it as years pass by. The aim of including music and movement exercises is to make learning fun and teach kids the importance of healthy living. It is good to balance active and quiet times in the classroom. Leaning on one side too much is destructive and does not motivate a child to learn new things. Moreover, the attention span of toddlers is short, and they want to move their bodies. The good thing with music and movement exercises is that it is not a must that you play an instrument or have a good voice for toddlers to have fun. Teachers can play a CD and ask the children to move around. Music is a crucial part of the toddler curriculum and should be adopted by every education program. Music and movement exercises are good because they promote physical development, creativity, improve language and communication. They also promote active listening and social interactions. Children cannot stay for a long time.

Playing music is a great way to get calm or quieter children to get involved in in-class activities. Toddlers can do the plate dance or walk in the jungle while listening to music. Another great way to make music enjoyable for toddlers is to have them bang on drums. Drums can be made from recycled tins and used during music and movement exercises. Have a movement break for a few minutes so that the child can relax. Children who have musical instruments at home can carry them to school for practice. Music and movement exercises should not be monotonous or restrict a child's movement. The teacher should create space where children can jump, dance or run freely.

Chapter 5: Practical life activities

Parenting can be very frustrating at times. And it takes a lot of patience to learn the best ways to raise a toddler. The Montessori way offers the best guide in bringing up those kids with a range of activity-based processes that help in creating a good bond between the two of you. However, many parents find it difficult to pinpoint where to start from or the areas put the most emphasis on. As a Montessori parent, you should not forget to center your concentration fully on the utmost essential area of a Montessori classroom; the practical life area. This area encompasses the day-to-day exercise and undertakings of your toddler and is a very crucial part of the development of the toddler.

Introduction to Practical Life activities

Practical Life activities are the daily drills aimed at helping a toddler to understand the events in his/her daily life and learn how to do basic things in a resolute manner. Additionally, practical life activities help in enhancing the growth and development of a toddler by aiding in the harmonization of movement of body parts and imparting a sense of independence and order. As a result, a toddler is enabled to adapt to the environment and develop a good intellectual understanding of the surrounding and concentration skills.

Categories of the practical life activities and the target age bracket

Practical life activities are applicable for young toddlers of up to 5 or 6 years old in the various classroom settings (home, church, school, etc.). The activities are classified into five main categories namely; preliminary activities, self-sustaining activities, activities that enhance care for the environment, activities that enhance the elegance and good manners, and activities for control of movement.

1. Preliminary activities

Preliminary activities are often the baseline activities that are introduced in the first days of the toddler. They are important for the orientation of the toddlers to the environment. These activities are always done with definite materials that do not require an introduction. Ideas made known are grouping, pairing, matching, and three- dimensional relations, and the content is mostly dimensions and outlines. The materials help develop coordination and physical skill. Preliminary activities can be categorized into two;

The first category involves activities that isolate motion related to certain objects in the environment or movements within the environment. Examples within this category are; carrying a book, moving an object, etc.

The second category of activities is one that isolates a specific but important movement from a more complex order of work. For instance, opening a bottle.

- **Carrying objects (for example, a book)**

This activity is aimed at developing a voluntary movement of the arms by teaching the toddlers how to cope up with the necessary movement of the arm in lifting and setting down a book. The activity is best for toddlers aged two and a half years and above.

Step by step

The parent/teacher should prepare the material, in this case, a book, by placing it on a flat surface (table). Make the toddlers comfortable (seated) and make them aware of the book on the table. Introduce your presentation by saying what you are going to do.

- **Lifting**

  i. Have one thumb over the book cover with the rest of the fingers underneath it. Note that you should always use the hand you are most comfortable with.

ii. Lift the book by swinging your arm from the elbow until it is at a vertically level higher above the table where the toddlers can clearly observe.

iii. Move the book towards the toddlers noting to maintain the vertical distance above the table.

- **Setting Down**

Remember to remind the toddlers about the activity you are about to teach. The introduction makes the alert and ready to observe and learn.

- ✔ Carefully lower your arm towards the tabletop.
- ✔ Let the book rest on the table by removing letting grasp of it.

At this point, ask the toddlers to do what they have observed.

- **Opening and closing a door**

You are required to draw the attention of the toddler towards a door with a door handle. The handle must be at a height that the kid can reach for this activity to be effective.

Step by step

i. Grasp the handle and turn it downwards.

ii. Pull the door gently towards you or away from you depending on the direction that it turns to when opening.

iii. Once the door is open, and the toddler has observed carefully, push the door gently to close it.

iv. Invite the toddler to open and close the door by following the steps you have shown.

- **Rolling and unrolling a carpet**

The activity is essential in developing coordination, movement of the body, and attentiveness. You only need a carpet and the attention your kid for the activity.

Step by step

i. Lay down the carpet on the floor.

ii. Put your palm beneath the carpet and roll it slowly, showing the toddler all the motions.

iii. To unroll the carpet, put your hand on one edge of the carpet and slide it open on the floor.

iv. Invite the toddler to participate in rolling and unrolling the carpet.

- **Folding Clothes**

For the exercise, you require pieces of clothes and a cloth-basket. Prepare for the presentation by inviting the toddlers to the workstation. Place the cloth-basket where all the toddlers are able to observe clearly. Remind the toddlers that they are about to learn folding clothes by observing how you fold the clothes. The purpose of the exercise is to help the toddlers learn well-developed control of their hands in preparation for geometry by intuitive engagement in, and observation of, the lines of the folded clothes. The activity is recommended for toddlers aged between 2 ½ - 4 years.

Step by step

Note: Make sure that every toddler has a tray of cloth.

Folding

i. Place a flat piece of cloth on a tabletop.

ii. Have your palm underneath the cloth and fold into half

iii. Repeat the second step until the cloth cannot be folded anymore.

iv. Slowly slide out the palm from beneath the folded clothing.

Unfolding

The easiest way to unfold a piece of clothing is pinching one corner and lifting it. The clothing will unfold automatically. Alternatively, you can slide your palm into the half fold of the clothing and lift the other half towards you until it is flat on the tabletop. Once the activity is complete, and all the toddlers have folded and unfolded their pieces of clothes, replace the clothes in the basket.

- **Opening and closing a bottle**

The exercise is intended to strengthen the hands and wrist of toddlers and also help them learn how to handle the task of opening and closing a bottle well by themselves. The main point of interest is to feel the rotational effect of the lid of a bottle when it is opening and closing. The age bracket that is best suited for the exercise is 2 ½ - 3 ½ years.

Step by step

Opening

i. Wrap the lid of a closed bottle with your fingers.

ii. Twist the lid of the bottle in an anticlockwise direction until it opens.

iii. Raise the lid for the toddlers to observe.

Closing

i. Hold the bottle on one hand

ii. Wrap your fingers around the lid and replace on the opening of the bottle

iii. Twist the lid in the clockwise direction until it cannot move anymore.

iv. Lift the bottle up for the toddlers to observe.

Let the toddlers try their hands in opening and closing their bottles.

- **Turning the pages of a Book**

The gentleness required in this activity helps in creating awareness among toddlers on how to treat their books. It is good for toddlers between 2 ½ - 3 years.

Materials

A book, a chair, and a table.

Step by step

i. While seated at a central position, put the thumb of your hand on the edge of the book cover.

ii. Lift the cover slightly just enough to put your palm beneath it.

iii. Move the cover page to tilt leftwards. Do the same for other pages.

- **Siting and standing from a chair**

The exercise requires a chair and the attention of the toddlers. Slowly demonstrate to the toddler how to seat gently on the chair and how to stand up from it. It is purposeful in aiding the toddler to advance the necessary movement skills to avoid missing the chair.

2. Self-sustaining activities

Activities that enhance care for one's self are highly regarded in a Montessori classroom. It is essential to help the toddlers identify their physical needs and learn how to meet those needs. Parents often act hastily by trying to do everything for their toddlers. However, it is recommended that we slow down and help the toddlers do certain things on their own. This creates a sense of impartiality and builds self-esteem among toddlers. A Montessori teacher or parent is required to guide toddlers in caring for themselves in a certain way.

- **Make the materials easy to get to (the accessibility factor)**

The most important aspect of helping a toddler to care for himself/herself is by availing the essential materials and making them easy to access. Always try to keep the resources required for the physical care of the toddler within their reach.

- **Take your time**

Parents need to bid their time when dealing with toddlers. Yes, it takes a lot of time for the kids to master the skills required to do things on their own. A lot of patience is required to guide them. Give them room to grow and develop the skills. Take your time and think about it as a time investment. It takes longer now, but when they finally learn, they make it easier for you.

- **Create awareness**

At this early age, toddlers are not aware of certain aspects of their lives and may fail to notice the need to help themselves. Use a neutral voice to remind them when their hands are dirty or their nose running and try to guide them in fixing their mess. Make your choice familiar with the skills you would wish them to possess.

- **A little help is just enough**

The key principle in this section is to help the toddlers acquire the necessary skills for self-care. Try doing things with them instead of doing things for them. Monitor your kids carefully and give them a little help required to be successful. At times just, sit back and watch them struggle a bit before jumping in to help.

After taking the above steps into serious consideration, it is time to try out the following self-care activities with your little one.

- **Nose blowing**

It is important to set up a station within the Montessori classroom (your house) that has a tissue basket with tissues in it, a mirror, a dustbin, and some running water and hand wash detergents. These are required in helping the toddlers blow their running nose.

Step by step

i. Show your toddler how to blow and wipe her nose.

ii. Remind her to check her face in the mirror to confirm if it is clean.

iii. Throw the used tissue in the dustbin.

iv. Using water and the handwashing detergent, help the toddler wash her hands after blowing her nose.

- **Hand washing**

There are many ways to integrate this activity into the lives of your toddlers. First, you can start by providing wet wipes or hand towels and letting the toddlers help wipe their hands after activities that make their hands dirty, before eating and after having a meal, etc. the second method involves teaching them how to wash their hands using soap and water. In case your sink is raised above the reach of toddlers, consider providing a stepping stool. Note to use warm water to encourage the toddlers to wash their hands most of the time. Show your toddlers the necessary hand washing steps like wetting their hands in water, applying soap to the wet hands, rinsing the hands with clean water, and finally using a towel to dry their hands.

- **Helping with diapers**

Toddlers like to get involved with their stuff. For starters, encourage the toddler to hold the new diaper as you prepare to put it on. Lending a hand creates awareness to the baby about the environment. Additionally, you can show your kids how to pull wipes out of their containers. This activity amuses kids and helps them learn.

- **Dressing and undressing**

A Montessori mom is encouraged to help the independence of the toddler by helping them to learn how to dress and undress on their own. At an early stage, your toddler can help by pushing down his pants or taking off the socks. For the purpose of learning this activity, moms are encouraged to use simple clothes that are easy to pull off.

- **Buckling and unbuckling**

Provide a set of a buckle, considerably on a dressing frame. The end goal is the toddler to acquire the skills needed to buckle or unbuckle on her own. The activity helps coordinate movement and create self-awareness.

Step by step

i. To unbuckle, Pinch the strap and pull it out with one hand as the other hand holds the mettle buckle loop.

ii. Buckle up and let the kid unbuckle. If successful, proceed to buckle.

iii. For the buckling lesson, pinch the tip of the strap and guide it with your hand through the loop.

iv. Pull the strap to fit the desired size.

v. Position the pin into the hole on the strap that corresponds to it. Invite the toddler to demonstrate the activities simultaneously.

- **Hooking and unhooking**

Some of the clothes we use on our kids have the hook and eye. It is, therefore important to show them how to hook and unhook safely. The activity supplements dressing and undressing in toddlers. For the exercise, you need a pair of hook and eye mounted on a dressing frame or a piece of cloth in the house that has a hook and eye.

Step by step

i. To hook, hold the hook in one hand and the eye on the other hand.

ii. Insert the hook into the eye slowly for your toddler to observe effectively.

iii. To unhook, put the hook side on one hand and the eye side on the other slide the hook slowly out of the eye.

iv. Invite your toddler to do the exercise as you observe to correct an error.

- **Brushing hair**

For this activity, make sure that a smooth hairbrush and a mirror are easy to get to. Show your toddler how to brush her hair from the top downwards checking in the mirror to find out if the heir is neatly done.

- **Brushing teeth**

Babies are capable of brushing their own teeth at a very tender age. Make sure to brush your teeth as the kids observe and help them brush theirs for a start. Later on, you can let them brush on their own and even teach them how to apply toothpaste on the toothbrush.

- **Getting a drink**

It is important to make water easy to get to for your kids. Set out a specific station for a water jug and glass, notably on a table or shelf in the kitchen where they reach. As they grow old, they can use the water dispenser. Putting a towel or a mop in the station is essential as it helps the toddlers to dry water spills on the table and floor.

- **Preparing food**

This activity is very important in refining fine motor dexterities and attentiveness and is very engaging to the toddlers. Start by showing your toddlers how to prepare simple food such as peeling a banana. As time goes by, you can show them how to spread butter on a slice of bread. Toddlers can also learn by arranging spoons in a container

- **First aid**

Simple first aid skills can be mastered and done by the kids. If the injuries are not serious like a simple scratch, show the toddler how to clean the affected area using alcohol swabs. You can place the alcohol swabs and first aid bands in a tray at a place that is easy to get to.

- **Applying Lotion and sunscreen**

This activity can be very simple if you show the toddler what to do. Provide a small bottle of lotion or sunscreen and show the toddler how to squeeze the bottle gently and applying the lotion. Do not forget to provide a mirror for this activity.

- **Shoe polishing**

Showing your toddler how to polish his shoes refines concentration through preparation and order and the advancement of a well-developed control mechanism of the hands. Take on the steps one by one, as the toddler observes. Alternatively, you can provide two pairs of material each so that the toddler does what you are doing concurrently. Do not forget to put on an apron and help your toddler put on one too as the activity can get messy for starters. Once you are done, put everything away in its rightful place and invite the toddler to wash his hands.

- **Zipping and unzipping**

As part of showing your toddler how to dress, zipping and unzipping is very important a skill in the development stage of the toddler's life. For starters, you should provide a dressing frame with a zipper to make an observation and practice easy. Commence the presentation by placing your thumb beneath the zipper and your index finger over the zipper so that the fingers nip with the zipper in between. Move the zipper up and down as you tell your toddler that that is how to zip and unzip. Since you are using a frame, remember to ask the toddler to show you where a zipper is in his clothes. The activity is vital in enhancing coordination of movement.

3. Care for the environment

Our planet should be taken good care of to ensure that the limited resources last longer to benefit us all. There is no recommended age to start teaching your toddler how to take care of the environment. Care for the environment should be introduced into the life of the toddler as soon as they start to recognize things around them. A Montessori parent is urged to impart the skills to reduce, reuse, and recycle in the toddlers to help maintain a cleaner and greener environment.

The activities that foster care for the environment are meant to help the toddlers take part in making their surroundings clean and relate freely with the things in the environment; nurture the interaction of the toddler with the environment. Additionally, as the kids interact with their environment, the activities refine their sense of responsibility.

The activities need a lot of patience, depending on the age of the kids you are dealing with. They may not be able to make a big difference but don't they say that baby steps are still steps? Introduce the undertakings slowly and integrate more complex ones as the toddler grows. In no time, you will realize that the toddlers can make a remarkable difference in your home.

- Outdoor Sweeping

Your kids can help you do outdoor sweeping from the age of three. Helping your toddler to develop environmental awareness is the primary aim of this activity. It also improves the controlled movements of the body. Using a broom show the toddler how to sweep, moving the dust to collect in one place before scooping the dust and putting it in a bin. Remember to put on gloves when picking up the dust. Ask your toddler to sweep another section of the driveway.

- Washing a Chalkboard

The materials required for this activity are a sponge of a piece of cloth, water in a bowl, and dry cloth. The purpose of the activity is to aid the toddler to identify the buildup of chalk-dust on the chalkboard and show him how to clean it independently. For the presentation, soak the sponge in the bowl of water; squeeze the sponge to drip off excess water. Place the sponge on the chalkboard and wipe the board clean. Once the entire board is wiped clean, dry it using the extra piece of cloth. Let your toddler take his turn in doing the cleaning.

- Polishing Glass

Nothing beats the joy of seeing your toddler lend a hand in doing the household chores. Well, this is made possible by teaching them how to do simple tasks like polishing glass. Using a piece of cloth apply some polish on the mirror and let it dry. Once dry, remove the polish by wiping the mirror surface with a clean wet cloth. Dry the mirror and let your toddler polish another mirror. Put everything away and wash your hands as your kid does the same after the activity. It is crucial to put on an apron for this and other cleaning exercises.

- Setting a table

You are required to set aside a table for this activity. Alongside the table have a stool with a mug, a bowl, a small serving dish, a table knife, a teaspoon, and a tablemat. The activity not only creates a sense of independence but also integrates the toddler into the social structure.

Step by step

i. Ask your toddler to pick one object at a time and show her, by pointing, where you want it placed.

ii. Once the table is set, ask the toddler to help carry food to the table. Remember to start with light and cold items only.

- **Dusting a table**

The required materials are a duster or a piece of cloth. Place the duster on the tape and wipe the entire top of the table. You can also add soapy water but dipping the duster in the water and using it to wipe the table. In case you used water, rinse the duster, and use it to dry the table. Alternatively, you can use a separate dry cloth to dry the table. Ask the toddler to do the same.

- **Arranging Flowers**

The improvement of aesthetic sense through isolation is very possible at an early stage. Your toddler can absorb how to cut the stems of flowers and arrange them neatly in a flower vase. Pour water in a vase until it is ¼ full. Using a pair of scissors cut the tip of the stem of the flower such that the remaining tip fits nicely in the vase. Ask the toddler to cut the other tips and put the cut flowers in the vase. Use flowers that are just enough for the vase. Once the flowers are neatly arranged, tell your toddler to move the vase to a desired spot in the house. Clean the workstation.

4. Grace and courtesy

The activities in this section were introduced to bring order in the life of the toddler. It is fundamental that the toddler gets acquainted with the social structures in place to understand his/her surroundings well. The activities on elegance and good mannerism build the vocabulary of the toddler along with helping in improved awareness of the surroundings and the receptiveness of the people around the toddler. As a result, the toddler gets oriented to the natural and social space.

The improvement of courtesy skills begins at an early stage as the toddler gets to know how to associate with the people and the surroundings at large. As a parent, it is your role to use the right words, clear-cut activities, and presentation steps as you assist the toddler to develop a good indulgent of himself as well as others. At the right time, the toddler will get a grip of the hows, the whens, and the where to apply the terms for a more satisfying life for others and him. In the long run, the toddler learns to integrated good mannerism into his life on a daily basis.

- **Introducing one's self**

Show your toddlers how to introduce themselves when they meet someone new, for instance, "Hello my name is Leah." Remind them that they can shake your guests' hands while introducing themselves.

- **Greeting a Person**

For this activity, you need to show your toddlers how to greet each other while maintaining eye contact. You can shake their hands as you say "hello Lisa" or "hello Jimmy" and teaching them how to respond. Other great words to use for this activity are "good morning," "good afternoon," etc.

- **Showing gratitude**

It is important to teach your toddlers to show gratitude and appreciation by saying thank you. Ask them always to say thank you if someone gives them something or does something nice to them. You can integrate this activity during meals when you pas the salt or help them tie a napkin.

- **Interrupting**

As much as it is never polite to interrupt someone, we sometimes have to get their attention, and in so doing, we should use the most polite way. In the case of dialogue, you should teach how to take turn politely.

Words such as "excuse me, can I have your attention for a moment" or "I'm sorry to interrupt but really need to speak to you" are important to help the toddler develop polite vocabulary when interrupting others.

- Coughing

It is important that a toddler knows what to do when coughing to avoid coughing on other people. For the activity, you should tilt your face slightly away from the toddler, place your fore a close to your mouth, cough then close your mouth before removing the forearm and turning to face the toddler. Explain the steps to the toddler and have them exaggerate a cough as they do what you have shown and explained

- Yawning

What you need to do when teaching your toddler how to yawn is already explained in the activity above (coughing). Just for clarity, you can repeat the explanations to the toddler and have them practice yawning the right way.

- Control of movement

As the kids grow and master new skills, they tend to move around grabbing items they can get to. With time, the kids develop more skills and can do a handful of activities. This sequence shows that toddlers are always in learning mode as they try to discover their bodies and how to control their movements.

This period is very essential in the development of the toddler. They find a lot of excitement in doing certain tasks successfully, like scooping grain without a single spill. The activities at this stage of growth are very important.

- **Walking on the Line**

From the age of three, your toddler should be able to exercise, better, and fuse the movements of the body. Walking on the line activity is a good exercise for this. The activity helps the toddler to have better control of the body, improve stability and balance along with developing the action of the mind in controlling the movement of the body. For the activity, the line denotes a continuous path in the environment. The distance between the lines should be just wide enough to accommodate the shoes of the toddler. The line should not be hidden or concealed. For a group, place your toddlers on the line midway between each other. Ask them to walk in the line while maintaining the distance in between and to stop when you ask them to.

Walking on the line activity can be supplemented by other advanced ideas;

- **Hopping over a log**

Hopping over a piece of the log may seem easy and simple, but the amount of concentration and coordination required to perform the task is essential in the development of the toddler. Additionally, the energy level required to jump over, again and again, is enormous. The activity not only keeps the toddler fit by enhancing the growth of muscles of the legs but also makes them sharp and attentive.

You can also challenge your toddlers to walk on the log. This gives them the outdoor version of walking on the line and is an adventurous upgrade to the traditional walking on the line activity. The log activity requires additional balance as compared to the line.

Note: To avoid injuries, never let young kids do this exercise on their own until they have mastered the skills very well.

- **The silence game**

Everyone needs a moment of tranquility and peace of mind to have a rest and meditate. Endless noise may lead to petulance, obstruction, misperception, and even drowsiness. Dr. Montessori observed that a profound level of consciousness and thoughtfulness could help in creating a more advanced and elusive environment. For this purpose, the silence game was introduced.

During this activity, the toddlers are expected to stay quiet. Staying quiet means that the toddler has to have great control of the movements of the body and connect with the mind. The toddler must have a decent synchronization of body movement and the brain, possess a solid resolve and have pronounced responsiveness of the things and people in the surrounding.

Chapter 6: Sensorial activities

Sensorial exercises are activities that sharpen up the senses of the toddler; visual, auditory, tactile, olfactory, and gustatory. Toddlers are predominantly open to refining their senses from the early age of two, thus the importance of integrating the Montessori sensorial activities into their lives. The materials for these activities should be prudently designed to meet the basic principles set out by Dr. Maria Montessori. The Montessori sensorial materials aim at sharpening the senses of the toddler to isolate and categorize materials distinctively in his/her environment. As a result, toddlers are offered the chance to refine their intelligence in regard to the surrounding.

The Montessori materials for refining the senses of toddlers are specifically designed to;

i. Help the toddler to concentrate on isolating and identifying one quality at a time.

ii. Help the toddlers in making their own corrections through the control of the error feature of the material.

iii. The materials are physically attractive to call in the attention of the toddler and help in maintaining focus and concentration.

iv. The sets of materials are usually complete to help the toddler go through the exercise to completion without having to pause in between the activity to find a misplaced part.

v. The materials are meant to turn theoretical ideas into substantial concepts.

Sensorial Activities for Toddlers

Note: for the activities in this section, toddlers are defined as toddlers under the age of five. Nonetheless, the activities are not for a specific age group only. Monitor your toddler to know what he/she likes and can do with ease because they develop at different paces.

- **The coin box**

The coin box, or alternatively a domino box, enhances the hand-eye coordination of toddlers. The material is designed with closing and opening slots and a hole in the top lid. Toddlers are encouraged to fit certain objects in the box, which is opened when full to remove the objects. The disappearing and reappearing of the objects in and out of the box refine the concentration of the while the exercise of fitting objects into the hole improves accuracy.

- **Straws in a cup**

This activity involves putting colored straws in different containers, and the toddler is invited to empty one at a time then put the straws back. To upgrade this exercise, a Montessori teacher is encouraged to use colored containers so that the toddler can sort the straws according to colors when putting them back into the containers.

- **The texture basket**

The texture tray or basket is a guileless activity that draws the attention of toddlers into isolating the texture of materials. For the exercise, you are required to assemble different materials within the house and put them in a tray or basket. Invite the toddler to feel the items by turning them over their hands and help them identify and isolate soft, in one basket, and hard, in a different basket. Note that you should use simple words for this exercise.

- **Sound cylinders**

Sound cylinders are stress-free and the most charming materials to make and use. Toddlers are always delighted to hear the different sounds produced by the cylinders. For the activity, use a control cylinder (say a yellow cylinder) to make the first sound by shaking it. Proceed to the next cylinder (say red). Shake the second cylinder and ask the toddler to differentiate the sound from the first one. If the sound made is the same, the cylinders are put in one tray. Different sounds are put in separate trays. Invite the toddlers to shake the cylinders and sort them according to the sound they make.

- **Color marbles**

This activity helps learners to differentiate colors. Toddlers are invited to sort the marbles according to their colors and putting them in a matching container. For a start, consider using simple or primary colors like red yellow, white and blue. In the presentation, remember to read out the colors of the marbles and the containers to the toddlers as you match them. Once all the items are sorted, return them in a basket and invite your toddlers to sort them. Additionally, you can upgrade this activity by increasing the range of colors and playing the color hunt game where you ask the toddler to point a certain color in the house.

- The grain box

This activity involves providing a variety of grains in different texture and size. Pool different grains, like rice, beans, sand, stones, beads, etc. in a tray, basket or box. Invite the toddler to feel the texture, isolate the color, or isolate by size. For safety purposes, bear in mind the age of the toddler and the grain provided. Always keep watch when carrying out this activity.

- Spooning ice

This activity is best suited for a hot day. You are required to provide ice in a bowl, an empty bowl and a pair of tongs or a spoon. Show the toddler how to scoop and lift ice with a spoon or tongs from one bowl into the other. Invite the toddler to try his hands on the activity. You can also ask the toddler to feel the temperature of the bowl with ice and the empty bowl by wrapping their palms around the bowl. This activity can be upgraded once the ice has melted by transferring the water from one bowl into the other using a syringe.

- Sorting by shape

For his activity, you should begin with a sample pack of simple shapes. For the start, provide the same shapes in the same color. At this point, your toddlers can sort according to color. Advance by mixing the colors but maintaining the shapes. As you progress, introduce tracing the shapes on a piece of paper or board. For the presentation, name the shapes as you sort them first before inviting your toddlers to do the same.

- **Fabric board**

This activity is very crucial in introducing texture to toddlers. The activity involves presenting different fabric squares of different textures and inviting the toddler to feel the difference. The textures are described in simple words like rough, soft, and silky, etc. the toddler is expected to match the fabrics with a similar texture. A homemade fabric board is made by cutting a piece of Styrofoam placard into a good size that fits into your basket or tray. Next, you glue different fabrics on each placard.

- **Simple puzzle**

This activity is essential in helping toddlers to decode size and shape. The best puzzle for starters should be a 1-3 shape puzzle. The puzzle can be made by cutting a placard into one shape (say triangle), then drawing a puzzle in the shape. Cut out the drawn lines. Using a different piece of paper, drawn a rough draft of the puzzle to be used as a control. Invite the toddler to set up the cut pieces to form a complete shape seen on the control paper.

- The Pink tower

A complete pink tower consists of ten cubes of different sizes. For this activity, invite your toddler to help you carry the cubes to your play station. Starting with the largest cube, construct the tower by piling the next largest cubes on top until all the cubes are used. In case the toddler is not able to identify the next largest cube, help them by pointing out the cube.

- Knobbed cylinders

The knobbed cylinders are meant to help the toddler differentiate height and diameter. Each block consists of roughly five cylinders decreasing in height and diameter. Show the toddler how to carry the cylinders from one station to the other from the biggest to the smallest, which help them in arranging the cylinders inside one another. Once the entire block is done, replace the cylinders in their original station.

Hanging Ball Activities

The set of activities in this section involves the use of a suspended ball. The ball is suspended to save you the time of chasing after missed balls as the exercise goes on. Set up the activity by putting a ball in a net and tying it with a rope. Suspend the ball on a hook, taking note to make it a level chest of the toddler.

- Racket and ball

Help your toddler to hit the suspended ball using a ratchet. The point is to let the ball swing back and forth without missing a hit. Make the activity more challenging by using smaller balls and ratchets.

- Push and Catch

The exercise requires the toddler to push the ball and catch it as it swings back without missing or letting it bang against their body. This helps in refining concentration by carefully watching the ball swing from and to the hands. Upgrade to more challenging series by asking the toddler to clap in between the catch and the push.

Hand-eye coordination ball games

- Rolling a Ball

For this activity, sit opposite to your toddler. Have them sit with legs apart facing you. Roll the ball towards the toddler and ask them to catch the ball before it hits the body. The activity requires the toddler to watch the rolling ball prudently and synchronize the hands into stopping the ball before it reaches the body.

- Ball Relays

This activity is good for many kids. The process requires that you provide a basin or basket full of balls. Make the kids line up behind each other and place an empty basket or basin at a good distance from them. The exercise is picking a ball and running to the empty basket to put it there. Once the kid has put the ball in the basket, she runs back and lines up behind the other kids. This arrangement ensures that every kid has a turn to pick a ball, run and put in the other basket before coming back. Alternatively, the kids can line up in between the baskets with each kid keeping their position permanently. The kid closer to the basket with balls picks a ball and passes it to the next kid until the ball reaches the last kid who puts it in the empty basket. The activity goes on, once the other basket is full. To introduce more challenges, you can increase the distance between the toddlers and ask them to toss the ball to each other or pass it overhead.

- Tossing and passing a ball

This activity requires a lot of focus and concentration from the kids to toss the ball overhead to one another without missing a catch or overpassing the ball. Position the kids at a distance from each other. Give them a ball and ask them to toss it to each other. Increase the challenge by making circles on the ground and asking the kids to stay in the circle when tossing and catching the ball.

- **Ball to wall toss and rebound**

This exercise follows the toss and catches activity. Once the kids can pass the ball and catch it successfully, you upgrade to the ball-wall toss. Here, you show the toddler how to toss a ball against a wall and wait for the rebound. The toddler is expected to catch the ball as it rebounds back. Keep a record book to note down the number of successful tosses and catch before the ball falls down. Always encourage your toddler by offering a present every time they break their record.

- **Toss and catch**

One of the best hand-eye coordination activities is tossing the ball up in the air and catching it again. The exercise becomes more challenging when you introduce a circle that the toddler is required to maintain standing in when tossing and catching the ball. Additionally, as your toddler makes progress, encourage to toss higher.

- **Threading and Lacing**

Another activity that enhances hand-eye coordination is stringing beads or lacing up cards. For a start, use beads with larger holes and reduce the size of the holes as the toddler makes progress.

- **Beads in a straw**

This activity requires a lot of concentration and supervision because of the size of beads used. You are expected to present colored straws and small beads of different colors. Help the toddler fit the beads in a straw of the same color.

- **Tasting bottle**

This game is fundamental in helping a toddler to isolate the four major tastes; salty, sweet, bitter, and sour. The game also helps improve the responsiveness of the toddler to understand the connection between palate and scent. The activity involves presenting different bottles, each containing a different taste. The game is to taste the contents of the bottle and identify the taste.

- **Smelling jars**

Just like the taste bottles, the smelling jars are presented containing different scent. The toddler is invited to smell each jar and differentiate the odor in each jar. This activity helps in building the ability of the toddler to isolate the odor.

- **Matching thermic tablets and bottles**

The game is aimed at refining the thermic sense of the toddler. The materials required are a set of thermic tablets in a box. For the presentation, remove all the tablets and place them on a tabletop. Invite the toddler to feel the temperature of each with the back of the hand. Due to the difference in heat conductivity, the tablets will have a varying range of temperature according to the material they are made of. For the game part, you can ask the toddler to close the eyes and feel one table. Ask the toddler to find a tablet that feels the same without opening her eyes. Once done, have the toddler open her eyes and see if the tablets have been sorted correctly.

- **Maracas and clatters**

Put some maracas and clatters in an enclosed container. Invite the toddlers to shake the container as they listen to the sound produced. You can put on some soft music for the toddlers to shake the maracas and clatters along as they dance to the tunes.

Chapter 7: Language activities

This chapter explores the materials and activities that enhance the language development of a toddle. It is hard to isolate the materials that are categorized as language materials clearly. However, the descriptions are derived from the purpose of the material for the material to be considered a language material. For the start, any material that helps in strengthening the grip of the toddler is essential in helping the toddler develop writing skills thus the material is considered a language material. Furthermore, any activity that develops the visual isolation skills of the toddlers is categorized under language material and helps in reading and identifying letters, shapes, colors, etc. lastly, any activity that encompasses naming of objects in the toddler's surrounding is a language material.

The language materials in a Montessori classroom are specifically intended to demonstrate to the toddlers the ins and outs of both the inscribed and oral language. The ability to understand both the written and spoken language enables the toddlers to develop intellectually and improve their academic levels. The Montessori language materials are used to learn basic letters, resonances, sharp handwriting, and in due course writing and reading.

There exist a range of activities that help in building the language of toddlers, along with their ability to communicate both orally and in writing.

Relationship between the activities and language development

It is important to understand how the activities listed in this chapter relates to the development of language before presenting the activity to your toddler. For a start, it is import to note that all of these activities are meant for visual refinement. From this point of view, it can be argued that writing and reading involve the ability to decipher refined shapes in the form of letters and transferring them on a paper or surface or resonances and words respectively. Therefore, any activity that refines the visual ability of a toddler is directly related to language.

Good mastery of language commences with aural knowledge; toddlers isolate ideas and objects around them according to how they hear the sounds they make or how we speak of them. The silence game requires toddlers to close their eyes and pay attention to the sounds around them in silence. The game helps sharpen up the auditory sense of toddlers. The more the kids practice this activity, the more they develop sharp hearing skills and can isolate different sounds around them. The silence game raises the alertness of the toddlers to viva voce sounds and the desire for knowledge of things around them.

Pre-Writing Activities

- Picking up objects.

This activity requires chopsticks, a pair of tongs, or a spoon. The end goal is to strengthen the grip of the toddler. As a language development activity, it makes the toddler familiar with the requirements of grasping writing materials at an early stage. The activity also guides the movement of the hand.

- Pressing the bulb baster

The exercise of squeezing bulb basters works the same way as picking up objects. The firmness of the material helps in building muscles of the hand that is necessary for writing. Alternatively, you can guide your toddler to use a syringe or eyedroppers to transfer water from one container into the other.

- Knobbed puzzles

For the activity, present pieces of a puzzle with handles. Help the toddler arrange the puzzles to create the required shape. This activity is the last step in developing pre-writing skills.

Writing Activities

- Sandpaper Letters

Toddlers should be introduced to letters and sounds from an early stage. The activity helps the toddlers in isolating the consonants, vowels, and sounds. The presentation part of this activity involves constructing the alphabet by mounting sandpaper letters on board. Different boards are used for vowels, consonants, and sounds that cannot be represented by a single letter. Invite the toddler to take on the shapes of the letters and the sounds and to isolate them.

- Tracing Metal insets

The metal insets are basic in enhancing the fine motor skills required to write. Also called letter tracing, the metal insets come in a range of shapes and sizes. The metal insets can be of letters or shapes. For the presentation part, place one piece on a paper and using a pencil to trace the outlines of the piece of metal. Remove the metal and move to the next one. Invite your toddler to do the same. This activity strengthens the grasp of the toddler and helps in molding handwriting. The toddler can use the metal insets in many ways, such as tracing the inner and outer outlines, assembling a new shape.

- **Matching Vocabulary Cards**

Also called the three-part matching cards, the vocabulary cards are used to teach reading at the beginners' stage. The vocabulary cards consist of three parts. The first part shows the image; the second part has the word that describes the image while the third part consists of both the image and the word. The third part is used as the control. The activity involves matching of images or shapes and colors with the words that relate to or describe the images, shapes, and colors. The toddler is allowed to check the control card when stuck. This activity should come after the toddler has mastered letter and sound identification.

- **Writing and drawing in Sand tray**

Present a sand tray to the toddlers and invite them to write letters in the sand. Shake the tray to erase the letter as the toddler progresses to the next letter. Drawing shapes in the sand is also a good activity for toddlers.

- **Movable alphabets**

The moveable alphabets are used to complete the activities discussed above. Additionally, they can be used to label images or build word puzzles. As an activity, the moveable alphabets can be used to match written letters, words, or colors. Word formation at an advanced stage is an essential language activity that involves the moveable alphabets.

Reading activities

- **Graphic Symbols and their Key Sounds**

This activity can be used at a very tender age. The toddler is introduced to alphabets and the key sounds that the letters can represent. The most common material here is the reading alphabet chart. For easier understanding, the charts are made with a letter of the alphabet, an image or a symbol that the letter may represent and the word for the image. For instance, in the first box, you can have letter A, an image of an apple and the word "Apple." For the activity, the toddler is supposed to point a letter and read it like, "A for Apple…B for Boy…C for cat…until you reach letter z."

- **Sound Boxes**

The sound boxes, baskets or trays are filled with objects or the cards with images drawn on them. Along with the objects or small cards are moveable letters. The exercise is all about separating the letters on a flat surface then picking n object or card randomly from the basket. Every object picked should be placed above a letter that represents the object (say A for apple. This implies that an apple is placed on top of letter A). As the mastery of this activity is noticed, upgrade by letting the toddler spell out the entire name of the object using a set of moveable letters. At an advanced stage, the toddler is expected to write the names of these objects

- **Sorting Rhyme Cards**

The rhyme cards are language materials that consist of different words. For the activity, toddlers are required to identify words that are almost pronounced the same (rhyming words). Read each card and allow the toddlers to identify the rhyming cards. Cards with rhyming words are put together. This activity is good for toddlers to identify the relationship between sounds in the words.

- **Using the phonogram dictionary**

As the reading ability of your toddler advances, he/she needs a phonogram dictionary to help in pronunciation and knowing the meaning of the words. A phonogram dictionary consists of symbols that represent words. For example, the word dog can be represented by a picture of a dog alongside the word. This helps the toddler to identify the word easily and helps make reading enjoyable.

- **Playing the activity word game**

The exercise involves reading a word that can be acted upon, for instance, simple doing words like jump, clap, etc. read a word and ask the toddler to do the action. For instance, if you read the word "clap" have the toddler to clap. Once the toddler has mastered the game, introduce word cards. Ask the toddler to read the card and do the action. At an advanced stage, do the action and ask the toddler to guess the word then find a card with the word.

- **Matching pictures to real objects**

Give your toddler a set of cards with images on them. Ask the toddler to observe the image and identify where that object is in the house. For example, a cup.

- **Reading picture books**

Picture books are effective in refining the reading skills of young toddlers. The book consists of different pictures on each page. Go through the pages one at a time asking the toddler to name the object drawn on that page.

Handwriting activities

- **Writing the alphabets**

This is the first step in actual writing that helps in developing good handwriting. Give the toddler a task book to write the alphabet in uppercase and a lowercase version just beneath it. Repeat the activity repeatedly until the book is full. You can introduce another book for numbers 1-10.

- **Spelling game**

For this activity, present cards with written phrases like great quotes. Have the toddler read the card then turn it down so that she can write without looking. Once done, turn over the card for the toddler to self-evaluate. Let the toddler repeat writing the line in the entire page. At an advanced stage, you can read out the lines, and the toddler writes without having to look at the card completely. Writing the line, repeatedly, helps in molding handwriting.

An additional activity that is suitable for building the language of the toddler is;

- **The sound game**

For this activity, toddlers are expected to classify objects into broader groups like animals, parts of the body, etc. invite the toddlers to sit down and choose a group for them. Ask them to give you the names of the objects that fit into the chosen group. As they progress, let them play this game by challenging each other.

Chapter 8: Music and Movement Activities

Music is considered to be the most important aspect of life that connects the senses and engages the body more than any other form of activity; thus referred to as a global language. Everyone is said to possess inborn abilities to isolate different kinds of music. However, the preference for music varies according to culture, tunes, tempo, and musical instruments.

The notion every toddler possesses the musical ability and can interpret musical knowledge as well as manifest their emotions musically underpin the Montessori Method of raising toddlers. In Montessori learning, music is considered an equally integral aspect in the education curriculum like any other form such as academics. The incorporation of music in the curriculum helps in supplementing other forms of learning like reading. Parents and teachers are thereby advised to consider using music to teach, teaching music itself and combining music with other activities.

As a parent, you are required to incorporate activities that help in developing body movement and enhancing the coordination of the body with other things in the environment of the toddler. Exercises that involve music and movement gives toddlers a chance to manifest their exceptional dexterities.

The connection between music and movement

Music has a strong connection to movement. We all get the urge to move to the tunes of music every time it is played. It is for this reason that movement is considered a fundamental part of the learning of music. For every music activity, there should be a movement activity that accompanies it. The activities should correlate and connect well for better understanding. Movement brings some energy into music activities, and toddlers often find this very enjoyable.

Rhythm stick activities

The music activities that involve rhythm sticks are essential in muscle development in hands, thus an important tool to prepare the toddler for writing activities. The rhythm sticks can be used together with a variety of songs. The correlation is very calming and exciting to young toddlers.

For the first stages of teaching how to use the rhythm sticks, you are advised to use the 3 phase lesson arrangement. As a parent, you should show the toddlers how to hold the sticks, how to put them in a rest position, and how to use the sticks to make different tunes.

Phase 1: in this phase, you introduce the material to the toddlers. Identify the materials by their name, for example, rhythm sticks. Make sure that the toddlers can say the name with ease.

Phase 2: the stage after introducing the material is teaching how to use them. Once the toddlers can distinguish the material from others, you proceed by showing them how to play the rhythm sticks. You can also show the toddlers the rest position.

Phase 3: you have introduced the material and taught how to play them. The next stage is letting your kids play the rhythm sticks freely. At this stage, you can now begin to introduce different songs and patterns in play. Challenge the toddlers to listen to different songs and copy the beats.

Rhythm sticks are the most versatile set of musical instruments for your toddlers. The set can be used in very many ways to teach music. The following activities can be exercised using the rhythm sticks;

- **Tapping the rhythm sticks together**

This activity is very easy but it can be challenging when tapping to the beats of a specific song. The goal is to create unique sound patterns. Younger toddlers can start learning how to tap their sticks to the tune of rhythm sticks waltz. The song requires toddlers to tap three times in a reaped sequence. You can add more fun by asking the toddlers to count as they tap.

- **Hammer and nail tapping**

For this music activity, toddlers are required to tap the rhythm stick with one held vertically on the floor like a nail and using the other stick to hit the top, like a hammer. The toolbox song is the most suitable song for this activity, as it requires toddlers to think deep to produce a replica of sound patterns in the song.

- **End to end tapping**

The activity involves tapping on the end of each rhythm stick simultaneously. The intensity of each tap can be varied to produce different sets of sound and cues.

- Tap and scrap across each other

One of the most advanced methods of using the rhythm sticks is tapping then scraping across each other. The sequence can be used to produce fine cues. For a more enjoyable experience, use the clatter, clatter, clackity clack song for this activity. The song is good for creating replica sound, enhancing responsiveness, and paying attention to lyrical cues.

- Drumming

The rhythm sticks can be used as drumsticks by tapping them on the floor. This method applies to any given song. You can generate a sequence of beats with your toddler using the drumstick method.

- The echo game

The echo game helps in refining listening skills, retention skills, and synergy. The game requires the parent or teacher to make a rhythm and letting the toddlers copy using their rhythm sticks.

- Playing the miniature music box

A music box is a set that produces fine sounds according to the speed of the rotations made on the knob. A miniature music box is made with a transparent material to help toddlers see through the instrument. To play the miniature music box, the toddler should rotate the crank using the knob on the side of the box. Ask the toddler to release the knob after several rotations and listen to the music produced. The miniature music box can be used along with other activities such as walking on the line.

- **Wrist and ankle jingle bells**

This set of musical instruments is perfect for young toddlers. Give your toddler wrist bracelets and anklets fitted with tiny jingle bells. Every time they move the jingle, bells make a sound. For older toddlers, you can show them how to make different sound patterns by clapping and stamping their feet rhythmically.

Movement activities

Movement is also important in enhancing the growth of the toddler as well as the development of balance and equilibrium. The control of the entire body depends on the movement of the toddler and the connection with the environment. It is, therefore, important to make movement part of the daily activities of your toddler. The most exciting part is that with or without the outlined activities, your toddler will still move voluntarily or involuntarily.

- **Doing the alphabet yoga**

For this activity, you need to be creative enough to

form a list of simple yoga poses from the 26 letters of the alphabet. Unroll a mat on the floor and invite you toddlers for yoga exercise. Challenge them to pick a random letter and guide them to do the activity that the letter depicts. For instance;

A – Airplane (stretch out your arms and mimic the movement of the airplane).

B – Banana jump (do the banana jump).

- **Foxtail softie**

There are several ways to use the foxtail softie to develop movement activities of your toddler. The best way is the volleyball game. In this game, have your toddlers' partner up and take sides on either side of the net. Every toddler takes a turn in throwing the foxtail softie over the top of the net to the toddlers on the other side of the net. The goal is having the other team fail to catch the foxtail softie. On the other hand, the toddlers move about their side of the net as they try to catch the foxtail ball. If the ball land on one side is uncaught, the other team is awarded a point.

- **A ball over the net**

The ball over the net activity is similar to the foxtail softie. The only difference is defined according to the rules you set. For instance, you can play an elimination game where a toddler is eliminated is he fails to catch the ball. Alternatively, you can introduce a tennis ball that the toddler is expected to softly hit against a wall and catch the rebound. The game can be played by two where one throws the ball to the wall, and the other one waits for a rebound and vice versa. Progress to a more difficult level by introducing rackets.

- **Playing the scavenger hunt**

The scavenger hunt is a versatile game that supplements other activities. The most appropriate way to do the scavenger hunt is by doing the "find and label." In this method, you challenge your toddlers to find an item within the house or outside the house and put a descriptive or name label on it. At an advanced level, you can write descriptive notes and hide beneath certain objects in the house. Ask the toddlers to find the note by describing the object without naming it.

- **Target toss**

For this game, you are required to provide a basket and some balls. Have the kids line up equidistant to each other. Ask them to toss the balls in the basket. You can introduce the challenge mode by asking the kids to stand on one leg before tossing.

- **Play with balloons**

For this activity, blow up some balloons for your kids. You should keep some spare ones in case the first set gets popped. There are many balloon games that enhance gross motor skills to choose from. For a start, you ask the kids to balance the balloon on their heads as they walk a short distance in the house. As they make progress, ask them to toss the balloons in the air as they walk on a line.

Chapter 9: Art and craft activities

The Montessori activities on art and craft can teach a thing or two about organization and order. Toddlers' materials for these activities should be; easy to get to, well organized, striking, suitable for their age, appealing, and guileless. The most important aspect of art and craft material for toddlers is their simplicity. The materials are expected to enhance creativity, hone fine motor abilities and improve coordination and sharp focus.

For these activities, it is essential to avoid the compilation of clutter and waste. The following steps should guide parents and teachers when teaching art and craft activities.

i. Use a few materials. It is important to present the toddlers with few materials at a time. The fewer materials presented to the toddler the fewer chances of waste and mess.

ii. Present a manageable number of activities. Do not overwork the toddler with loads of activities.

There still is time for the toddler to master the concepts. Rotate the activities as much as possible but not engage the toddler with a lot of activities at the same time.

iii. Use baskets and trays. Always provide the art and craft materials in a basket or a tray. The containers help in making the materials easy to get to and keep the materials safe and orderly. The only exemptions would be water or paints.

iv. Make the materials suitable for the age of the toddler. Suitability, in this aspect, means material that is not dangerous to the health of the toddler. Do not use toxic materials or very complicated materials.

v. Present materials that encourage clean-up. Provide sponges, wet wipes, mops, etc. to allow the toddler to learn some cleaning after exercising the art activities. Small bins are also important for discarding paper wastes.

With all this in mind, now let us take a look at a host of art and craft activities for your toddlers.

- **Drawing**

Materials

For this activity, you need to present some color pencils in a box with a sliding lid, a paper, or canvas surface. Take note to rotate the color selection from time to time depending on the type of paper or surface you are using.

Step by step

i. Show the toddlers how to use their color pencils or crayons by drawing some simple patterns on the paper or canvas material.

ii. Let the toddlers take turns in drawing the patterns you have just showed them.

iii. Remember to show the toddlers bit by bit to inspire them to explore more, without being rigid, which may hinder their imagination.

- **Watercolor painting**

Materials

Provide watercolors, brushes, a jar of water, and a plain surface (paper or canvas), and a pallet for mixing colors.

Step by step

i. Smear the desired color on a pallet.

ii. Wet the bristles of the brush in water provided in a jar.

iii. Mix the color on the pallet using the wet brush.

iv. Paint some patterns on your flat surface.

v. Keep a piece of cloth to help in cleaning the area of exercise.

- **Cutting**

Materials

Sturdy cards and a pair of scissors.

For this activity, teach the toddlers how to hold the scissor by the handle and remind them that the blades are sharp. The activity is recommended for age group 3 and above.

Step by step

i. Hold a piece of sturdy card on one hand and a scissor on the other.

ii. Cut a thin strip off the card.

iii. For younger kids, hold the paper for them as they use their two hands to hold the scissors and cut.

iv. As the kids advance, start creating straight lines on the paper and cut along the lines. Let them repeat the process on their own.

- Sewing

Materials

For this activity, you are required to provide sewing cards, cross-stitch needles

In a case and sewing threads.

Step by step

- Hold the sewing card while showing the toddlers the holes in the card.
- Show the toddlers how to sew the holes and rotate the card after each hole.
- At this stage, let the toddlers pull the sewing thread through the holes and push the stitching needle through the next hole on the sewing card.
- Cut the thread at the end and let them learn how to make a knot at the end of the thread.

- Prick work

This activity is aimed at helping the toddlers learn how to control the movement of their hands.

Materials

A piece of paper, pricking object.

Step by step

- Make patterns on the piece of paper. Start with simple patterns as you advance to complex drawings.
- Let the toddlers prick holes along the patterns.
- If possible, show the toddlers how to make holes all along with the shapes you have drawn. Help them pull out the shapes.

- **Punches**

Provide paper punches on varied shapes and sizes like hearts, diamonds, or Christmas tree. Let the toddlers punch a piece of paper that you have provided and pull out the shapes made. This art activity helps the toddlers develop creative skills and learning about different shapes.

- **Gluing**

Materials

Provide different shapes of paper images in a bowl, a small pot of glue and a brush. A separate flat paper is also required.

Step by step

i. Spread the sheet of paper on a flat surface, preferably a tabletop.

ii. Using the brush with the bristles immersed in the Pot of glue, spread the glue on the back of the shapes and images provided.

iii. Slowly spread the shapes on the flat sheet of paper.

iv. Let the toddlers try doing this on their own.

- **Modeling clay**

This activity should involve toddlers in making different shapes using clay.

Materials

The supervisor should provide some modeling clay, a rolling pin, and some cookie cutters. Also, remember to provide a wet towel for cleaning once the activity is complete.

Step by step

i. Guide the toddlers in modeling different shapes using clay.

ii. For flat shapes, place some clay on a flat surface and flatten the clay using the rolling pin.

iii. Using the cookie cutter, cut the clay into different shapes.

iv. Guide the toddlers in repeating the process.

As an alternative to the modeling clay, you also use colored playdough or kinetic sand.

- **Color Collage**

This activity involves sticking different colored papers into matching colors on the flyer provided. Creating color collage helps develop creativity in toddlers.

Materials

Colored construction paper, bowls, flyers, scissors, and glue.

Step by step.

i Cut the colored paper according to the color arrangement. Put different colors in separate bowls.

ii Pick one bowl containing cut pieces of paper of the same color. Read out the color to the toddlers and ask them to identify the color in the flyer you have provide.

iii Using the gluing skill you had taught earlier, let the toddlers stick the pieces on the flyer with matching colors.

- Making a color booklet

Materials

A sketchpad, labeled colored papers, glue, and crayons.

Step by step

i. Cut the labeled colored papers into one shape, preferabl y rectangle.

ii. On the sketchpad, label every page with a different color on the top part of the page.

iii. Let the toddlers identify the colored papers and help the stick every paper on the matching page of the sketchpad.

iv. Leave a small margin on every page for the toddlers to paint the matching color using their crayons.

- **Handprint fall tree craft**

This activity requires you to provide some bottles of paints and cotton swabs. Trace the outline of a tree on a piece of paper and let the toddler finish the leaves by dipping her fingers in paint and leaving her prints on the image. Random prints can give the image a very appealing look. The cotton swabs are used to clean the fingers to change to another color. After the activity, have your toddler wash her hands.

- **Paper shape collage**

If your toddler can draw, ask them to draw a random shape, say a triangle. Now have them introduce another shape in the triangle, say a circle. Tear colored papers of different colors and have your kid glue them to the image. Note that every shape should be given a different color of paper.

- **Creating Paper plate animals**

Your toddler can make paper plates by finger-painting them. To create the paper plate animals, guide them in fixing paper faces and limbs. The activity offers the environment for nurturing creativity and awareness of the surrounding.

- **Sticker word activity**

This is among the simplest art and craft activities for the toddler. Have them write their name on a manila paper (offer help if they cannot write on their own). Offer the toddler a set of colored stickers to put on the name or word written. The stickers are put along the lines of the letters.

- **Colored straw necklace**

For creative and elegance have your toddler exercise this activity. Provide colored straws. Help the toddler cut the straws using a pair of scissors to the desired size. The sizes may vary. Using the threading technique you have taught, let the toddler thread the straws together, and alternating the colors to give the necklace a beautiful look. For more designs, you can tie a knot after every straw. Join the ends of the string by tying them together. There you, your toddler just made a beautiful straw necklace.

- **Squirt gun painting**

For this activity, hang a canvas on a board or use a sketching pad. Fill a squirt gun with watercolor and let your kid spray the canvas randomly. You should consider mixing the colors to give the paint an appealingly unique look.

- **Palm painting**

Have your toddler dip the palm of their hands in paint and put a print on a piece of canvas. You can have a whole pad full of your toddler's prints with a different color on each page. Apart from enhancing artistic skills, the activity provides a good source of toddlerhood memory. This method can also be used to make fingerprint flowers.

- **Making paper rainbow**

What is more beautiful than using craft to teach science? Here is how. Give your kid a card with the rainbow image as control. Now give the toddler a set of colored paper strips. Let the toddler arrange the colors of the rainbow as observed on the control card. You can add more learning lessons like naming the colors in the correct order and gluing the strips on a placard and hanging them in your kid's room.

Spray paint craft

Avail a variety of spray paints. Write any word on a placard, cover the word with a tape such that the tape fits every letter, and can be read. Invite your toddler to spray paint the placard using different colors. Once done, remove the tapes to expose the word you had written.

Conclusion

Raising your toddlers, the Montessori way at home can be very hectic. Unlike Montessori teachers, parents do not have the necessary skill set of knowledge and special training for the Montessori curriculum. This makes it hard to know the areas to polish as a parent and how to polish them. Furthermore, creating a Montessori environment at home is not easy. For these reasons, parents find it difficult to inculcate the Montessori philosophy at home. However, with simple tips, you can find teaching your toddlers the Montessori way and turning your house into a Montessori classroom very simple.

As much as teachers are required to possess a well-versed and comprehensive understanding of the Montessori curriculum, there are no set rules for you as a parent on how to run your home. All you need to do is follow the simple steps below and ensure to ensure that you are in line with the requirements that make the activities Montessori.

i Promote the freedom and independence of your toddler.

ii Respect the abilities of the toddler.

iii See things the way a toddler would.

iv Use a soft tone.

The Montessori Home

How to Create a Montessori Toddler Environment at Home

Introduction

Congratulations on purchasing *The Montessori Home*, and thank you for doing so.

The following chapters will discuss the amazing philosophy of the Montessori system of education and a practical way of implementing it as a friendly atmosphere in a home setting. The concept of a Montessori pre-schooling is primarily focused on early years' formative development as a whole. The toddlers aging from 2.5 or 3 to 6 years are mainly the learners of this scientific-educational approach. This book will touch the historical significance of the Montessori method and further delve into the important aspects of this philosophy, which has a child-centered pedagogy and curriculum.

The later chapters will explore the Montessori-friendly traits of a pre-school home setup that can facilitate the holistic development of a toddler. Subjects in the Montessori system along with Montessori-specific lessons and exercises are mentioned in detail to help provide a distinctive guideline to the parents and teachers alike to raise their toddlers at home, *the Montessori way.* The role of the parent and the importance of educating the toddlers as preparation for life are important ingredients to ensure their proper development and enhancement as *makers of men.*

Furthermore, positive experiences at home can help your toddler in avoiding obstacles to growth which are also a major problem in untrained adults nowadays. The child's right to choose the purposeful work preserves his independence, confidence, curiosity, and inner satisfaction. It leads him towards the path of normalization, away from any possible deviations that may come his way otherwise. To provide your toddler with a nurturing, prepared environment is a crucial step in setting up a Montessori-friendly children's house to raise him in.

There are plenty of books on this subject on the market, thanks again for choosing this one! Every effort was made to ensure it is full of as much useful information as possible. Please enjoy!

Chapter 1: Montessori System of Education - Some History and Present

At the start of this book, we have discussed the Montessori system of education and pedagogic philosophy in great depth. To understand any educational system, we must learn the basics of it. The foundational facts and the driving forces behind a particular theory makes it all the more effective to implement and put into practice. Setting up a Montessori at home and providing a perfectly prepared environment consisting of all the necessary ingredients to raise a toddler, may seem like an overwhelming task. As normally, parents tend to assign this sort of responsibility to conventional preschool settings, shirking the burdensome notion. But the truth of the fact remains the same.

A Montessori-friendly home is immensely beneficial for a child's holistic development in his formative years, however much challenging it seems to be. The more we learn about the historical perspective of this scientifically approachable educational system and the correct ways to incorporate it in our toddlers' lifestyle at home, the easier and less challenging it would become in the eyes of the public.

Montessori System of Education:

Education is the process of learning or getting the acquisition of language, skills, and abilities from resources around you. Most people believe that experiences educate a person more than anything else, but it is also a fact that education takes place under the guidelines of educators. Self-education can also be learned, but it will need more effort and mental stability than the education provided by a proper educating system. From this its extracted that education can be formal or informal. Informal education involves self-learning, and formal learning can be attained by following a variety of pedagogic approaches of which Montessori is a remarkable scientific approach.

Beginning Of Montessori Education:

The Montessori educational system followed around the globe is an extraction of the theories given by the great scientist and physician that the world knows as

Dr. Maria Montessori. She was born in Italy, in Chiaravalle (Ancona), in the year 187. She belonged to a middle class but educated family. Gender preferences are always there from the start of mankind, and as Maria Montessori was growing up, Italy also had gender preferences and a conservative approach to the women's role in society. But Maria Montessori was not concerned about the thinking of society. What mattered to her was the love for getting an education and for serving the nation. She was 14 when she moved to Rome, and there she attended boys technical institute, there she developed her thought process towards math and biology. Her father was against her higher education, but with her mother's support, she went to medical college, and she became the first female doctor in Italy.

Birth of Early Childhood Education:

Pediatrics and psychiatry were the major field subjects of Montessori as a Doctor. In the period when she was teaching at a medical school, Montessori served many poor and socially unstable people at the free clinics there. She was the woman of great observational potential, and while serving these economically unstable peoples, she noticed a peculiar sense of intelligence among their kids. In 1900, Montessori became the director of the developmentally disabled children. Their she started research on early childhood development with the help of theories of two other French physicians from the 18th and 19th-century namely Jean-Marc Gaspard Itard and Edouard Seguin who worked with the disabled children and wrote theories based on their research. Maria Montessori worked on these theories further and made theoretical methods to be implemented following these theories. All these methods she invented were tested through hands-on scientific observation at the school. She saw great results from her research on children, and she started to promote her findings all over Europe through her speeches. She wanted to make the women aware of their rights, and she also acknowledged this topic in her speeches.

Educational traditions:

It was not long before that Montessori realized that the methods she has been experimenting with disabled children begin to show remarkable results. A thought-provoking question came to her mind, what if she uses the same methods on the normal children? Her thought soon became a reality when the Italian government offered her 60 students from the slums and shanty dwellings in 1907. Their ages were between 1 to 6. These schools became the basis for the establishment of *Montessori Children's Houses.* The schools allowed

Montessori to create a prepared learning environment for the students so that she can observe the working of the conceptual methods she created to explore the creativity of the children with disabilities with normal children as well. In the same period, she also made changes in her methods according to the findings of research to get far better results from the children who were given the right to choose and initiate their activities out of interest and desire to practice purposeful work.

Strength Gained by Montessori:

In a very little time, Montessori proved her methods workable. She spread her findings all over Europe. Her school captured attention from all over the world. Officials around the world travel to Rome to see the proven results of concentration, attention, and discipline on the children Maria Montessori worked on. Montessori method attracted so many educators to learn the strategies she has developed scientifically. Soon her methodology became so popular that students from Chile and Australia also came to learn Montessori courses. Within years Montessori schools were established in 5 continents.

Montessori's first book was published in 1909, in Italian, which was later translated into ten other languages. In

English, the name of the book was "Montessori Method." Europe adopted the Montessori method efficiently, and until 1910, schools with Montessori's method can be found all around western Europe. The first of the Montessori schools in America was established in 1911. Maria Montessori was highly praised by the magazines and educational literature of that time, around 187 articles were published by the news agencies praising Montessori's remarkable work in early childhood education. Her detailed work in producing the special, didactic material according to the scientific pedagogic approach of education having a built-in control of error and stimulating points of interest, gained further recognition as well.

For the successful results with the students ranging from 1 to 6, Maria Montessori started to focus on the elementary level students in the year 1916. She, through her speeches and lectures, promoted the findings she gained from the material she has introduced on the elementary level. Montessori's second book named "The Advanced Montessori Method" was published in 1917, focusing on the materials and methods created for the elementary level students.

A Unique Verge:

An observational mind never stops observation and thinking. Same was the case with Maria Montessori as after her successful implementations of Montessori and elementary schools all around the world it was high time that she turned her focus towards the most crucial age of the person that is adolescence in the year 1920. Her observations about the children of this stage were crucial, and she explained the need for the practical activities for the students of this age to learn and develop the sense of basic norms of the society. She also wanted the students to explore themselves through these activities. So that they can give the best of themselves to the betterment of society.

She opted to open residential schools where children can learn and get educated by some real-world activities like farming, marketing, etc. According to Montessori, "it's all about learning to behave independently. She wanted to educate the young learners about the rules of the society in which they have to survive in an organized manner through learning basic self disciplines and rules to face the challenges they will face after starting of the practical life.

Though Montessori's main focus was to educate people about the methods she has invented, she also wants them to learn the importance of the upbringing of a child from the toddler stage till adolescence. She wanted people to recognize the rights of the children and their status in the society and for this, she with her son Mario established International Montessori Association in 1929 to carry out her thoughts and creational methods as she wants them to.

Montessori Movement in America:

After capturing Europe and other parts of the world, Montessori changed her direction towards America, where she was welcomed open-handedly. She established the first Montessori school in, New York, America in 1911. When Montessori started her work she was given students from the slums to work with but the time was changed, when she established a school in America, her school was filled with the students from the cultured and prominent families who wanted their kids to have the best education available at that time. Americans praised Montessori for the work she has done to make the children more bright and self-confident.

Exceptional Classroom Design:

Maria Montessori conducted her first international training, to train the teachers specifically when she returned to the U.S in 1915 at Panama International Exposition in

San Francisco. At the exposition, the world saw a new way to make a classroom by Montessori as she constructed a glass classroom in which three sides of the room were made of the glass where people can come and observe the exceptional progress of the students. The glass classroom design was a huge success. It was unique and worth constructed. It gave Montessori exceptional appraisement for the helpful and thoughtful methods she has developed for children all around the world.

Wreck In Progress:

Due to the invasion of world war 1, Montessori's work went in derailed due to the language issues and anti-immigrant sentiments. Extremists got the opportunity, and they started propaganda against Montessori work as not up to the standard of the educational system. Prominent figures of the society of that time like William Kilpatrick was the most active person who criticized Montessori's book Montessori Method openly in his book The Montessori System Examined. He was the most popular scholar of the 20th century who criticized Montessori's efforts, inventions, and her overall method of early childhood education. He believed and made other Americans also believe that the education system which Maria Montessori has created is nothing but a myth, and she is fooling around with the people all around the world. His criticism was widely accepted by the Americans, and by the year 1920, Montessori education faded away from American society except for the few schools.

Rejuvenation:

After the collapse of the Montessori educational system from America, there was no chance of rejuvenation of this educational system again. After 1950, the U.S was looking for some new ideas or substitutes for an emerging educational system. In those days for seeking change, there was an aspiring young, and talented teacher who lived in New York named Nancy McCormick Rambusch. She happened to come across by the books written by Maria Montessori, and her idea fascinated her.

She felt the freshness in Montessori's methodologies and traveled to Paris to attend the Montessori congress conducted by Mario Montessori, son of Maria Montessori. She met him, and Mario Montessori asked her help to bring back Montessori's educational system in America. She got so influenced by the inventions of Montessori that she made vigorous efforts for the establishment of the Montessori educational system in America again. Her efforts didn't go in vain, and very shortly results can be seen in the educational system in America. People became profound for this amazing method for the upbringing of their children in a prepared environment. In 1960 with Nancy's proven efforts Montessori educational system established and American Montessori society came into existence.

Present Day Montessori:

One hundred years ago, Montessori started her work with a bunch of students from slums and poor families. She took her stance and promoted her methodologies through her speeches and courses worldwide. Her work in the educational field has no words of praise. Montessori has given her best what she could, to her country, society, to the world. Thousands of Montessori schools are running across the globe, taking care of children's educational needs in a guided and independent manner. Children from infancy through adolescence are being catered with the rules of Montessori with love and affection.

International Montessori council working hard to cater to the needs of children from different cultures and different societies. They aim to give the children the best education possible in America and also out of America. China is also in particular interested in the Montessori educational system for Her kids. They are seeking to train the teachers according to Maria Montessori methods also creating an environmental schooling system just as Montessori proposed.

When it comes to education, two forms, come in mind traditional method and Montessori method. In the traditional method, you don't get a prepared environment, whereas the Montessori method provides an education system in a prepared environment in making the child learn independently yet in a safe environment. Another difference is in the traditional system the child always has a passive learning system like memorization, tests, etc. but if we follow the Montessori method, the focus is on the creational mind of the student to make his mind strong enough to act independently. And most importantly, the role of teachers in both systems.

In traditional system teacher don't interact with her students individually, she delivers the lesson, do some exercises and finally take the test to know the memorization skills of the child. Whereas in the Montessori system teacher interacts with the student on one on one basis. She gives every student individual time to learn the things accordingly, she doesn't have to focus on how well her student has memorized her major concern is the ability of her student to work independently and with the concentration he needs for his future.

Present-day schooling systems are divided into these forms mentioned above. Scholars and researchers are working on the peoples to make them aware of the rights of their children. Education is the right of every child, so why not the best one? We have to come out from the cocoon of the traditional system for the better future of our children. We have to make them independent, strong, and positive thinker who gets along well with society and cherish the world with their abilities.

Chapter 2: The Child as a Hope and Promise for Mankind

"The greatness of human personality begins at the hour of birth." – Dr. Montessori

If the notion of education is just deemed to be the mere transmission of ideas and knowledge, then there is much to be considered for the betterment of society and reconstruction of the world to eliminate warfare and present the holistic concept of child development. This concept will help in realizing the totality of education of the child from the moment he is born and raised, educating both the mind and the senses. This sort of developmental education will help the children in emerging as the social personalities, members of the workforce, and psychic entities of this world. Endowed with hidden powers and unknown potentials waiting to be unveiled through the correct sort of guidance and direction, these children are the *makers of men.* They are the promise of the future, a hope for mankind.

According to the research and observation of various psychologists and their special observational findings regarding the newborn babies, the conclusion has been drawn that the first couple of years of the child's life are crucial in his growth and development. So it can be extracted that education must start from the moment the child is born. This special embryo transforming into a miraculous being at birth holds great importance and bears an elemental role in utilizing his inborn psychic abilities to bring a revolutionary change in the future. It all depends upon the way the infant's early years and their fruits are cultivated. As it is the most precious period of his life at this stage, it must not be wasted. The loss of these years can never be compensated in full. The child himself guides the adult to unearth the fruits of his cultivation. He starts showing the impressions that he has taken unconsciously or consciously from the environment. He lays his path of growth and development, setting up his own pace. He just needs the facilitation and direction wherever and whenever necessary.

Once the adult starts paying attention to this wonderful creation of mankind, he begins to unearth the dynamic power of the constructive energy that has been pulsating inside the child's psychic personality. These hidden talents and rich abilities may have remained hidden if not for the longitudinal observations and researches that dug up the truth and made us all realize the importance of the period of infancy and the spiritual miracle that has been bestowed to us as a gift in the form of the child. This self-teaching and self-cultivating concept can be truly demonstrated and understood by the way the children learn their languages perfectly in babyhood and retain them until their old age. This happens without the assistance of any language instructor or training courses because at that particular age of infancy and toddlerhood they can only observe and take impressions from the environment; no formal teaching can be done at that stage. So, it means that they actually self-learn and both unconsciously and then consciously acquire the skills to speak fluently by gradual succession.

As the development occurs by leaps and bounds, this process of absorbing information and learning on his own is also the child's way of teaching himself about the surrounding environment and the world's affairs. This is not a linear process; this demands a dynamic approach which is exactly what the early years' education is all about.

Under the age of three years, a sort of an unconscious inner teacher is present inside the child. It helps him understand the world in his own way. His attempts are real, unguided, and quite natural. The adults, however much they try to influence him at this stage, the child seems to have a mind of his own, taking intricate impressions and storing up as many details as he can in his cognition. After the age of three years though, the child is more ready to put a conscious effort in understanding the adult's guidance and contribution to make him learn more about adult's reasoning on different aspects such as their social, emotional, religious, and cognitive perspectives. He has now built his formative structures of the personality and can take input from the adult without biasing his own thoughts and can distinguish between his own wishes and the will of an adult which may have been imposed on him.

As the intelligence of the older beings may prejudice his creativity and instinctive potential, adults must refrain from snatching away the free will of the child and his right to choose the work he is interested in doing. Psychologists say that, due to the astonishing accomplishments of the child in terms of creating his psychic personality and acquiring skills unconsciously, the child may well have been considered as a *mini adult, or little man*, at the age of three when he starts going to school. Yet this, by no far comes close to what he still can do.

The child's power of absorption makes him capable of doing more hard work than a sixty years old man. Sometimes his untiring efforts and unstoppable activity may amaze you. Such are the traits that distinguish him as a hope for mankind. Whatever impressions he takes from the environment; he returns in full as he grows up. His promise to mankind is to repay what he has been given, what he has been taught to learn, and what he has been shown to adapt and follow. By virtue of experiences gathered by him in his early life, he promises to deliver on the basis of a spontaneous education that he himself has learned by observing material, people, and overall surroundings.

The facilitation of a proper, conducive environment and enlightening resources will help build the child's personality in such a way that he would not be a burden to the society or an empty receptive vacuum to be filled by an adult's wisdom, otherwise helpless and utterly clueless to play his part in the progress of a nation. The teacher's supervision and provision of guided freedom will help the child in growing up as a man with clarity of vision and ambition. He, who will be not a victim of fate or events but a tailor of his own future, able to mold and direct the future of not only himself but in the process, influencing the future of mankind as well.

"What the mother brings forth is the baby, but it is the baby who produces the man." Dr. Montessori actually depicts an inevitable truth in this statement. She says that the mother is not the one who actually forms the personality of the child or teaches him how to eat, walk, or learn. It is, in fact, innate ability of the child which compels him to learn and grow up on his own accord. If the parent was to die, would the child stop growing? No, he would still form his personality finishes his work of making himself to be a man of the world. Many would think that the native language or mother tongue must be learned while living with the mother, but if an American child was to live in an Arabic foster care in his early years, he would be able to speak Arabic like a native regardless of his actual mother tongue being English. This is because he, himself, has been absorbing information from the surroundings, learning and adapting.

However, recognizing the efforts of the child as a mini adult does not vouch for overlooking the role of a home environment and a parent's authority. Once the role of the parents becomes as a facilitator and partner in education instead of a dictator and builder of the child's personality, they are far better collaborators in preparing the home as an effective, nurturing environment where the child cultivates his personality as him building the inner structures of his psyche depends greatly on the suitable home environment and timely help from the adults when need be.

The parents are the essential source of help and guided supervision in his life, enabling the creative work and purposeful activity, but the role of society is also important. The society must be able to cherish this gift and hope of mankind bestowed by nature. By recognizing his true potential, enabling him to exercise his rights, and providing for his psychic needs, the society is answerable to taking care of this secret of mankind. The child since the moment of his birth awakens a sense of unselfish love, care, and protective instinct in the adults around him, especially the parents. This idealistic love is the one that should be actually prevalent all around the world among mankind. Nature teaches this sort of love as a lesson that how the selfless, pure form of love and devotion that the parents bestow on their child without an ounce of sacrificial, compulsive feelings can be a sort weapon to conquer the world without violence.

The kind of joy and contentedness that the parents experience while taking care of their children can influence people to be loving, eliminating hatred and learning to be gentler beings as even the most savage animals become tamely gentle in front of their offspring. This is a real side of nature, much more approachable and happier, free from antagonism and vengefulness. The child, therefore, can be a negotiator of peace for mankind. There are normally two sorts of instincts that are followed by not only humans but also other forms of life, such as birds, etc. No matter in what way they choose to socialize, their response to their young ones is always protective. The more we study how children affect the adults' behavioral patterns and how it might differ from the way they normally act in other peoples' companies, the more we can understand human nature and its intricacies. It also asserts the important role of the child in transforming mankind.

The long period of infancy and gradual succession of periods of growth and development makes a man quite different from other forms of life. It creates a distinguishing barrier between him and other creatures as it separates him as an individual is capable of accomplishing what others can't. The power of a child is not derived or continued from a previously halted stage of some ancient life form. The power of a child is actually created from scratch when it is just a fetus in his mother's womb. His appearance as a spiritual embryo was actually an initial point from where the life started, and the making of the man began. What distinguishes a creature from another is always what is new, not what is similar; never the likeness but the novelties. So the jump-start of a child's life became the beginning for newer, upcoming destinies.

The child has a wonderful ability to adapt and conform. However, he also has the instinct to turn the events in his favor as he starts to grow. The inner ability and power of adaption let him succeed in adapting to civilizations and their customs according to the present level of modernism that they have reached. He is able to act on the constructed behaviors of adaptive nature that helps him in either conforming to the customs of a particular area or building his own pattern that may influence his surroundings. He becomes a link or union joining the customs and preserving the culture of various periods of historical civilizations. Therefore, the child's historical and cultural enlightenment is very crucial in the early years as they are the hope for us in preserving our culture, traditions, and values.

As the newborn being, the infant does not have a predetermined goal or aim in his life. The proper nurturing and right kind of guided freedom will help in realizing his potential and interests. It will, therefore, help in determining the direction of his life and desired goals to be achieved. The path he chooses to achieve these goals will mark the shape his future will take. As the promise to participate in the betterment of the world and helping mankind, the child's aims must reflect positivity and hope. The creative sensitivities that the child possesses are not hereditary models of personality. They are actually the influencing periods of focusing on a particular set of skills or traits. These bits and pieces of sensitivities can awaken attributes in a child that may become helpful in shaping up his future growth as a dynamic whole.

The development is considered as a long path paved with experiences that a child must walk through in order to reach maturity. It cannot be taught. It has to be experienced with freedom and willful pace. However, this freedom and will must not be misunderstood as letting the children experience whatever they feel like experiencing without providing guidance and supervision. As this sort of destructive freedom will result in the deviated personality of a child. Too much prohibition acts as a floodgate on the child's compulsive need to get freedom. Similarly, too much freedom without putting a loose rein and observational eye can result in leaving the floodgate ajar to pour out the uncontrolled impulses in a very disorderly way as the child has not yet developed the ability to control himself fully.

As soon as the adult's will becomes eliminated in controlling them, they start acting on a pure impulse that mostly leads to more deviation than normalization. Thus the work becomes not an action but a reaction, destroying the constructive abilities of the child who is on the path of self-discovery. He is, under the misguided notion of loose freedom, is left alone to cope up with the world and his inner demons. He will not be using the resources provided to him. Instead, blatant misuse may occur. How would this child be materializing as an adult then? How would he become an addition to mankind, a positive integration, or a negative accessory?

The motives or objectives of an activity must be provided to a child by an adult so that he is able to concentrate on the work and realize its purpose and usefulness. In this way, normalization is achieved, eradicating the chances of increasing abnormalities or developmental delays that may be caused by irregular, aimless activities and behaviors. The supervising adult should provide a chance for exercising the work that arouses interest in the child. It should call the child towards action and performance in such a way that his personality as a whole becomes engaged in it.

The Montessori perspective of education deals with such exercises that can influence the personality of the child on a holistic level of sensorial perception and development. The details of these activities and exercises will be discussed in the later chapters of this book. Normalized children acquire such wonderful traits of a stable personality that help build the future man in all his independence, positive attitude, and confident approach towards the workings of this universe. These traits include sympathy, social sentiments, spontaneous discipline, and the love for purposefulness and continuous work. These traits produce an individual with a hardworking core and an emotionally intelligent being as a whole.

The child's transformation into a grown-up, normalized adult, gives hopefulness to mankind and tangible evidence that there is a possibility of a better humanity. As an adult, we see these miraculous masterpieces of nature's creation undergoing a constructive journey to acquire goodness, discipline, order, and self-control. This reinforces our belief in the possibility of a better world and the possibility of mankind being capable of improvement, growth, and change in order to transform themselves into better human beings.

The hope keeps man striving for the aims, and the promise makes it all the more worthwhile. The hope is a mindset while the promise is the motivation behind that mindset. Being both the hope and promise for the future, the child has to prepare his personality in a normalized, constructive way. This is because he has to achieve the set goals of the future in order to fulfill the promises made to mankind upon the birth of a child.

However, the beauty of this subtle promise is that the child is never compelled or feels obligated to fulfill it; instead, he chooses his own destiny and does it on his own accord.

By choosing the learning opportunities and experiences, the child maximizes his chances of growth and creative potential that in the future would be a driving force in letting him build his own place in society. Therefore, in educating a child, focusing on the purpose is very important. The purposeful and rational actions can give strength and life to the performance and help bring order and concentration in the child's work.

As the children must be acquiring growth in both the physical and spiritual aspects, the aspirations must be clear. Both the mind and the spirit must gain sufficient food or nourishment from the environment. The child's mind is like a hungry being intent on feeding itself with all available means. The spirit is also a starved inner child who longs for a proper diet that can adhere to its spirituality in an effective way. The environment provided to the child is prepared to keep these factors into consideration, then the development occurs smoothly, without any conflicts.

Spirituality is actually the essence of Montessori educational pedagogy. It is prevalent in all the teachings and philosophies of Dr. Maria Montessori. The home environment can be a perfect prepared arena to develop the spirituality of a child. His motivation can be derived from the relationships of his family members, his parents, and their love, his siblings, his sense of belonging and feeling of shelter and protection, etc. He can grow up as a man who values customs, morality, good deeds, and habits. He would be able to believe in faith, unity, peace, and freedom of expression. He can also be good at reasoning, logical questioning, exploration, and sensory perception if provided with a stimulating environment that triggers his cognitive abilities. A good, adequate space for physical work and play can facilitate necessary movement and help in learning to exercise balance and coordination. These all virtues of a prepared environment can help develop all the parts in an integrated manner i.e., mind, body, and soul.

There are always two sorts of work on the part of the child: the internal work and external work. The internal work is never at rest. The child must be given rest from external work in order to The basic time for internal work i.e., cognitive or sensory functions. The child's mind is busy developing his schematic structures that form his personality. This is what intelligence means, and this is how the auto-formation of his mind happens. He is actually preparing himself to adapt and associate himself with the world he has been born into.

We call it the *work of the child.* If he is exhausted due to loads of external work or activities, he may unwillingly shirk the internal workings of the mind resulting in slowed cognitive progress, development delays, hindered thought processes, poor memory, etc. There are other factors that influence the cognition of a child and prove to become obstacles in the way of growth and development. We will be studying them in detail in one of the upcoming chapters of this book.

Chapter 3: Education and Learning - Preparation for Life

Learning is one of the most important parts of human experience. Without education, humans are mere animals. It's our ability to learn, grow, and differentiate between good and bad is what makes us superior to other animals. Thus quality education is vital for a life worth living.

If you want to become a physician, you need to study day in and day out. There's no other way, other than this long, difficult journey. Having a dream to become a physician is incredible, but the majority of us in our modern corporate world only think of education as a way of making money or get a decent job. This is a crisis; if our future generations think in this dangerous manner, mankind will lose the true essence of learning as a whole. If this attitude towards education remains this way, we will have scientists who know how to experiment and discover great things in the name of science but don't know how to solve daily life problems, like how to treat your wife with respect. This example can be said for politicians, professors, engineers, and so on and so forth. Remember, education is what makes us human and we must learn to improve ourselves, improve as human beings, to make positive changes in ourselves.

You need to train your child for life, not for a b. The process of learning starts way back; it doesn't start at the Montessori. We start to learn the moment we are born, babies look around and observe everything. If all the baby has ever seen is violence and hear profanity, then you shouldn't expect that the baby will behave other than that. On the other hand, if the baby seems father caring and being generous to needy people, the chances are you will find the same qualities in the father baby.

Teach your child to be nice with people around, to help people around who are in need, to stop any kind of abuse if you are witness to it. If you believe that the toddler will learn when he or she gets older when they're about 8,9,10, you're making a huge mistake. You need to start focusing on the child learning from day one. It's just sad to see people nowadays what they are doing to their innocent children. You might have seen people shove their children in front of screens from mobile to laptops to television. The content they are watching is having a mental impact on them, which might stay there throughout their life. The television shows filled with graphic violence and just complete nonsense are ruining your child's mental health. Gone are those days when parents used to spend with their newborns and teach them life values themselves.

The goal of Montessori education is to create a baseline for learning. Something we can later work on to make the children grow from. To have a foundation at which a beautiful building will be created. You shouldn't think your toddler will learn how to program and design a video game at that age. That is expecting something way out of reach at that age. You should let the toddler free; his curiosity and imagination will teach him things by itself. Children are curious by their very nature and don't fear to try out things as adults do. Just leave them and let nature do it's by itself.

I think it's time for me to rant on our education system. Here we go. Our education system is broken and in dire need of fixing. It teaches us to become another labor in society. The difference between an educated person and an uneducated person is more or less the latter is skilled labor, and the other one is none skilled labor. Think about it; an engineer is just a skilled labor; he doesn't do any sort of critical thinking, maybe besides the work given by his boss. Same with the physician, he's skilled to help you get better health. Now you're getting my point. Our whole education system is designed for making skilled labor for our massive companies and corporation and so on and so forth.

Montessori education is different than traditional education simply because of the fact that it gives freedom to the toddler to experiment and society himself in an organized manner. Children learn by doing with their own hands rather than consuming words shoot at them. There are special materials also for learning in the Montessori system which helps the children learn by themselves. Specially trained teachers are alongside the young ones in the organized environment to help aid the young one in his learning path. Montessori system teaches children a desire for learning, helps them concentrate better, and builds there self-discipline.

Another thing to point out about our education system is that it doesn't care for the student's development. We are creating a workforce that doesn't know how to deal with real-life problems. The education we're providing doesn't help the student discover himself in an ever-growing and complex society. They don't know how to deal with poverty, climate change, racism. These are real-life problems just waiting to be solved. Yes, these are complex issues and not easy to solve. But until and unless we teach in such a way that our children are at least able to solve these complex issues, we shouldn't expect these problems to be solved any time soon. As the great Maria Montessori, herself said: "the world of education is like an island where people, cut off from the world, are prepared for life by exclusion from it."

According to Maria Montessori, all children pass the stages of development, but everyone is different and have their paths, so to say one child might be sharper and faster in one activity while the other in another activity. The Montessori system has a multi-age class setting which makes the younger ones in the group look up to elder ones for guidance and the elder ones act as role models. This philosophy clearly shows Maria Montessori's system has the society in it as its center stage for learning rather than school laws and rules which do not actually help the child in real-life scenarios.

John Dewey once said, "Education is not preparation for life; education is life itself." This popular quote sums up this whole chapter in a beautiful manner. It dawns upon you as an individual once you are out of a conventional education system and out in the real world that how much it means to learn life skills and gain education as a life matter, not as a vocational prerequisite. Once you start facing practical problems and challenges in real life, then you start to see the actual quality of our education system. Education is about making a well-rounded person, not to get a distinction or get a "good job." Our education system should be helping our young ones in preparing them to solve problems that are to come while walking the uneven road of life.

If you ask someone today how much significant do you think your education was in your success? Or do you think your education in school was useful in your life in any way we're probably going to get the answer "yeah little bit" or "maybe," but no one would be able to answer with positive conviction. During the middle ages, children were taught the Trivium method at schools. This classical education was much more effective than what we have today. Trivium enabled the human mind to break the natural shackles, which limits one ability to think critically and communicate much more effectively. Montessori in our age does the same what Trivium did; it enables the enablers to think critically and solve real-world problems all through cooperation, integration, and sensory perception.

Pioneers of the Montessori system talk about its effectiveness as an education-for-life philosophy and pedagogic approach by exemplifying famous people who been raised in a Montessori educational environment or participated in its propagation in some way or the other. Larry Page and Sergey Brin, co-founders of Google, Jeffrey Bezos, founder of Amazon, Katherine Graham, owner of Washington Post, Anne Frank, Author and Prince William and Prince Harry, Members of British royal family. Also, Graham bell helped Maria Montessori financially to create the first two Montessori classrooms in the USA and Canada. Thomas Edison also helped to create a Montessori school.

Chapter 4: Development at Home - Absorbent Mind and the Sensitive Periods

The periods from age 0 to 3 years and from 3 to 6 years are vitally important in the development of a child. The newborn has an innate ability to take in emitting vibes from the objects around him. He is so curious and sensitive to the happenings of his surrounding environment that every single thing leaves an imprint on his mind. His mind is hungry for knowledge, eager to engrave the impressions that are provided by the environment. This quality of absorbing information is the true essence of an absorbent mind, a term devised by Montessori to represent the *sponginess* or capacity of the brain to store the gained knowledge.

The first three years of an infant's life are quite similar to how he has been living in his mother's womb till now. His mind is still in an unconscious, naturally developing stage where a conscious effort is not yet exerted. It is called an *unconscious creation* of cognition. The child has this period to create his knowledge box or prepare his memory structures. However, still, it happens so naturally that after growing up, he himself becomes quite oblivious of the details about how it all happened at the very beginning. This also happens in his embryonic prenatal life when his sensory organs are taking shape, developing his powers, but as it is an unconscious period, he forgets about its happenings after birth. This is because still, the personality and its structures are not unified as a whole. Each organ is forming gradually, separately. The mind has powers that are not operated as a holistic system yet. Thus the unity and harmony can only be possible when the formation of each part has been completed.

The age of three starts with a conscious rebirth. The infant enters a toddler, and this marks a new beginning of creative consciousness in his life. He seems to remember things in all their detailed glory. The personality becomes unified, and the urge to create and perform the work consciously becomes all the more prominent. Thus the *unconscious creator becomes the conscious worker.* The creation and formation of functions and senses are accomplished before the age of three and from then onward, their development continues.

Experts in psychoanalysis express that it is quite hard to track the memories before the age of three and harder still as we go beyond the age of two. The three years' onward, your toddler is a complete stranger to you in terms of his nature, memories, and interests. He is a curious creature focused on gathering as much information as possible to feed his mind and fill the void that has become evident after passing the unconscious period.

The adults should be aware of the potential danger of destroying his conscious creativity due to their lack of tact and care. The adults tend to forget the demarcation of the boundary between these two separate states of the absorbent mind. After three, the child has left behind his dependency on the adult. He is more eager to explore his freedom of choice and act upon his inner urge to satisfy his consciousness. He experiences a vital, internal force within himself that urges him to conquer his sense of independence. He is experiencing the *Horme* or will-power, which is an internal drive present in every child that governs his sudden impulses to perform an activity or desirous action.

Beware, your toddler needs to be functionally capable of performing a fruitful task now. His days of oblivion are over; he is quite energetic to explore everything; his motive is to self-explore and self-achieve. Although we loosely compare the *Horme* with will-power, the former is general in a sense relating to life and its experiences, whereas the latter is a somewhat restricted concept. If the *Horme* of a child is liberated and satisfied, it gives way to his perfect externalization of thoughts into actions and desires into accomplishments. This awakens in him, a special kind of joy and enthusiasm to explore and achieve more, making him always cheerful and active. The happiness of becoming independent enables the basic achievement of normal development or a child.

The paths or stages of normal development are closely related to levels of independence climbed in succession by your toddler. Enabling this at home makes your implementation of the Montessori method throughout the conscious period of the absorbent mind quite easier. Each domain of development whether it is physical or emotional, language or cognitive, moral or spiritual, social or cultural, all of them has these successive planes of independence governed by the inner urge called *Horme*.

The powers of consciousness empower him to defend himself against the oppressive behaviors or imposing nature of an adult. Your toddler may play pranks on you, runs away mischievously, etc. to express his protest against the undesirous treatment. You as both his teacher and a parent must direct his internal urges and energies toward a purposeful task. In order to channelize his energies, provide expressive paths or channels. Let him become calm by concentrating on the activity at hand. Enhance his interest by adopting a cheerful tone of voice. This sort of attitude is what a *Montessori directress* adopts to ensure that the children are directed toward the normalized path of development.

Your toddler wants to master his surroundings and explore his means of development within his environment. The question is, what does he want to develop indeed? As a newborn, the child who had started formation from scratch has now started searching for every possible means to develop the powers which were created. The senses are now accompanied by hands, and their active participation has accelerated the process of absorption. Dr. Montessori has called the hands of the child as *prehensile or adapted organs of the mind.* The almost compulsive urge or tendency to touch everything makes a child no longer just a gazer or observer of the universe. His intellect is not merely an existing feature now; he needs to enhance it further by means of all the possible learning resources and conscious exploration. There is a couple of major tendencies involved in this stage of three to six years. First, the child is extending his conscious efforts to perform worthwhile activities to enhance learning; then he tends to indulge in perfecting and enriching the powers already acquired and formed. The knowledge gained is perfected by repetition and reinforcement of the activities and exercises. This marks the period with *constructive perfectionism.*

Your toddler may feel constant urges to touch wet sand, dirty his hands in the paint, run his hands across the surface of your beloved satin dress, etc. These urges are a testament to his explorative nature. If you have been implementing proper Montessori activities inside your home learning environment, you will be able to satisfy his curiosity by means of *fabric boxes, geographical features' molds,* and other similar sensorial and cultural exercises. We, as adults, often exhibit little or no patience to bear the consequential, messy remains of his several little forays into clay-play, water activities, artsy trials, etc. However, we must realize the importance of these natural activities as both a fun and realistic way of developing his senses and sharpening his skills better than synthetic, artificial toys, and electronic gadgets.

Montessori's idea of a little world created at home, or your toddler's benefit previously seemed like an otherworldly concept, yet so fascinating and wonderfully astonishing that it could not have been imagined by the people at that time. Then it materialized into reality, and people saw a beautiful, small haven set-up and proportioned specifically for the toddlers. Small chairs and tables, small utensils, small brooms and dustpans, small aprons, brushes, etc. Everything has to be prepared by keeping the child in mind, presenting him with real-life situations to deal with, all this inside your home.

If we go back a little in the past, American society was quite unaware of the importance of small-sized real objects, specifically synthesized for use by the children. As the prevalent approach was to create and mass produce vain toys like dolls, mythical objects, fairy-tale storybooks, etc. John Dewey, a pragmatic educationist of his time search vainly for child-appropriate, real items in the city of New York but found nothing of the sort. The market vendors did not realize the need to sell them, nor the toy factory owners felt their manufacturing a matter of instant importance. Even though the children demonstrated their preference to socialize with their counterparts in real, instead of playing with fake dolls. The child, as considered in these circumstances by Montessori, was a lost citizen, forgotten by the masses. He was living in a world where every person had something to do while he was considered idle — no purposeful activity for him, no custom-made object and utensils appropriate for his age. To seek satisfaction, he used to breaks the toys, trying to get a real response from them, but the adult remained oblivious to his frustration and needs.

The advent of the Montessori system came with a revolution in the learning material and the teaching method. Once the child is provided with a world that is according to his own size, he takes ready possession of it. Your toddler becomes the active learner limiting the role of the parent as an observer. He is no longer idle; he is no longer frustrated. He has numerous things to do, to run his world, to master his environment, and to learn to survive independently.

Now, that the psychologists are paying closer attention to the period of infancy and toddlerhood, they come to observe various sensitive periods of growth and development concerning the child. The sensitive period is *a pattern followed by the absorbent mind to gain knowledge.* During the period of birth till the age of six, these periods are most evident. The child is interested in developing a particular skill or area of his intellect. During these periods, the sensitivity to a particular object or skill is heightened, and these sorts of sensitivities come and go sporadically. For instance, if the sensitive period of movement has started, it means that the child is particularly responsive to the activities involving movement and is quick to learn and develop his fine and gross motor skills.

The sensitivity to a particular skill ensures that the child:

- *will demonstrate his interest and fixation to a particular object or activity*
- *will tirelessly repeat and reinforce the task until he perfects his ability*
- *will be stimulated by any display of relevant objects related to that particular sensitivity.*
- *will be able to maintain his focus and attention for prolonged time-span*

It happens like a cycle of metamorphosis, when a sensitive period is at its peak, the absorbent mind of a child accumulates more information about a particular skill than any other time possible in the child's life. Once it reaches its maximum level, it starts to diminish or be replaced by another sensitive period, and the cycle goes on. The constructive cycle or rhythm of vitality is demonstrated through sensitive periods. There are main characteristics that remain at work during these periods, the motive or aim of the activity, the inner urge to complete the task, the repetition to perfect it, and the closure or winding up of activity to restore order and peace. Major sensitive periods evident till the age of six years in the period of infancy called the first plane of development, are:

Tiny Objects and Details:

This period occurs from 1 to 2 years. It can extend up to 4 years though, in some children. Here, the child is drawn to tiny objects and observes the minutest details of things present in his surroundings. He is able to spot them and observe, while others who are not going through a similar sensitive period are oblivious to them or tend to overlook them. The child who was often lying on the bed previously; once he starts to move around, crawling and walking, he begins to explore the environment. He is seen paying attention to small insects on the grass, fallen tiny buttons or ornaments. Even a thinnest of threads on the clothes would catch his eyes.

Order:

This period occurs mostly from birth until age four. This marks the need for organization and coordination in each and every task that is performed around the child. The child's need for absolute control and order makes him a planner, categorizer, and an organizer of things and events. The child needs a peaceful, harmonized environment where each thing has a place, and each place is allocated for a specific thing. His mental tranquility needs to be maintained in order to facilitate smooth development. His sensitivity to order makes him restore the chaos, compels him to sort out the conflicts or avoid the noisy commotions. You would have often noticed your toddler becoming agitated by shrill shouting and scolding. He might even put his hands on his ears to block out over-the-top shouting voices that disturb his peace of mind. He also becomes quite sensitive to particular people, familiar places, and preplanned organization of things. If something is expected to be found in a particular place in his room, and he has become familiar with this particular setting, he will always expect it there. If someone changes this setting, his mind may not accept the change that easily. He will experience chaos in his thought process due to unfamiliar people, strange things, or unexpected places. At that time, his upset and disturbance would be quite evident because his orderly world would be disrupted.

Movement:

This period occurs right after birth and sees through 5 years mostly. You can see your toddler so excited at the prospect of every single activity that involves movement. He may start playing physical games, walking for a long time, or running without tiring. He begins to love all things mobile. He himself cannot remain seated for long and requires to externalize his inner urges in the form of some sort of movement. He begins to achieve balance, coordination, and control in his gestures, postures, and physical stance. He is motivated by activities such as washing, squeezing, pouring, rolling mats, etc. He even derives pleasure in jumping or hopping at the same spot instead of just standing. You can also see him climbing up and down the stairs just to count the steps or repeat the same action in order to do it better. He also becomes quite fond of jumping up and down the bed or a sofa, and you might have scolded him on various occasions for doing so, without realizing that he is going through a sensitive period of movement.

Refinement of Senses:

From the initial moments of his birth until well beyond the age of 4, the child is in a sensitive period of sensory perception. He is, at first, only capable of seeing and hearing clearly, then he begins to develop his other senses such as smell, touch, and taste. He further refines his perception of sensory organs by collecting sensory impressions from the exploration of everyday objects and classifying them. After that, he starts to relate these concrete sensory impressions to more abstract concepts, and this is formulated through his sensorial memory of previous concrete experiences. The parents find it difficult that the child needs to explore his surroundings in order to refine his senses. He needs freedom with guidance. If he is constrained, inhibited to move and explore, his sensory development gets hindered. Your toddler does not need a child seat or a playpen. He needs an environment that encourages his muscular intelligence, sensory perception, and stereognosis sense.

Language:

It goes on actively from birth until six years of age. It is the longest sensitive period. This period is important for all sorts of intellectual competence. The writing, speaking, and reading, all are developed and refined here. Your home environment must be a language-enriched environment. The toddler must be exposed to the language properly. Anecdotes, storytelling, questioning, and rapid-fire games to enrich the vocabulary must be played on a regular basis to help ensure the accelerated pace of learning and language development at this sensitive stage. The conversation is the main source of enrichment of vocabulary at this time. Adults should talk and let the child participate in the conversation as well in order to learn new words and phrases.

Social skills or Grace and Courtesy:

It may start from 2 or 3 years onward and continue till the age of 6. When the child starts interacting with other kids in the learning environment, he becomes aware that he is a part of a social circle. He realizes that there are other similar aged kids in the world who talk, walk, and act like him. He notices that he is not the only mini adult living in this society. He learns to socialize and acquires basic social skills. He learns to give importance to grace and courtesy. He says sorry and thank you at appropriate occasions and says his greetings well. He learns proper ethics and table manners too. This sensitive period enhances his good manners and etiquette. At home, your toddler should not be isolated while being raised. He, as a Montessori toddler, should be given ample opportunities to interact with other children, eating, playing, working, and socializing with them regularly.

Reading and Writing:

The writing starts at three and a half years and continues till five, while the sensitivity to reading starts at four years, continuing up to six. This also shows that the sensitive periods of development are often running parallel to each other. The child is intensely fascinated with writing patterns, symbols, and tracing the letters. He learns the formation of alphabets quite easily too when presented to him at the right age and in right order i.e. learning to hold the instrument for writing, creating lines, shapes and patterns through metal insets, tracing the sandpaper letters, writing on the green board, then writing between the lines on the paper, etc. Similarly, the reading is also easily learned if presented at the right peak of the sensitive period of reading, and at the time when indirect preparation for reading has already been completed through prereading games and oral exercises. Your toddler can learn to read much quickly when he is passing through this sensitive period as his cognitive senses are more responsive, and his intellectual powers more enhanced. Firstly through phonics by sandpaper letters and making small three-lettered or four-lettered words through movable alphabets, then introducing phonetic words and phonograms through object boxes, also the puzzle words, etc. the child learns to read efficiently and systematically. There are several other reading exercises to practice and reinforce the act of reading, such as all the word study exercises (Phonogram booklets, story cards, Dictation cards, etc.).

These exercises and activities will be described later in this book, in the chapter dedicated to Montessori-friendly lessons.

Chapter 5: Obstacles to Development at Home

The child, in his early years, is like a flexible clay or Play-Doh. They can be made without breaking. However, if over the years they are hardened into set structures, their personalities are quite difficult to change. Therefore, at home, the preparation for creating or setting up an environment to raise the toddler must be a careful, thoughtful process. It should involve not only the child's own efforts to learn but the adults' efforts and consideration to facilitate that learning too.

Considering the example of language development, the child firstly put efforts to speak in the form of exclamatory expressions, or mumbling sounds that are incoherent. Then he proceeds to the next stage where he starts to join sounds and syllables in order to articulate a small word altogether. This further leads to the formation of sentences.

However, these stages are not such a linear, serial process. It happens as an explosion. The explosion of newer vocabulary makes him speak the newly learned words in a fluent manner. This explosion of words occurs and is shortly proceeded by another explosion of thought which results in forming the words into coherent order to utter them in a meaningful way. This stage helps the child in getting his message across and his desire known.

These explosions require some prerequisite preparation. If the proper environment and facilitation are not present to equip the child with enrichment of senses and clarity of cognition, he may have difficulty expressing himself. Similarly, the proper strategies and oral preparation for the enrichment of vocabulary in the home environment is a powerful preparation method to facilitate the child. There is also some kind of hidden preparation that the mind itself starts working on the way before that. The evidence of its absence can be seen when the child starts showing signs of extreme vexation and inability to properly express himself in front of adults.

Some mute children are often seen troubling with anger and frustration issues. Their lack of ability to externalize their inner thoughts and freedom of expression leads to an increase in their quarrelsome behavior.

Similarly, some children may be seen easily provoked and show sudden rage at not being able to succeed in completing a task or their request not being heard. It can be because there is a certain gap of communication and understanding between an adult and the child, which often results in the child not being understood by his parent or teacher. This may also happen due to the lack of attention and care on the part of an adult. Some adults even put their children in the care of the governesses or maids who might speak to them in an uncaring tone and treat them with a harsh, unfeeling attitude. The children are very sensitive toward these sorts of behaviors. They can develop a special sensitivity to traumatic incidents if exposed more than once. Even the cold and calm tone of voice can reflect a sort of calculated ruthlessness to them. This can escalate quickly into ugly depression and fearful, traumatic experiences that put a massive lock on the door of development and shuts the windows of opportunity close.

People think that giving birth to a baby is a wonderful thing; it sure is; however, the first difficult phase of adaptation starts for the child, right after his birth. He, who has been depending solely on his mother till now, has to learn to adapt to this alien world. He has to learn to sleep, eat, and express himself through gestures and cries. He has to survive on his own, yet he needs immense care at that stage to smoothly transition from this period of infancy without having to go through any negative experiences that might prove to be obstacles in his future development.

The second major adaptation he has to go through is when in toddlerhood, he must cope up with all the limitations or lacking in his powers and the environmental obstacles. If he is able to cope up with both the adaptations smoothly, he goes straight on the journey toward independence and self-reliance. This is what we call normalization.

The child not only retains the positive effects of his powers of adaptation and developmental experiences in early years' till the later age of his life, but he also remembers the unfortunate struggles that he went through to survive his childhood. Therefore, the deviations also originate in the period of infancy or toddlerhood and can be deeply rooted in the personality becoming serious as time passes.

Certain reasons cause delays in normal explosions sometimes. This can happen without any apparent physical defect. For e.g., a child may not start speaking at a right age even though his sensory organs for speech are in order. This is due to a sort of *mental dumbness* which happens as a psychological condition triggered by environmental obstacles or disturbances or some sort of inner conflict or fear. This has been proved as certain cases of children were observed speaking suddenly and miraculously after a long delay. It was concluded that a particular obstacle was removed from their surroundings or inner personality to stimulate the explosion of words.

Even some adults can be seen showing the deep-rooted effects of these obstacles by having a lack of confidence in public speaking, stammering on stage, clogging of the throat, lack of proper articulation and sentence formation, etc. Unfortunately, most of the time in adulthood, these effects turn into lasting inferiorities that are very difficult to get rid of. Dr. Maria Montessori says that *"Each different period of acquisition in childhood, has its own kind of regression."* That is why a parent as a teacher is not just a caretaker, but an observer and discoverer too. They must be able to psycho-analyze their toddlers to track any possible obstacles in their path of development.

You, as a parent to a toddler being raised in a Montessori environment, must analyze the child's sayings to read between the lines and understand even the implications behind his words. Keep in mind that your toddler is already in a struggling age were expressing his thoughts and desires clearly and effectively seems to be a challenging task. Help him, facilitate him, and be patient with him.

The children love those adults who are quick to interpret their minds and wishes. When you become apt at understanding your toddler's choice, words, and expressions, you will win his heart. And this will happen when you spend quality time with him, pay closer attention to what he is doing, letting him express his desires, letting him choose his own mode and type of activity. It will let you know what sort of interests and potentials he has and what sort of learning he prefers. Adults must stop imposing themselves on their children so that their creative will survives and their right to self - discovery is not deprived.

Chapter 6: Importance of Movement

Movement is a vital part of every living creature. Life is all about mobility. Movement is responsible for every other major process in the body like digestion, respiration, metabolism, and immunity. External movements of the body like swimming, walking, running are the locomotional movements responsible for the better internal functions performed by the body. Movements help us to locate ourselves from one place to another. Mostly living creatures locate themselves for survival by seeking food and shelter.

Movements help us to survive in a society in a better and effective way. The human body is designed in a way every movement of the body creates different postures for sitting, standing, walking, etc. The body maintains its equilibrium against the gravity through these postures. External movements help us to gather the information of the surroundings, internal movements like the circulation of blood digestion, etc., are performed by the movement of special muscles designed to make organs of the body perform efficiently. Muscles, bones, joints, and tendons are the major components joined together to make the body move adequately.

Locomotion in the human body works with the help of two main systems that are skeletal and muscular. Both these systems are interrelated with each other. The absence of any one of these components can lead to immobility. The skeletal system consists of bones and joints, which give the body movement for postures and aligned.

The muscular system consists of tissues, ligaments, tendons, which helps the skeletal system work effectively. All the internal organs and limbs of the body can work because of the muscular system. Circulation of blood throughout the body also occurs due to the muscular system. Apart from these two systems, there is the main system that is responsible for the working of the whole body. It is called a Vegetative Nervous System or Autonomic Nervous System. This system is present in vertebrates; there are certain internal organs present in the body which works with involuntary movements. Like heart, spinal muscles, and gland cells. These organs work on the vegetative nervous system. This is comprised of sets of nerves that connect the internal organs to the brain, increase of blood flow, heart rate, etc. are caused by these nerves. The vegetative system provides a person with a healthy life with pleasant moments. This gives the pleasure of the impressions and perfection of thoughts.

There are mainly three types of muscles in the body. Skeletal muscles are also known as voluntary muscles as they are controlled by the body. These muscles are attached to bones with tendons. Tendons help in the locomotion of different parts of the body and skeleton. These muscles are organized in the form of stripes, also termed as Striated Muscles. Smooth muscles are also called involuntary muscles which are not controlled by the body directly, but with some special system which we have discussed above, that is the vegetative system. These muscles are present on the outside walls of the internal organs work through the tubular form. The autonomic nervous system helps these muscles to work at a certain pace and makes sure these involuntary movements take place accurately. Cardiac muscles are also called involuntary muscles. They are present in the form of branches, found in the heart of the body. These muscles are comprised of muscle fibers.

The skeletal system is the framework of the body. It's made of cartilages and bones. It gives a basic shape to the human body. Soft muscles like lungs and brain are also protected by the skeletal system with the help of skull and rib-cage. Bones of the skeletal muscles are supported by strong tissues are known as ligaments. The skeletal system provides a rigid surface to attach the muscles to the tendons. The basic purpose of the skeletal system is to provide locomotion to the body.

Importance Of Movement According To Montessori:

Life depends on movements, mostly directed movements. Directed movements are controlled and guided movements which helps the person to act consciously. These movements are also made to understand the children's work and to guide them better. Movements can be educational, according to Montessori. She emphasized that movements should consider an education point of view. In today's world, traditional parenting and teaching concepts are of a child who sits silently listens and follows instructions accurately; furthermore, they consider this attitude under disciplinary behavior. In the traditional method of parenting and schooling, the movements of the children are not GUIDED; they are restricted. Restrictions cause damage to personality development, but according to Montessori, she denied this theory of restricted movements but gave the world concept of guided movements in a well-prepared environment.

There are lots of research and articles published on this vary topic that states about the concern of parents and teachers about a child's physical and intellectual development. According to theorists, most of them are agreed that still- movements can make a child learn more and with concentration. According to parents' views, "children who can't sit still learn that being disruptive gets them attention. They learn to get in trouble, and this behavior causes long term disciplinary problems". Some parents also believe that "sitting still and paying attention with silence are the building blocks of success." It's a teacher's dream that she gets a set of students who follows instructions obediently. Stays still on their seats and listens with concentration and understand what is being said. It's high time that people realize the power of movement in the intellectual and physical development of the child.

Dr. Montessori was a woman of great observation while going through research on the children she was working; she smartly sensed the relationship between the brain and movement of the body. She was a visionary researcher who thought that it would be a loss if we will separate the work of movement from intellectual development. She also agreed with the idea that body movements also strengthen our cardiovascular system. Until today all educationists believe that movements of the muscular system only aid in the functioning of respiration, blood circulation, etc. but the thought which Maria Montessori had given century ago that movement is important for mental development also. Now researchers are working on that thought, and most of them have agreed to this point of view that movements create intellectual brains. Montessori believed that the actions done by the child are connected with the mental activity of the brain.

Today, theorists don't deny the imperative development in children due to the physical movement. They are researching the children with activities and trying to find out the results from these activities. Some studies have shown the strong connections created by the brain with the movements of the body. When they attempted to work with the children in the classroom, they opted for some activities with less physical movement with one group, and with the second group, there was more working physically then sitting.

This research brought influential results. Those children with good physical movements we often associate them with the term Hyperactive, but in this study, those kids proved to have better mental skills and grasp of knowledge than the other batch of students. Secondly, children with more movements are more practical learners. Their decision making and independence define their mental stability towards themselves and their environment. They did not seem to be focused, but their observational skills can be seen from the work they did during the research procedure. The statement of Montessori about the movement that "movement is connected with activity going on in brain" got clarified with this short research by the educationists.

According to Montessori movements can do magic only if they get guided. Children have the inborn capability to take things out of their environment. A child's mind is meant to explore things present around him. Exploration is the process that leads a child towards successful learning. Adults can provide a child with an environment where he gets busy with purposeful movements. These purposeful movements will act as a building block for their success.

Activities should be designed in a way that a child learns about things around him with purposeful movements. Montessori, with her materials, worked on this thought and created materials like Red Rods, the child, physically brings the rods to and from the work area. He is learning mathematical orders not only with his mind but his body is also involved in the whole process of learning. "work is inseparable from movement" (Montessori) as she believes that a child's work is to learn so why not make him learn by incorporating guided movements in the environment to see the better results in his learning.

Development of Brain and Motor Skills:

Theorists now support the idea of learning through movements develops the brain in a more constructive and positive manner for life long. For such growth and improvements, well-prepared environments are needed. Rich environments create rich brains, and guided movements are an essential part of this environment. Researchers are more focused on the early childhood development process for the sake of children and society as well. To study more deeply about early education, science is working on the critical periods of a child's life.

Early life, especially infancy, is the most sensitive period of a child's life in the developmental process. As we already know that a child is born with billions of brain cells, and these brain cells are connected with strong wiring, which makes the human function effectively. The stimulation caused by the electrical signals created a hard-wired connection, and this connection is the main part of the working of the child's brain. The stronger the wiring the strongest will be the development of the child both physically and mentally. As the brain cells work on stimulation, the child's physical activities enhance these stimulations and making the brain at its peak. Multiple organs get involved in a simple activity performed by the child, but this activity will give an enormous amount of beneficial results in the early development of the child's brain.

Research has shown both the positive and the negative results shown by the children due to the environmental factor. Optimization of brain development surely depends on motor and sensory development. Both the developments can be done and lead to the success of the child though guided movements under a safe and enriched environment full of activities. A child's mind behaves differently at different stages of his age, so it's important to observe the child according to his age keenly. In some circumstances provides due to some external factors, a child shows delayed development, which is a reversible process if given a healthy environment.

Scientist who has worked on the children's mind believes that a child is born with the window of opportunities, precisely, when a child is in his mother's womb he is automatically taking the information of the outside world through this window which nature has given him, when he gets born this window get narrow and as he grows up this window gets narrower and narrower. This is the reason scientists have given this sensory windows the term "window of opportunity." Opportunities don't come to a person; he creates an environment that waits for the right time for the right to grab. The same is the case with the child's mental development, a healthy environment, and guided movements are the best opportunities given by the adults to the child for optimized development of his motor and sensory skills.

Basic motor skills of the child through windows of opportunity appear from the prenatal period till the age of 5. The brain works at its peak during the age, and this is the age in which we put a foundation of the child's success towards life. It is done by giving him the moves he requires for his brain to get developed at an optimized pace. The window of opportunity gets narrower by the age of 10. So, keeping this fact in mind gives your child the best of opportunities or experiences for him to learn and grow healthy.

What an Adult Can Do:

Windows of opportunity is a scientific term; it is not approved yet. But to make people understand the concept of how the child's brain and its wiring structure work at different stages, they needed a term. It is mostly agreed by the theorists that early childhood development depends mostly upon the movement of the child.

In the infancy stage, the more the child moves his hands and legs, the stronger the process of myelination will take place. Myelin is the sheath-like proteinoid coating around the nerves that accelerates the transmission of cognitive impulses. A child is born to explore, so let him do that. His physical and mental health depends on the activities he performs in his daily life. He needs his brain to work at its peak through his movements. Make sure that these movements are positive and safe.

Activities should be designed in a way that they create positive stimulations in a child's mind. They should provide the child with a lot of motor and sensory experiences. It is human nature that the child learns more from what he sees than from what is told. That is why learning opportunities, through visual sense is a crucial type of development. The physical development opportunities also must be planned in such a way that they provide the child with different activities to enhance his visual sense quite well. Activities like kicking, catching the ball are the best examples of the whole-body movement with also the strengthen of visual sense. Gross motor activities help the child to control his posture and maintain his equilibrium. His movements get more enhanced with these activities. Intense and vigorous activities like jumping, rolling on the floor increases blood flow in the body, which automatically triggers the brain and thus making a child healthy from inside out.

Activities like singing and dancing can also be fruitful if added properly. Actions on poems will help the child involve his body through movements and brain on concentrating on the words of the poems the adult is singing to them. Again a great activity for brain enhancement. There are many more activities an adult can start from the age of infancy, toddlers, and preschoolers for the early childhood development of the child. Parents and teachers both are responsible for the children's growth of mind and body. They should consider the fact the child will not be able to make his brain and body strong if not provided with different opportunities. He needs to develop with the movement of his body through positive physical activities designed just to make his mind and work efficiently.

The environment is the key factor for early childhood development, and if physical guided movements are present in that environment, they will boost the capabilities of the child in an affirmative manner. A child will grow as an independent, disciplined, mentally, and physically aligned.

An adult should observe the needs of the child on every stage of their development and provide them with what is best for them. A child is the future of society; he needs to be both mentally and physically strong to fulfill his responsibility as a grown-up. His actions will reflect the learning he got from his childhood. We must cater to the child's development sensibly for his and our better future.

Chapter 7: Language Acquisition

Language is a medium of communication. Verbal communication takes place through speaking listening and writing. On the other hand, nonverbal communication takes place through signed language, body gestures, and facial expressions. Initially, when the man was self-discovering himself, he wanted to communicate with others for his survival. Evolution took place and signed language was replaced by sounds and syllables. This further led to the forming of words and their meanings.

We develop the process of communication through language, which is a spontaneous process, and we can't interact with each other if no language is available. Nature has given man indicts to Brain is the vital organ of the human body responsible for every work done by it. The human nervous system knows how to react and adjust with different tasks going around him. Neurologists who studies the nervous system defines us the when the baby is born he has billions of brain cells already placed by nature he will need all Each brain cell has dendrites which are the adjunct of the cells connected with other brain cells, the point of connection of these cells is called a synapse, brain cells make connections to transfer the information from cell to cell through electrical signals.

In today's world of advancement, science has proven the process of "hard-wire." In this process, synapses are accelerated repeatedly, and the pattern on which cells are connected creates electrical signals. The process gets stronger, efficient with each signal that passes through the cells network to transfer the information required by the brain quickly and accurately. Nerve cells present in the brain cortex are responsible for the development of the language. These nerve cells are divided into two parts the one is responsible for the hearing process and the other one for the formulation of the speech. The ear receives the sounds in which the brain can relate through the nerve cells. Then the brain sends signals to the organs involved in the speaking process to make the language development work.

Learning the language process is different in grown-ups than in a child. A child learns language from the depths of his unconscious mind. There are certain kinds of activities to be done, both physically and mentally by the child for the speaking process to get completed.

Sounds in the environment stimulate the child to mimic them and try to reproduce them as heard. Production of speech is a natural process; there is no logical reason for that. It seems that nature is being logical. When we study nature, there are so many logics we see around us that in the end, we believe that there is some A child's brain reorganizes the connections of the brain after birth and these connections get highly impacted by the environment the child is living. Repetition of positive experiences before the child can make his brain development strong.

The physiology of the ear is very complex and different from the anatomy. Sound waves travel in the air in the form of vibrations around us; these vibrations are caught by our brain and send it to the ear canals. Eardrum gets vibrated due to the sound waves; the eardrum is the most sensitive part of the ear; it can detect faintest and most difficult vibrations. The eardrum has vibrations brought about by sound waves move the chain of little bones (the Ossicles – Malleus, Incus, and Stapes) in the center ear moving the sound vibrations into. This happens because the remainder of the three bones in this chain, the stapes, sits in a layer canvassed window in the hard divider which isolates the center ear from the cochlea of the internal ear. As the stapes vibrates, it makes the liquids in the cochlea move in a wave-like way, invigorating the infinitesimally little 'hair cells.'

Strikingly, the 'hair cells' in the cochlea are tuned to react to various sounds dependent on their pitch or recurrence of sounds. Piercing sounds will animate 'hair cells' in the lower some portion of the cochlea and low-contributed sounds the upper piece of the cochlea.

What occurs next is considerably progressively wonderful because, when every 'hair cell' identifies the pitch or recurrence of sound to which it's tuned to react, it creates nerve motivations that travel quickly along the sound-related nerve. These nerve motivations pursue a confounded pathway in the brainstem before touching base at the conference focuses on the mind, the sound-related cortex. This is the place the surges of nerve driving forces are changed over into important sound. The majority of this occurs inside a little portion of a second, promptly after sound waves initially, enter our ear waterways. It is consistent with the state that, at last, we hear with our cerebrum.

Maria Montessori strongly believed that a child is born with what he needs to develop language. And according to this statement, adults around the child can help him to enrich and develop his verbal skills with a positive attitude. Adults should create a prepared environment for the child to develop his language according to the environment created for the enriched language skills. A child's mind grasps language much faster at an early age if exposed to the language properly. And this vocabulary needs to get visualized in the forms of alphabets and words for the child to learn reading and writing.

It is necessary for the child that he should develop the language skills in a curate and prepared environment enriched with opportunities for the child to obtain his language. We all know that in the early stages, the child learns the language unconsciously from the environment. He hears the sounds and then vocalizes them in to form different words. It's the responsibility of the adults around to make sure that the words the child is learning are being repeated for the sake of the child's speaking clarity and making him.

"Language is the central point of difference between the human species and all others. Language lies at the root of that transformation of the environment that we call civilization." ~ Dr., "a child's mind is like a sponge," said Maria Montessori in her well-known book "The Absorbent Mind." The acquisition of the language by the child is behind this idea. She worked on this subject extensively that how the mechanism of the language process works in the mind of the child. She focused on the idea of the unconscious development of the child's language through his environment by simply listening to the adults talk. This absorption of the words takes place during the first three years of his child's life.

Dr. Silvana Montanaro, who is the pioneer spreading insights of Montessori, also acknowledged this idea of a child's language acquisition. As her subject was to study the development of a child during pregnancy and 3 years after birth, she quoted that, "From the moment of birth, infants know that spoken language comes from the mouth, and if we allow them the time, we will notice that when we talk to them, they try to move their mouths correspondingly. Studies have shown that from the stage of infancy, children's brains can encode and decode the information they gather from their surroundings. According to Montessori in the first three years, childhood memory is in an unconscious state that is whatever he learns during these years will eventually fade away with time and after three years he will enter into the conscious state of memory.

Learning in the unconscious memory period doesn't mean that he will lose his memory afterward; it's just that he will remember the words unconsciously but not the environment from. As this is an unconscious process, he will forget the environment but not the language acquisition. Another theorist like Vygotsky has also mentioned that language is a social-based activity.

Children learn through interaction with the people around them. Having people around in a good social environment child gets motivated to speak and visualize a meaningful part of their social lives.

She says that *"The child must create his interior life before he can express anything; he must take spontaneously from the external world constructive material to 'compose'; he must exercise his intelligence fully before he can be ready to find the logical connection between things. We ought to offer the child that which is necessary for his internal life and leave him free to produce."*

We can find other prominent theories about language development by great researchers. Noam Chomsky's creational approach about language is that it is an inborn capability in a child to learn and explore words around him. Noam does not focus on the environmental impact on language. He emphasizes the fact that the brain leads a child to learn the language.

Guidance of adults makes this process quicker, but if adults are not around, he will still acquire the impressions as learning any language is a cognitive and lingual process, and it happens automatically. However, the interactions of children with the people in society help him learn to strengthen the connections between the adults and his acquisition of language through a mutual bonding present. She emphasizes on the thought that the environment should be enriched with the activities for the well, the prepared environment was the term first given by Montessori to her classroom for the children to develop their skills in a prepared and guided environment by the teachers. She believed that a well-prepared classroom would give a child the freedom to work independently and at his own pace. Giving children the freedom to explore enhances the capability of their auditory sense and also their sense of judgment.

And research has shown proven results of the kids who worked independently in a well-prepared environment. We should all know that we have to develop the language of the Material based learning methodology invented by Montessori enabled the child to begin his learning skills through practical life activities. These activities help the child to build concentration focus and confidence. By doing these activities, he eventually starts loving and caring for himself and the environment. He gets curious about the sensorial area after the practical activities where he can explore more deeply. Materials and activities in the sensorial area are more profound to give the child a chance to explore his world more deeply.

Working with the sensorial materials helps the child to speak of his experience with more desire. Language in infused in all areas of the environment. Fine motor skill activities like pin punching, knobbed cylinders, etc., creates a child's brain to attempt to start writing. A classroom should have writing activities present so that he gets the opportunity to practice his writing skills as he explores the different materials from the sensory area. Flashcards of different categories also help the child to memorize the pictures letters through visualization. Language material helps the child to read and write at his own pace. The child must be able to make his own decision, not the adult on his behalf. A child reads and writes letters according to his developmental skis he is acquiring through an exploration of materials around the environment. It's really important that at this stage of development, the child practices to learn how words sound. He practices more to reproduce the accurate sound, and by the time he begins writing, he should know the sound and letter names accordingly.

Language is the way of communication through which the child expresses himself with confidence, only if the adult allows him to do so. The concept of language material is to give children directions to interact with the environment. Learning words and vocabulary enhancement allows children to label objects and people accurately. In a well-prepared environment, we focus on the activity-based learning process of reading and writing rather than pushing the child through traditional teaching method the most beneficial part of material learning is that the child develops the reading habit for the rest of his life.

Working on sandpaper letters is an example of learning the letter with the phonetic sound with the help of the combination of a two-way process that is of hand and the mind using sensory developments in making the child learn the language properly. And if we take the example of practical life exercises when he pours rice from one bowl to another, he hears the sound which gets echoed through his auditory sense. It's a fact that visual teaching is more impactful than just giving the child an imaginary thought.

For example, if the child is tracing the letter on the sand, he involves his muscular education which trains him for writing, he is seeing the letter and pronouncing the sound as well this activity fixes the image of the letter quickly with the coordination of multiple senses. The teacher of the Montessori environment should not stop to guide her students just through prepared materials but also incorporate similar activities which enhances the learning process of the child. Poems and songs are also a common way to engage the child's attention and build up his language.

When it comes to phonetic learning misspell is a common hurdle that comes during the learning process, but it's not the main issue; this can be overcome by the passage of time when they will be able to spell the words correctly. An adult has to show patience since it's not sensible to correct the child on and off; we have to wait until he corrects himself. Not correcting the child is a difficult task for the adults but to make children learn by themselves, the adult must have to behave accordingly. This is the method for the trilogy process at a time or 3-period lesson. For example, in stage one, we introduce the name of the object like "this is a table." On the second stage, it's for the child to identify what is just being introduced to him. He recognizes it. You may assess him by saying, "Put your hands on the table," and in the last stage, a child needs to remember what has been introduced, “where is the table.” The three-period lesson is the most effective method to work on three areas in a single go i.e., naming or introduction, association or recognition, evaluation, or confirmation.

The most common misinterpretation is that a child will learn his reading and writing skills by a certain age. Adults fail to realize that the developmental process is different with every child. If due to pressure and force the child will able to learn reading, but that will not be lifelong. Language is a developmental process that needs patience and prepared to In the first three years; every child reacts differently so the parents should know the abilities of their children at certain ages.

Childs first schools are his mother's womb; parents should realize that a child develops his skill right from his birth; all he needs is a good environment to develop his.

Parents should incorporate poems, little stories, learning phonetics in their home environment so the child can learn the language more easily and effectively. Top of Form No production of words can be done without good auditory senses. Adults should first focus on the hearing capabilities of the child. With too much little sounds around the child will be able to mimic them then will reproduce them. First, the sounds and utterance of words will be improper, but eventually, the more the child will practice, the more he will begin to grasp the language accurately.

Chapter 8: Setting up a Montessori Environment - A Children's House and its Traits

Dr. Maria Montessori states the traits of the Montessori Children's House in great detail in her own handbook of Montessori educational philosophy. She says that the children's house acts as an environment that offers maximum developmental opportunities for the child. This is a special house in which the conventional, strict concept of schooling is not in practice. Instead, it caters to the individual differences of the children and facilitates the learning opportunities accordingly. It has a flexible angle to it in a way that adapts to the availability of financial resources at hand and the strength and learning pace of the children.

In a Montessori environment, there are no restraints on the lessons and activities due to lack of financial affordability as normally happens in conventional schools.

Montessori suggests that it ought to be a real house that can serve as a suitable children's house; it also should have a garden and open area for a nursery or pet keeping. An adequate space can facilitate convenient areas for reading, resting, eating, sleeping, and playing. The shelters or shades in a garden such as gazebos or benches for sitting and some age-appropriate play equipment installed in a secure courtyard or back compound can offer several developmental opportunities for the young ones.

The importance is given to an open air space that is rich in fresh sunlight, natural views, and proper ventilation, along with being protectively shielding from rain and dust at the same time. There should be shaded areas to protect from scalding sun and heat. As the name suggests, these houses should be prepared by keeping the children in mind instead of adults. The children's house is a Montessori-friendly home environment that is specifically child-centered. It serves as a learning and developmental haven for the toddlers created purely to facilitate maximum opportunities for growth and progress.

Specific Rooms, their Furniture, and Other Wall Equipment:

Following points must be considered while selecting the equipment for the environment:

- ✔ All the equipment such as toys, furniture, learning resources, shelves, cupboards, chairs, etc. must be according to the child's age, size, and developmental level.
- ✔ The color of the furniture must be light so that dust and dirt can be easily spotted and cleaned right away. Children should be able to wash and scour it with soapy water.
- ✔ The weight of the furniture must also be light so that the children can carry the chairs and move around, or navigate the tables, etc., as per the need.
- ✔ Several low tables in various shapes should be present in the environment so that the children can form small and large groups during material presentations or reinforcement exercises or conversation time. Some individual or combined lessons can be performed using small round tables or large rectangular ones.

- ✔ Wooden material is preferred or wicker or chairs or table, etc and stone or wooden flooring is also better. This is to increase familiarity with nature instead of artificial or synthetic materials such as plastic, carpet, etc.
- ✔ There should be some small couches, cushions, or sofas as a reclining seat for retiring or relaxing.
- ✔ The room for work and activity must contain cupboards and shelves suitable for placing the apparatus and other learning material in order. The didactic material is commonly shared and owned by the children.
- ✔ Each child has his own drawer to keep personal items. These drawers must be installed in such a way that they remain in reach and at the level of the children's height.
- ✔ Work-room also should have different large and small rugs to be laid when presenting floor exercises. These rugs can be vibrant in colors to differentiate each area of ongoing activity in the room. This room should have adequate space to serve as a free-spirited activity room or multiple workstations.

- ✔ There should be low hooks installed to hang aprons, table cloths, dressing frames, etc.
- ✔ Some corner tables should be there to place vases in which flowers are arranged. Children can gather fresh flowers from the garden and help in the arrangement of beautifully aesthetic table baskets, etc.
- ✔ Some soft boards and black or green boards must be hanging on the walls at eye level to the children. This way, they can jot down whatever they want to or attach pictures or artwork, etc.
- ✔ There can be a pedometer or stadiometer placed in a corner to help measure the child's height. Each child can himself stand on it and see the growing difference after each regular measurement.
- ✔ A shoe rack must be there at the entrance of a classroom so that each toddler learns to place the shoes in order and also be comfortable while working.
- ✔ Another room can be prepared as a sitting room or a parlor. This room can be like a sunroom or club used for candid talk among the children, playing games, etc. The tasteful and

particularly relaxing furniture in this room such as comfy toddler settees, couches, play instruments, round tables with illustrated books, walls decorated with scrapbooks, photo albums, story charts, etc. The adults can entertain the children with some interesting anecdotes too. The children can also place their small pots with seeded plants as an indoor activity.

- ✔ The walls may contain small alcoves to display small artistic crafts, or catchy pictures, or educational material.
- ✔ The dining room is another particular place to prepare in a Montessori-friendly environment. It should have small-sized tables and chairs to facilitate appropriate sitting arrangement for the toddlers.
- ✔ There should be a low cabinet in the corner to place cutlery in the right order and accessible manner for every child. They should be able to help themselves by picking and placing the plates, spoons, napkins, etc. on their own.
- ✔ The glasses and plates must not be of plastic or less appealing material that may disorient the child's aesthetic sense and self-esteem. The

material of glass or chinaware should be used instead.

- ✔ There is also a dressing room or a washing area. It should have a sufficient number of washing basins and soap bottles or containers.
- ✔ The dressing area also must have appropriate chests with drawers to serve as lockers for each child where they can put their pouches containing toothbrushes, hairbrushes or combs, napkins, etc.
- ✔ The equipment in a Montessori environment can be quite vast yet very diverse. It happens because the toddlers are being trained in not only the academic or physical side of the development but also the social and practical aspects of life. They learn to sweep, wash, dust, clean, polish, pour, fold, wrap, and even cook some snacks, etc. Every single task that they do require age-appropriate material and equipment.
- ✔ Each area or learning corner of the Montessori classroom has a distinctive color and apparatus especially the set of material in specific exercises can be color coordinated to help the child in remembering the tools used in a particular activity.

- ✔ The walls must not be painted too bright, or equipment in too many bright colors. The neutrality of decoration and paint will help the child focus more on the didactic apparatus displayed on the shelves on the walls instead.
- ✔ The didactic material placed on the shelves must be in progressive order according to the learning sequence in each subject area.
- ✔ There is a nook serving as a library or reading corner. It should have bookshelves accessible to the child.
- ✔ Then there is also a pet corner or pet house. The pets can be present both as indoor or outdoor companions. For indoors, some fish or parrots or birds can be placed while in outdoors, rabbits, peacock, etc. can be present.
- ✔ A small kitchen area can be prepared to teach cold-ingredients' recipes like making a fruit salad, cheese sandwich, juices, etc.

Your home environment can be a familiar place for your toddler, yet it still can be without order and proper format to ensure maximum learning opportunities when you are opting for homeschooling your child. The careful tips provided here are based on the pure Montessori concept and will facilitate systematic, individually- catering, creative environment to the child. Raising him in this sort of development-friendly atmosphere will help you and all other parents to realize the full potential of your child along with keeping track of his learning pace.

As the Montessori method states that the prepared environment is like a triangle. The material and resources or class are at one corner while the adult and the child represent the other two corners. This way, every three corners are interdependent for the optimum developmental outcomes. The absence of any one of them will result in a vain effort on the part of the remaining two. All three of them shape up the most powerful opportunity of revolutionizing the learning and system of education, in a most positive way.

Another very distinctive trait of a Montessori children's house is its discipline while catering to even mixed-age groups of children. The calm, peaceful working of small toddlers ranging from 2.5, 3, 3.5, 4, 4.5, 5, 5.5, 6, etc. , mesmerizes the onlookers. Children are so indulged in satisfying their internal urge to accomplish a meaningful activity that they don't even want to argue or waste time making noise or causing a disturbance. Choosing their activity, taking out respective material from the right place, sitting on their choice of rug or table, calmly paying attention to their work, then winding up properly, replacing the material to its corresponding place, this all requires some extent of absolute control, sense of order and responsibility, and innate discipline. These children being raised as Montessori toddlers also exhibit a mutual sense of respect and are inquisitive in nature.

Children in Montessori also learn to share the common material and become patient at waiting for their turn to use it. They are provided with enough resource activities and material exercises to engage in and do something constructive without wasting their time. Each exercise has a purpose, set of direct and indirect aims, and point of interest. Most of the Montessori material tends to be self-exploratory and can be quite easy to handle. All the equipment is according to the size and age of the child, and he learns it at his own pace individually. There is no concept of a mainstream classroom lesson or combined lecture, etc. Actually, there are some group lessons, but they are for the oral practice of language or have pre-reading games and in no way are they just passive listening sessions on the children's part.

The environment also has historical timelines, interactive calendar displays, and cultural maps or globes, etc. to enrich the children with geography, history, and cultural information. Each of the Montessori subjects, including Exercise of Practical Life, Sensorial Education,

Language and Literacy, Mathematical Concepts, and Cultural Subjects, are described in detail in the later chapter of this book.

Chapter 9: Montessori Subjects' Presentation and the Didactic Material

Montessori system has a unique scientific approach that can be seen in the way it focuses on self-teaching material that is manufactured in a perfect size, color, and proportion. The Montessori subjects are also carefully selected and integrated through a broad curriculum that encompasses not only academics but social life skills as well. By following Montessori subjects in a parallel and systematic way so that each domain of development is integrated efficiently, your toddler can be raised in a perfect manner.

The didactic material is a special-purpose material intended to be a pedagogic aid or teaching resource, yet it can provide a pure self-learning experience for a child as well. The Montessori methodology is not just scientific in its aim but in the substance too. That is why the didactic material is also called scientific material. It has some special characteristics that ensure the maximum training of the senses, and possess definite shape or dimension. Objects in the same activity group often show the same quality in gradation or sequence. They include the extremes of high and low and the medium-graded objects in between. The child chooses his own material activity according to his interest and inner urge or sensitivity. The graded contrast sharpens the sensorial perception of a child and teaches him the intended quality in vivid detail.

The child is exposed to the material first by being given a proper presentation. The teacher or an adult acting as a directress shows him a constructive way to use the didactic material and the aim of the related activity. This helps him explore the material purposefully. The following characteristics are the essence of scientifically prepared, Montessori didactic material:

A Single, Isolated Quality:

Each set of material has a specific quality isolated in it, such as weight, color, height, length, size, form, roughness, etc. This way, the material ensures that the child learns only the thing that is intended to be learned through a certain material, nothing more, nothing less. The concentration of a child is maintained, and this helps make the learned concepts clear and concrete. For example, the red rods or long rods are presented to teach the concept of length. So the child will only realize the length while arranging them. All other qualities are the same in these rods such as color, height, form, breadth, etc. Only the length is changing in each of them because it is the intended focus of learning for this particular presentation. Similarly, in color tablets, the intended quality to be taught is the colors and their degrees of lightness and darkness, also called gradation. Thus, the structure, form, size, etc. of each tablet remain the same except its shade of color because it is isolated in this material.

The Control of Error:

The control of error ensures that the child realizes the mistake of the instance he makes it. The errors are self-corrected due to this characteristic of the didactic material. The child instantly realizes that something is wrong in his way of performing the activity or handling the material due to the apparent visual disharmony of the object. For e.g., the set of cylinder blocks. Each cylinder in a block must be inserted in its respective socket in order to be in proper order and proportion. If the child tries to insert a thinker cylinder in a thinner socket, it would not be able to go inside. Similarly, a shorter cylinder may go inside the taller socket, but it would not get fixed appropriately. Thus the child will notice his possible error of judgment and would correct it on his own accord. This proves to him that each hollow in the block is built exactly according to the size and dimensions of the cylinders that are going to be deposited or inserted in them.

Purposeful Activity:

The material in a Montessori environment is not just for decoration. It is also not just consisting of certain attributes only to become interesting for the child within its own self, but it also must lend a meaningful, motor activity for him to maintain his interest. He must know that the material can be *used* in a purposeful manner to achieve a particular task in order to learn something. For e.g., however much the child seems to like the pink tower and its cubes, he will eventually begin to be bored by just gazing at them. He will be eager to touch them, move them around, explore their dimensions or form, and make a tower out of them or else he will lose interest. He would feel immense joy in carrying each cube in his hands, feeling it, weighing it, and even playing around with it purposefully. Thus his activity can be prolonged, offering numerous opportunities or placement, arrangement, replacement, and rearrangement of the material to explore the possibilities. This is all possible if he knows how to use the material and for what purpose it should be used.

Limitations:

A very interesting pedagogic principle in the domain of education is that of the *limited quantity of learning material*. It applies to all of the material sets used in a Montessori classroom environment as it is a prepared environment setup for enhancing the qualities of patience, tolerance, sharing, caring, and mutual respect among the children. The limited quantity of material teaches the child to cherish it and realize its true value. He learns to patiently wait for his turn and also learns to manage his time well in order to be able to benefit from the material fully and letting others do the same too. Also, the limited quantity of material maintains order and clarity of understanding and remembering the details. It also makes it easier for the child to maintain concentration and develop an affinity with the material. Even though many would believe that an ample quantity of objects will help him learn quicker and explore further, yet it couldn't be farther from the truth. Instead, a multitude of various objects will make his mind perplexed and introduces a chaotic, disorderly state of affairs both internally and externally.

Aesthetics:

The attractiveness of the didactic material is an eye-catching attribute for the child. The color, the luster, the brightness, the clarity and harmony in the concrete material call to the aesthetic sense of the child. The clean, polished surface of not only the material but the environment itself appeals to him just like the bright petals of a flower appeal the nectar-sucking insects. The beautiful, 63 shades of color tablets. The appealing, prominent alphabet and number symbols in their holders, the lovely pink colored cubes placed on a small perch, the bright red rods, etc. Everything calls to his senses, saying: "*Careful! Use me or lose me.*" Your toddler, when presented with these aesthetically appealing objects in your home environment, will choose what appeals to his dominant sensitive urge at that time. This is similar to how so many pretty flowers are present in the garden having a variety of fragrances, shapes, and colors, but the bird or insect chooses what corresponds or relates to it the most.

Gradation:

This characteristic of the didactic material ensures varying degrees of the material exhibiting the same quality. The gradation offers the opportunity to understand the extremes and the degrees in between those extremes.

It is also one of the stages of presenting the material to the child. For e.g., after being introduced to the fabric boxes and a rough fabric and a smooth one, the child can be given a presentation regarding the grading of roughest to smoothest fabric by feeling the surface and texture of each piece of fabric.

Precision and Proportion:

The material is also precise in its color and has a fix proportion in its form or dimensions. For e.g., the brown stairs are always brown, and the child knows their precise color and distinguishes them from other materials easily. Similarly, their size and proportion are fixed too. All the prisms of the material set are similar in length i.e., 20 cm. As they are also called broad stairs, their height and width vary ranging from thickest (10 cm) to thinnest (1 cm) wooden cuboid or prism.

Point of Interest:

The point of interest is present in each material, and the directress must keep it in mind while presenting the exercise so that the child is demonstrated the activity with arousing interest. He can be stimulated to perform the activity himself or concentrate while it is being performed by another because of the underlying points of interest in that particular material presentation. For e.g., the child may get fixated on a particular part of the activity or material and engages in it more, repeating it again and again. Upon shaking up a particular soundbox, he may become so much interested in listening to the sound of shaken particles enclosed in the box that he repeats it again and again. The emerging, clanking sound is the point of interest in this activity.

Montessori Presentations:

The children of the future must be strong, free, and independent human beings. This is the true goal of Montessori lessons. Montessori presentation method is the source of learning the proper, aimful use of the didactic material. The child in these early years begins to imitate the adult. He even tries to substitute for the personality of his teacher. This imitation cannot be done without first observing and understanding the actions that are to be imitated. This is where the importance of presentations comes in, and this is what we call *setting a good, imitable example.* Sometimes he has to be prepared and inspired to act using the material at his disposal constructively. Oftentimes he can be more creative and purposeful than the adult himself while using the material. He just needs to be *directed* without being *dictated.* The material should be introduced in an easy-to-use, clearly understandable manner. It should be shown to him in order of use, sequence, or level of complexity. Three principles are to be strictly followed to facilitate proper understanding.

"Concrete to abstract, known to unknown, and simple to complex."

Your toddler can perform an activity once he sees you doing it in step by step, easily understandable manner. The activity itself is not the main aim, but the satisfaction of an inner urge to do something constructive and meaningful is. Similarly, the activity itself has prerequisite preparation called indirect preparation that leads to the development of many other integrated concepts for other future activities.

For instance; the activity of *pouring beans from one container to a number of containers* is a practical life exercise that is not performed just to play with the beans. It has a direct aim of learning a method to transfer some quantity of dry substance into another container. It also has indirect aims such as learning to divide the available quantity of dry substance into two or three containers in equal proportions. This leads to the preparation of mathematics and culture. Development and refinement of gross and fine motor skills, coordination of movements and control while picking the container and pouring the substance carefully avoiding any accidental falling of the beans, etc.

Some rules to present a Montessori material lesson or activity:

- ✔ Always introduce the name of the material and activity.
- ✔ Always invite the child and take his consent before involving him in an activity. Say: "Would you like to see or help, etc.?"
- ✔ Always maintain eye contact to show your consideration and attention as well as to maintain the child's interest.
- ✔ Make sure to not talk too much as it may distract the child from the actual purpose of observing the activity and following the method of presentation at each step. Remember, one of the most important principles of presentation is:

"Speak when you are not presenting and present when you are not speaking."

- ✔ Make sure that the child sits on the side to which he can clearly see the presentation without your hands' movements hindering the view. For e.g., the right-handed directress should always seat the child on her left-hand side.

- ✔ Always present with slow, precise, and deliberate movements involving controlled, planned actions. The child needs clarity and objectiveness in the presented method or else he will be distracted and confused by unnecessary or repetitive actions or steps.
- ✔ Make sure that the child himself repeats the exercise to reinforce the concepts.
- ✔ Complete the cycle of activity with proper introduction, presentation, and wind-up.
- ✔ Use of the three-period lesson is important whenever introducing a new object and naming it. The language of each material is also given through this method.

Three Period Lesson Example:

(Introducing the unknown miniature objects in the vocabulary basket)

Your toddler is shown some objects such as small bed, car, refrigerator, spoon, etc. He recognizes them all and names them when you ask. However, he remains silent when shown a mini wok, lid, and a lamp and asked about their names. You decide to give him a three-period lesson to introduce unknown objects to him.

First Stage (Naming):

- Align each object horizontally (wok, lid, and lamp) in front of the child who should be sitting beside you. If you are right-handed, make sure that the child sits on your left side.
- Let the child know that you are going to tell him something interesting.
- Once the child is attentively watching, slowly point your index and middle finger to the first object i.e., wok placed on the child's side and name it clearly two to three times saying: *This is a wok, a wok, a wok.*
- Similarly, name all the objects, clearly articulating the words a couple of times.

Second Stage (Recognition):

- After the introduction of the objects, the child is shown the way to recognize and associate the objects to their names regardless of their place.
- Interchange the sequence in which the objects are placed and after shuffling, ask the child to show you the position of any object and where

is it placed. Ask several questions by pointing toward the object and changing the position each time. *Where is the wok? Can you show me the lamp? Give the lid in my hand. Take the wok in your hand. Put the lamp beside the lid, etc.* This will also help in preparing him for an understanding of prepositions and memorizing the names without getting fixated on the places they were present at the time of introduction. This is important because you have to judge that he must know what each object is called instead of just associating the picture of the object with its place in his mind.

- The second stage is the most important and longest stage of the three-period lesson. It is the stage where the actual practice and reinforcement occurs. If the child is unable to connect the name to the object with the correct association, you must return to repeat the first stage or period to introduce the object again, this time more clearly.

Third Stage (Confirmation):

- After getting introduced to the objects and learning the association or recognition, the third stage is confirmation of the learned names.

- Interchange the position of each object and align it in a horizontal manner. Make sure that the child is ready to be asked and evaluated.
- Slowly point to the objects one by one and ask: *"What is this?"*
- Note the answer of the child, does he seem to state the correct names? Confirm and evaluate accordingly. If the child does not remember a particular name, resort to the first stage of the lesson to introduce again and repeat the process from scratch.

Chapter 10: The Development Areas or Learning Corners

The Montessori learning areas are essential curriculum domains that together formulate the prepared environment. These are described below as referenced by original Montessori pedagogy:

Exercises of Practical Life:

Certain simple tasks are included with proper, child-oriented material to let the child learn realistic ways to adapt to the society in which he lives. Through these everyday tasks and practical activities, he learns to develop his muscular coordination, normalizes his behavior, and achieves independence. He becomes a happy and calm individual who derives true joy and satisfaction by accomplishing realistic, domestic jobs that give him purpose and meaning and fulfill his need for work. This need is usually not satisfied in an adult-dominated household, so the toddlers need an environment specifically made for them. This learning area has the following major sub-categories:

- Basic Elementary Exercises Such as:
    - Holding a Tray
    - Carrying a Glass of Water
    - Holding a Jug
    - Holding a Spoon
    - Taking off or Hanging an Apron on the Hook
- Elementary Exercises Such as:
    - Pouring beans
    - Pouring water
    - Spooning
    - Sponging
    - Opening and Closing Bottle lids
    - Threading beads
    - Rolling and Unrolling the Mat
    - Folding and Unfolding the Mat
    - Pegging
    - Turning Pages of a Book

- Higher Elementary Exercises Such as:
    - Transferring Water from One Container into Multiple Containers through Sponging
    - Pouring dry substances into Multiple Containers
    - Carrying a Table or Chair
    - Use of Dropper
    - Using a Funnel
    - Cutting along the Line
- Care of Person Exercises Such as:
    - Washing the Hands and Face
    - Brushing Teeth
    - Combing Hair
    - Polishing Shoe
    - Cleaning the Nails, etc.
    - Some Custom Food-preparing Exercises (Using a blunt knife, peeling vegetables, using a grater, kitchen tools usage, making a personal breakfast consisting of a cheese sandwich or fruit salad, etc.)

- Opening and Closing Dressing Frames
    - Large and Small Button Frames
    - Hook and Eye Frame
    - Velcro Frame
    - Snapping or Press Button Frame
    - Zipper Frame
    - Buckle Frame
    - Bow Tying Frame
    - Shoelacing Frame
    - Safety Pin Frame

- Care of Environment such as:
    - Outdoor Environment
        - Picking up Dry Leaves in the Garden
        - Washing the Courtyard
        - Cleaning Windows or a Car
        - Care of plants, Watering and Weeding them
        - Care of Pet Animals, Feeding them, etc.

- Indoor Environment
    - Folding Napkins
    - Washing a Table
    - Polishing Metal Objects
    - Washing Clothes
    - Arranging Flowers
    - Dusting
    - Sweeping
    - Mopping

- Grace and Courtesy Exercises Such as:
    - Walking around Mats
    - Passing Pointed Objects such as Knife, scissors, pencil, etc.
    - Sitting on a Chair
    - Knocking on the Door
    - Opening or Closing the Door
    - Passing through a Crowd
    - Standing in a Queue
    - Use of Basic Etiquettes Such as Sorry, Thank you, Greetings, etc.
    - Coughing and Sneezing

    - Introducing Self
    - Receiving Guests
    - Table Manners
- Control of Movement / Advanced Grace and Courtesy:
    - Silence Game
    - Walking on the Line

Sensorial Education:

Sensorial area of learning includes refinement of the major senses of the child, i.e., Visual Sense, Tactile Sense, Baric Sense, Thermic Sense, Olfactory Sense, Gustatory Sense, Auditory Sense, and Stereognostic Sense.

Some major exercises include cylinder blocks, pink tower, brown stairs, red rods, color tablets, geometry cabinet, constructive triangles, touch boards, and baric tablets, thermic bottles and tablets, sound boxes, smelling bottles, musical bells, stereognosis bags, geometry solids, etc.

Language Education:

This learning area is of great intellectual importance. The main exercises are divided into three aspects of language i.e., Writing, Speaking and Reading. Some of these exercises are oral, pre-reading activities like a conversation, news period, question game, sound game, or I spy game, vocabulary basket, etc. While others are for preparation of writing such as metal insets, sandpaper letters, green boards, etc. Some are for reading like the movable alphabet, object boxes, etc.

Language exercises also include capital letters introduction, punctuation, and function of words exercises i.e., articles, verbs, adverbs, preposition, conjunction, pronouns, etc. There is a special grammar symbols box to denote the parts of speech used in a sentence.

Mathematics:

The introduction of the mathematical concepts should always follow a pattern in Montessori that is from concrete to abstract. First, introduce the concrete quantities, then their symbols, then associate the symbols with the quantities and show their relationship. It can be done by introducing, number rods, then sandpaper number, then both of them together, then spindle boxes to reinforce this concept. Other major mathematical groups include decimal group, linear counting & skip counting, arithmetic exercises, and abstraction group.

Area for Cultural Subjects:

A space in the environment must be dedicated to Montessori cultural subjects that include: Science, Art, Religion, History, Geography, Zoology, Botany, Astronomy, etc. The purpose of this area is to develop knowledge in children about the world they live in. The main cultural topics include simple science experiments about magnet, sound, water, etc., the creative exercises to produce child-appropriate art and craft, some knowledge about the animal and plant kingdom, the world and regional map, the geographic features and landforms like island, peninsula, etc., the historical timelines and comparison between modern and stone age, etc., the awareness of religious and national events and cultural celebrations, the solar system and the planet earth, etc.

Chapter 11: Some Important Montessori Activities and Lessons

❖ Exercise of Practical Lifc:

- *Sponging Activity to Strengthen Hands and Indirect Preparation for Writing:*

This activity is a great lesson to prepare your toddler for preliminary domestic work, increase sensitization in his hands' muscles and develop coordination of movement, patience, and skill to explore the environment further. This involves transferring liquid from one bowl to another by means of a sponge.

Age: 3 years

Aim:

- To develop fine motor skills.
- To transfer water from one container to another without spillage.

- To enhance focus, concentration, and control.
- To develop independence and reach normalization.
- To develop visual discrimination.

Point of Interest:

- The difference between the shape of a damp sponge and the squeezed one.
- Squeezing the water droplets out of the sponge while transferring and waiting until the very last drop.

Control of Error:

- Accidentally spilling the droplets outside the container.

Material:

- Two similar containers, one of them filled with water up to its half.
- A dry sponge.
- A Tray.
- A duster or towel cloth for drying in the end.
- A plastic mat or sheet.
- Aprons for the child and directress.

Presentation:

- The directress will introduce the activity and invite the child, taking his consent.
- She will take him to the place where the EPL (Exercises of Practical Life) material is kept.
- She will ask his help in carrying the material to the table for presenting it.
- Both of them will put on their aprons after taking them off the hook or hanger.
- The child will sit beside her.
- First, she will lay the plastic sheet on the table, then put the tray in which two containers are present, one is empty while the other is half-filled with water.
- Then she will start placing the material in order of use from right to left.
- She should arrange the bowls in such a way that the empty one is to the left in front of the child while the water-filled one is to the right-hand side in front of her. The sponge should be placed inside the tray beside the filled bowl while the duster should be on the top outside the tray, on the plastic mat.

- Telling the child to look carefully, the directress will pick up the dry sponge, put it inside the water, sinking it deep with both hands to absorb as much water as possible.
- Taking out the sponge she will wait patiently, keeping it in her hands to let the excess water spill in order to avoid falling of water droplets while transferring, and creating a mess.
- The child will observe how the sponge changes shape and color once being dipped and dampened.
- Then she will take the damp sponge towards the empty bowl and squeeze it carefully to let the absorbed water out so that the sponge reverts back to its original shape and color.
- Repeating the action multiple times will result in the successful transfer of all of the water from the filled container to the empty one so that the filled one becomes fully empty now.
- Put the sponge in the empty bowl once the task is completed. Make sure to wipe off any possible spillage with the help of a duster and interchange the position of the containers to let the empty bowl in front of the child again.

- Invite him to repeat the exercise if he is willing or else, dump the used water in the basin and after drying the material and folding the mat, put everything back to its proper place.

❖ Sensorial Education:

- *Mystery Bag:*

This activity is to enhance the stereognostic sense of the child by developing his muscle memory through tactile sense. The mystery bag is a fun and interesting way of learning the shape of familiar objects and recognizing them without seeing them.

Age: 3.5 to 4 years.

Aim:

- Refinement of Stereognostic Sense (Muscle Memory + Tactile Sense).
- To enhance the visualization power and mental imagination of familiar objects.

Point of Interest:

- Correctly judging the object and naming it just by feeling it inside the bag, without actually looking at it.

Control of Error:

- In the object itself upon seeing it after taking it

out of the bag, if it is recognized incorrectly in the previous attempt without seeing it.

- Also, if other children are watching, they can point out upon seeing.

Material:

- An attractive, decorative bag.
- Miscellaneous objects (approx 10) that are quite familiar and known to the child, to be filled in the bag. The objects must be very distinctive, quite different from each other, such as key, button, car, peg, pencil, sharpener, etc.

Presentation:

- Invite the child to perform the activity with you.
- Tell him that today's activity is related to a mystery bag and its objects.
- Show him the material and let him know that he should watch carefully how you are going to identify the objects inside the bag without looking at them.
- This activity can be done both as an individual presentation or group work.
- Bring the material to the table and let the child sit beside you on your left (If you are right-handed).

- Put the bag on the table between you and the child in such a way that the opening is nearer to you.
- Insert your hand inside the bag, feeling up the objects while the child must be looking carefully.
- Engage him by saying sentences and exclamations like; *Oh yes! Looks like I have found a key in my hand,* bring it out and let him see too.
- Similarly, each object that is felt and identified can be taken out and placed on the top left corner of the table in front of the child.
- Make sure that you say the name of the object clearly before taking it out of the bag.
- After that, the child can repeat the activity on his own too.
- If there are multiple children, let each child identify some objects in turns until all the objects are identified.
- After the activity, the material should be returned back to its place with the help of the child.

❖ Language:

- *Green Board:*

The green board exercise is a very effective way to trace and practice writing the alphabetic symbols. This is the very first time that the child actually writes with a direct purpose of writing. The color of the boards is an attractive, clear green that is neither black nor white. It is a striking surface for the child to express his understanding of the formation of letters. Here the most basic exercise is presented.

Age: 4 1/2 years.

Aim:

- Refinement of fine motor skills.
- Practical writing opportunity.
- Reinforcement of formation of letters by tracing the sandpaper letters.

Point of Interest:

- Trying to write in the exact way the tracing has been done.
- Working with chalkboard for the first time.

Control of Error:

- The child will know the incorrect formation instantly as he matches his written symbol with the corresponding sandpaper letter tablet placed beside the green board.

Material:

- A tray containing a blank green board.
- Chalk in a small bowl
- Damp sponge
- Duster
- Sandpaper Letter e.g. *c*

Presentation:

- Invite the child and take his consent to work.
- Bring him to the language area and introduce him to the material.
- Tell him that you are going to present the green board exercise today.
- Carry the material to the table and arrange in order of use.
- Let him sit beside you and watch carefully.
- Put the sandpaper letter in front of you, rub your fingers and trace it carefully.
- Then rub your finger on the damp sponge to increase the sensation before picking the chalk and writing '*c*' on the board. Repeat this two to three times.
- Erase the board with the duster and let the child repeat the exercise.

Chapter 12: Role of a Parent as Directress at Home

When it comes to education, there are two ways to get educated that are formal and informal. In informal education, the person gets self-educated without any help or guideline from a proper educationist. He gathers knowledge and information from his surroundings, makes self-studies his priority. While on the other hand, formal education comes by means of proper institutes and teachers. These institutes cater to the children according to their ages. Kindergarten, primary, elementary, high school, college, and universities are examples of educational institutes where a person gets educated. The role of parents and teachers goes parallel. Parent-teacher and the child are connected in a triangle. All three interlinked with each other. Both teachers and parents have some responsibilities they have to fulfill according to the needs of the child.

Montessori Directress:

The teacher is the one who serves and serves well. Montessori named the teacher Directress, not the teacher. There was a logic behind this term. A teacher is a common term given to a person who teaches her students. But as it comes to Montessori teaching, this teacher becomes the directress. Why because in a Montessori environment, the child is learning through guided instructions, not by the traditional method of learning. Directress is the person in charge of that prepared environment. She is the person who prepares a safe and sound environment with lots of physical and mental activities for the child to explore and learn. A child can feel the presence of the directress, her guided instructions also, but he will not feel the restrictions in the environment. Montessori believed that the restricted attitude of the adults could damage the personality of the child. The confidence he needs for his future life can get shattered due to this controlled attitude. Montessori worked on the two major components. One is the prepared environment, and the other one is the preparation of an adult as an observer and guide who knows how to prepare and take care of the child and the environment, and for that adult, she suggested the term, Directress. A role of a directress in a child's life is about guiding him through his ways and particularly to make him spiritually strong. A directress is a person who has to get trained for the classroom environment and for herself also to understand the needs of the child and the classroom. According to Montessori, directress is a scientist who connects with the child in a manner that the child explores the world around him with his maximum potential. She should not know how to teach. Instead, she should know how she could become a better guider and get the maximum from the child. She ought to be a refined observer; she should know her spiritual and scientific training approach and above all the directress should know her ultimate goal, that is to serve children, to help them to find out their hidden qualities at their peak.

Parent as a Directress:

Nature has given parents the toughest responsibility of raising a child. He is the one responsible for bringing the child in this world and taking care of his needs before and after his birth. Parents should acknowledge the fact that they are the caretakers of the child, not their sovereigns. It's their responsibility to provide a child with a safe and well-prepared environment for his potential growth. When it comes to learning and giving education to a child, the parent is the first formal educator in his life. From infancy till lifelong he stands by his side for the ultimate guide the child needs. Of course, we are talking about the parent as a guide, not an adult who forces his orders on the child. Restrictions, pressurizing, and controlling the child will not do anything good to the child and the parent as well.

A parent should realize the difference between guided instructions and forced behavior. It's a parent who should realize the power of independence. He should give the child enough opportunity to develop his confidence to survive well in society. Most parents are not concerned about giving their kids choices in their decisions; a simple act of giving a child a chance to decide what he wants to wear or what he wants to eat will boost a child's confidence at its best. Letting the child making his choices will help him in making a good decision-maker. He will observe from his decisions about the right and the wrong. And will eventually learn to make sensible decisions in the future.

Parents must stand by the side of their children like supporters and guiders. They should have to build a strong connection with the child so that a child can learn how to build trust in others. A parent ought to make sure the needs and wants of the child. If the child is hyperactive or stubborn, he needs a special care and sensible approach to make him a good observer and an explorer. Allow your child to have physical activities in a guided environment so that he can able to learn most through his physical activities. Parents should make sure that they design their home and activities in a manner that the child gets maximum from their efforts they are giving.

Parents should have to be keen observers so that they can sense the needs of the child and act accordingly. They must know how to control their temperament because anger controlling will lead them to develop trust and confidence with the child. Keep this in mind that the child himself is a very good observer; he senses the attitudes and then reacts towards the specific attitude. The positive attitude of a parent will give a child a positive environment to grow and explore with their potential. Parents should know how to love the child because love is the only thing that makes a person take care of another person in a beneficial manner. And child senses love differently than others. Make sure you let your child senses your love beautifully.

Conclusion

Thank you for making it through to the end of *Raising a Montessori Toddler*, let's hope it was informative and able to provide you with all of the tools you need to achieve your goals whatever they may be.

The next step is to map out your action plan to follow these suggested tips and carry out the informative guidelines to set up a Montessori-inspired setting. As this can be done in the comfort of your home, it will help you raise your toddler efficiently on your own. Most of the parents think that homeschooling is an impossible concept in today's world where even for preschool readiness, they have opened pre-preschools! Though you must be thinking otherwise after reading this guidebook.

The most interesting part is that however much the adults feel responsible and take credit for their toddlers' growth, learning, and development, it is mainly due to the astonishing powers of early years' mindset. The child happens to learn at his own pace, and while doing so, he only needs facilitation in the form of a properly set environment, positive attitude of adults, guided freedom to learn and explore. This alone can make a remarkable difference in his personality as he shapes it according to the opportunities given to him.

Properly implemented Montessori curriculum and scientific approach can be highly effective in producing men capable of not only reasoning and problem solving, but independently efficient in their work and deriving pleasure from it. This sort of mindset after being raised as a Montessori toddler shows that education is not just for task completion for vocational induction, but it is for life and is life itself. The Montessori toddlers are socially confident, emotionally stable human beings with spiritual love and a sense of responsibility present at their very core.

At the end of this exhilarating journey, we will leave you with a thought-provoking notion:

Do you think that the Montessori method can be used or upgraded to setup Montessori-friendly high schools or colleges as well? Think about it as your toddler starts growing into an adult!

Finally, if you found this book useful in any way, a review on Amazon is always appreciated!

Description

The most curious human being may well be those cute little toddlers. As they start to move around, talk, and pay attention, they become mini explorers of this magnificent world. The research has shown the hidden powers of an infant's mind; it further develops and retains those powers in toddlerhood. If the right sort of environment is provided, it can flourish and externalize these powers as wonders of developmental milestones. The Montessori method of education indulges the mind of a child aged 3 to 6 to enhance its conscious absorbent nature. This scientific approach, centralizing on the children's individual interests and learning pace, can be a massive turning point in early childhood educational reform. Transforming your home into a Montessori-friendly setup can help transform your toddler into a confident, normalized individual with a mathematical mind and intellectual power. The creation of a Montessori children's house is both a challenge and a pleasure. This book focuses on concise details of Montessori pedagogy with main focus on guidelines regarding Montessori subjects, learning areas or workstations, Montessori rooms and their traits, specific equipment and proper manner of setting them up, Montessori activities and lessons, adult's roles and responsibilities, etc. Bringing in the Montessori approach inside your home can be an enlightening experience. This book will help you realize the necessity of adopting a Montessori way of raising your toddler. The path to development is paved with unseen obstacles which may never materialize if your toddler is provided with a nurturing atmosphere for learning. However, the obstacles to growth may affect a child who has not been facilitated with a prepared environment or a trained adult who is patient enough to satisfy his curiosity, sense of wonder, and explorative instinct.

Imagine a toddler of three years, curious to learn or touch enough a particular picture he may have seen on the wall of a classroom. A busy teacher in a conventional school may not have properly responded to his inquisitive nature or allowed him to touch it, or the picture itself may even be hanging high enough, out of his reach. This causes hindrance in enhancing his tactile sense by touching and sensing the softness or roughness of the surface of the picture or visual and cognitive sense seeing it, remembering it and relating it to something similar that he may have seen recently. His sense of exploration and free-spirited flair slowly dies, and he becomes deviated.

Therefore, implementing the Montessori pedagogy in your home will help you raise your toddler without hindrances and deviations. This book will explore:

- The basic history and principles of the Montessori method
- The traits of an absorbent mind and sensitive periods
- The possible obstacles to development in the early years
- Importance of movement and language acquisition
- The preparation of Montessori-friendly home and the proper equipment
- Montessori subjects and setting up the learning corners
- Montessori inspired lessons and exercises to be implemented at home
- Details of the didactic material and its significance
- The parents as teachers of a Montessori toddler and their role
- *And much more...*

Made in the USA
Monee, IL
29 November 2019

17620680R00263